MY COUNTRY

ABBA EBAN

MY COUNTRY

THE STORY OF MODERN ISRAEL

Random House
New York

Library of Congress Cataloging in Publication Data

Eban, Abba Solomon, 1915–
My country.

1. Israel–History. I. Title.
DS126.5. E2   956.94   72–2725
ISBN 0–394–46314–5
ISBN 0–394–48256–5 (lim. ed.)

Designed by Alex Berlyne for Weidenfeld and Nicolson Jerusalem
Color photographs by David Harris

Composed by Keter Press Ltd., Jerusalem; printed by Japhet Press,
Tel Aviv; and bound by Wiener Bindery, Jerusalem, 1972

Contents

Acknowledgments

The author and publishers wish to thank the following institutions and individuals for their kind permission to reproduce illustrations and quoted material in this work: The Central Zionist Archives, Jerusalem, 11 (upper right), 27 (upper left, centre), 31 (centre); Keren Hayesod Photo Archives, Jerusalem, 21 (lower left), 51, 56, 62, 78 (lower left), 79, 81, 84–5, 93, 99, 111; Jewish Agency Photo Archive, Jerusalem, 31 (lower left, centre), 38, 43; Israel Government Press Office, 8, 57, 60–1, 67, 78 (lower right), 112–3, 122, 129, 136, 143, 150, 157, 159, 163 (above), 175, 178, 182, 185, 194, 207, 210, 217, 221, 247, 265, 277, 279; IPPA, 116, 261; the United Nations, 64, 98, 120, 140, 197 (left), 203, 211; Israel Museum, Jerusalem, 24, 27 (upper right), 39, 294–5; Werner Braun, 21 (lower right), 46, 102, 109, 152, 177, 199, 282, 284, 291, 292, 294–5; David Harris, 158, 163 (below), 173, 242, 271; Hazel Greenwald, 84 (lower left); Haifa Press, 11 (upper left); United Press, 197; Morris Kushilewitz, 224–5; Teddy Kandel, 229; quotation on page 228 from Michael Howard and Robert E. Hunter, *Israel and the Arab World: The Crisis of 1967*, International Institute for Strategic Studies, London; table on page 106 revised from the *Encyclopaedia Judaica*; maps and graphs drawn by Carta, Jerusalem.

Foreword

I have asked myself the familiar question: 'If a reader were limited to one book about Israel's story since May 1948, what would I like him to know?' Not only to know, but to feel.

The past decades have their taste and atmosphere, as well as their recorded facts. The facts will survive in records and documents, but no encyclopaedia can convey the sharp fluctuations of mood between anguish and relief. It is here that our contemporary witness is needed, and we should give it while we can. In 1973 the overwhelming majority of Israeli citizens cannot have a living memory of the day on which their independence was proclaimed; the perils that attended its early weeks; the combined burden and glory of the mass-immigration in the first crowded years; the pressures and scarcities of the early 1950's; or the tormenting rhythm of frontier violence before 1956. Thereafter, we come into a period that lives more vividly in the reader's consciousness. I have therefore given special weight and space to the earlier period.

I have undertaken no obligation to record everything of significance; selectivity is inherent in the task itself. I have considered that the main currents flowing into the formation of Israeli society and culture are no less decisive than the military and diplomatic battles which inevitably dominate most narrative literature on this subject.

My thanks go out particularly to Elaine Varady for her research and choice of illustrations, and Alex Berlyne has dealt tastefully with the graphic design. Finally, I express appreciation to Edna Marks, Nitsa Pines and Siegfried Brandler, who have tirelessly typed my manuscript through so many drafts and versions.

Jerusalem
July 1972

Abba Eban

I

A Single Day: 14 May 1948

*The eternal stars shine out as soon as it
is dark enough.* •Thomas Carlyle

*Accordingly we, the members of the National Council, representing the Jewish people in
Palestine and the Zionist movement of the world, met together in solemn assembly today,
the day of the termination of the British Mandate for Palestine; by virtue of the national
and historic right of the Jewish people and of the resolution of the General Assembly of the
United Nations; hereby proclaim the establishment of the Jewish State in Palestine – to be
called Israel . . .*

*With trust in Almighty God, we set our hands to this Declaration at this session of the
Provisional State Council in the City of Tel Aviv, on this Sabbath Eve, the Fifth Day of
Iyar, Five Thousand Seven Hundred and Eight, the Fourteenth Day of May, One Thousand
Nine Hundred and Forty-Eight.*

The words rang out, strong and defiant, across the humble museum hall.
Hatikvah, the anthem of hope, flowed through the radio channels into the
air of history. A few minutes earlier an older benediction had been heard.
'Blessed art Thou, our God, King of the Universe, who has kept us in life
and sustained us – and enabled us to reach this day.'

The thirty-odd signatories rose one by one and set their names to the
parchment scroll. The *Proclamation on the Rise of the State of Israel* had been
written into the life and law of nations.

One other deed was added to the brief solemnity. The Provisional State
Council appointed an executive of thirteen members to be known as the
Provisional Government of Israel, which now went into session. It immediately resolved that 'all laws enacted under the Palestine White Paper (1939) of
the British Government and all laws deriving therefrom are hereby rendered
null and void.' The Palestine White Paper (1939) was an odious document in
Jewish eyes. It had restricted the immigration of Jews into the country and
forbidden the purchase of land by Jews in all but five per cent of its area.
Palestine was almost the only country in the world in 1948 in which the law
overtly discriminated against immigrants or residents on the precise grounds
of their being Jewish. These cruel enactments had been applied when Jews

Tel Aviv museum hall, 4 p.m., 14 May 1948: David Ben Gurion,
flanked by leaders of the new state, reads the *Proclamation on the
Rise of the State of Israel*, 51 years after the First Zionist Congress

left Sir Alan Cunningham, the last British High Commissioner for Palestine, embarks from the port of Haifa

right King Abdullah was established as the ruler of Transjordan by the British in 1921. Most moderate of the Arab leaders, he nonetheless was unable to withstand pressure to go to war

far right The British Government was adamant in refusing the survivors of the holocaust entry into Palestine, but from 1946 to 1948 hundreds of small and unseaworthy vessels ran the British gauntlet bringing in 'illegal' immigrants

were being killed by the millions in Europe for want of a country to receive their flight. The new-born Government of Israel, in its first sovereign act, broke the lock and opened the gates. 'The State of Israel has arisen. The meeting is ended,' were David Ben Gurion's laconic closing words.

All in all it had lasted thirty-two minutes. The members of the Provisional State Council dispersed slowly into the sun-drenched streets. They had given Israel a dramatic birth; now the task was to ensure survival. Southwards, eastwards and to the north, the wave of Arab violence was mounting high; it was to break with redoubled force on Israel's head after midnight.

The seventh and last British High Commissioner for Palestine, General Sir Alan Cunningham, in the full uniform of his expiring office, was on his way by air to Haifa port. His flag had been lowered that morning on the mast of Government House in Jerusalem. At midnight he was to set sail in *H.M.S. Euryalus* with the last units of his civil government. There were still some British military enclaves in Haifa and in a few military camps, but they were to exercise no force or authority, except in their own defence.

Twenty-six years had passed since Britain had been charged by a Mandate of the League of Nations to 'ensure the peace and security' of the Holy Land and to 'facilitate the establishment of a Jewish National Home.' It had been a high vision with no precedent in law or history; and it had known some years of radiance. But it had long declined into what Winston Churchill had called 'a squalid war' between the British Mandatory Government and the Jewish National Home which it had been appointed to strengthen and sustain. Churchill's phrase was not excessive in its severity. Under the decrees of its Foreign Secretary, Ernest Bevin, Britain had found itself ruling by

whip and gallows with the aim of preventing the very thing it had been charged to promote. The National Home of the Jews was not to be 'facilitated' but curbed and stunted, and its hope of independence snuffed out in order that the number of Arab states might be increased from seven to eight and, eventually, to eighteen. And all this was to happen in an hour of agony for the Jewish people such as no family of the human race had ever known. Britain had been the first power to support the idea of national independence for a Jewish society in Palestine. It had now come to regard its own vision as a kind of pariah doctrine to be suppressed by righteous violence. The emaciated survivors of Hitler's dungeons had come in crowded, leaking ships within sight of the white houses and green olive-groves of Mount Carmel only to be forced back onto caged decks and escorted back to Europe. Indeed, in one case they had been expelled back to Germany, where the soil was saturated with their kinsmen's blood and haunted by memories of grief and havoc. Bevin was personally responsible for this particular brutality. Neither its own better conscience, nor that of mankind, could suffer that Britain, which had led the resistance to Hitler, should now be making war against his surviving victims. It was in the chasm of this moral paradox that the British Mandate sank down and died.

Israel's birth and the end of British rule were not the whole story of this single day. The Arab armies were poised to spring at Israel's throat. At sunrise Egyptian forces had crossed the frontier and advanced into the southern Negev. An Iraqi column moved in strength towards the Jordan River. The Transjordanian Arab Legion was arrayed along the river with its main encampment at Zerqa. On the upper reaches of the Jordan, a Syrian brigade was ready to attack the Jewish farming villages in the hot, green valley. Apart from the impetuous Egyptians, who had already printed stamps to commemorate the imminent victory, the Arab governments were awaiting the Mandate's last official hour before launching their armies in attack. The seven governments of the Arab League had concerted this policy at a meeting in Damascus late in April. Their aim was to occupy Palestine, subjugate its Jewish population and strangle Israel's statehood at its birth.

There could be no illusion about the imminence of the attack. It was known that Golda Meir, in Arab disguise, had crossed the Jordan a few days earlier, to attempt to persuade Abdullah, King of Transjordan, not to partake in the forthcoming war. He had rebuffed this proposal; it was plain that his purpose was to take the whole country and make its Jewish population, at the very best, a minority dependent on his tolerance. But he was the most humane of the Arab leaders, and it is doubtful whether his moderation would have had much effect if the Arab invasion had succeeded. It was more likely that if they lost the war, the Jews would have been sent to the kind of wholesale massacre being freely discussed in Arab rhetoric and poetry. Nothing but a promise to refrain from proclaiming Israel's independence would turn Abdullah from this path; and the news from Cairo made it doubtful if even this renunciation would deflect the other Arab governments from their plan of conquest.

The main target of King Abdullah's Arab Legion was Jerusalem, where it sought not only to frustrate any possibility of Israeli control, but also to thwart the UN plan to establish an international régime in the Holy City. The prospect of Arab victory seemed certain. In Cairo, Azzam Pasha, Secretary-General of the Arab League, looked at the maps, counted the forces on each side and spoke to the world in an exulting voice: 'This will be a war of extermination and a momentous massacre which will be spoken of like the Mongol massacres and the Crusades.' His words were shocking in their arrogance; but there seemed to be no logical reason why he should be wrong.

Israel was experiencing the joy of birth and the fear of death in a single taste; and the physical danger was deepened by political isolation. The UN General Assembly, which had proclaimed the Jewish people's right to statehood six months before, was now debating a proposal to set up an international 'trusteeship', instead of supporting the independence of a Jewish State. Shaken by the violence of Arab resistance, and sceptical of Jewish military strength, the United States had abandoned its support of the partition plan and was now urging the United Nations to endorse its own change of heart. Thus, from the shining hour of 29 November, 1947, Israel had slid back to weakness

and solitude. The moral force of international recognition was being withdrawn at the very moment when the enemy was massing for the assault. A
stunning aggregate of perils crowded in on Israel, and she faced them all
alone. Cut off from any sustaining contact with the world by land, sea or
air, her 650,000 Jewish citizens held one thing in firm resolve: the gifts or
blows of fortune would be met this time not by a nameless community, but
by a sovereign Jewish State.

To be sure, there was clear-headed calculation as well as courage in this
decision. Whatever dangers might come from proclaiming statehood would
not be avoided by recoiling from the proclamation. The Arab invasion would
come in any case. It seemed better to meet it with the Jewish banner flying high.

To the embattled Jews, it seemed that world opinion was no more effective than a Greek chorus, expressing eloquent and musical consternation
at events which it made no effort to control. Yet within a few hours, Israel's
independent decision was to create new currents of thought and action in
friendly lands, and especially in the United States. It appeared that if Israel
took sole responsibility for her independence, she would not long remain
alone. Those who were not prepared to encourage her decision in advance
might nevertheless endorse it once it was taken.

The main question-mark hovered over Washington. In November 1947
the United States had committed its policy to the establishment of a Jewish
State. Its influence had been the strongest factor in bringing the United Nations
to its decision. If the Jews of Palestine – putting their trust in a judgment of
which the United States had been the primary sponsor – were now to be
submerged in war, an intolerable burden would lie on the American conscience. American leaders devised many plans in addition to the trusteeship
device. Under each of them, Israel would have to postpone statehood in
exchange for a possibility – not even a certainty – that the Arab governments
would find it in their hearts to do without their 'Mongol massacre'.

But any belief that the Jewish people would now buy peace at the cost of
statehood was shattered on 12 May in a meeting of tense gravity with the
American Secretary of State, General George Marshall. Moshe Sharett, the
political representative of Palestinian Jewry, declared that the Jewish people
was about to fulfil the dream of centuries for which three generations had
striven in modern times. The prospect was at hand. 'History will judge us
guilty if we agree to let the hour go by.' Secretary Marshall, torn between
the strong impact of this affirmation and his own scepticism about the prospect
of the Jews holding their own in a military conflict, removed himself and his
government to the role of spectators:

'It is not for me to advise you what to do . . . If it turns out that you were right and you succeed in establishing your state I shall be happy. But it is a very heavy responsibility that you mean to take.'

This was not very valiant or encouraging; but it was far from the urgent negation expressed in Washington a few days before. The firmness of Jewish policy seemed to have given birth to new thoughts. Sharett's words to Secretary Marshall indicated that the Jews could not be persuaded to postpone their statehood. In that case, the question for Washington to consider would be whether the Arabs could be pressed to renounce their assault. As this thought took shape in President Truman's mind, a letter reached him on 13 May from the Zionist elder statesman Chaim Weizmann who for thirty years had led his people's dream of nationhood through a wilderness of which the end now seemed in sight. Since 23 April he had been acting on a hint that Truman would like to find his way back to support of the original plan for Jewish statehood. Weizmann's eyes were close to blindness, but in no other respect was his vision dimmed. And his was the only Jewish voice likely to sway Truman's action. He was now to be given the chance:

Letter from Dr Chaim Weizmann to President Truman
13 May 1948

Tomorrow midnight, May 15, the British Mandate will be terminated and the Provisional Government of the Jewish State . . . will assume the full responsibility for preserving law and order within the boundaries of the Jewish State, for defending that area against external aggression and for discharging the obligations of the Jewish State to the other nations of the world in accordance with international law . . .

It is for these reasons that I deeply hope that the United States, which under your leadership has done so much to find a just solution, will promptly recognise the Provisional Government of the new Jewish State. The world, I think, will regard it as especially appropriate that the greatest living democracy should be the first to welcome the newest into the family of nations.

The President had called an immediate conference with Secretary Marshall and his other advisers to consider Weizmann's request. The meeting ended inconclusively. But on the morning of 14 May, the opinion of Secretary Marshall and Under-Secretary Lovett moved slowly towards the idea of recognition. In a telephone call from the White House, Clark Clifford, the President's Counsel, told Eliahu Elath, the Washington representative of the Jewish Agency, that if notification came that the Jewish State had been established, recognition would be granted. A letter announcing in due form the establishment of 'a Jewish State' was hastily drawn up and sent to the

White House in a cab. By the time it reached its destination, it had become known that the new state was to be called 'Israel', and it was in this name that the act of recognition was declared.

At 6.15 p.m. Ambassador Warren Austin, the representative of the United States in the General Assembly of the United Nations, was instructed to stop arguing for trusteeship and, instead, to read a brief statement on President Truman's behalf:

This Government has been informed that a Jewish State has been proclaimed in Palestine, and recognition has been requested by the Provisional Government itself. The United States recognizes the Provisional Government as the *de facto* authority of the new State of Israel.

It was past midnight in Tel Aviv when the news from Washington came. The recognition could not save Israelis from their danger; but it gave new heart to their defence. A splendid gleam of friendship had lit up their solitude.

The UN General Assembly, meeting in New York, had first heard the news of Israel's proclamation in the museum hall at 2 p.m., which was 8 p.m. on the first day of 'Israel time'. The American Zionist leader Dr Abba Hillel Silver, seated at the committee table as the spokesman of the Jewish Agency for Palestine, had broken in on a lethargic discussion of the trusteeship proposal with the brief announcement of Israel's establishment:

Thus, what was envisaged in the resolution of the General Assembly last November, has been, as far as the Jewish State is concerned, implemented. Thus, too, there has been consummated the age-old dream of Israel to be re-established as a free and independent people in its ancient homeland.

The words about 'implementing the United Nations resolution' had their barb of irony, for the United Nations had been striving hard for several weeks to prevent its own resolution from taking effect. This had become strangely difficult. The United Nations had helped to plant a seed and had then tried to destroy it; but the flower insisted on growing day by day. Something like an independent state had grown out of the ruins of the British Mandate. Moreover, the American proposal for replacing Israel's statehood by international trusteeship had met such massive scepticism that its own authors were ceasing to give it any credit.

By now the trusteeship proposal was petering out. It corresponded to no reality on the ground, and it was hard to define what purpose it was meant to serve. The Jews had declared resistance to any postponement of their imminent statehood; and the Arabs would not let any 'trusteeship' plan prevent their invasion. Nor was Palestine a vacuum waiting to be filled at the will and disposition of the United Nations. The administrative framework of a Jewish State already existed in much of the country where British rule had virtually lapsed. The thought of the United Nations using force in May 1948 to prevent the fulfilment of what it had recommended in November 1947 was a little too bizarre, even for those hectic days. As the afternoon of 14 May wore on, the discussion in the United Nations became a race with time. The British Mandate would expire at 6 p.m.; and only up to that hour would Palestine be an international territory subject to disposition by the General Assembly. After six o'clock, Britain, by her own abdication, would have no authority in the land; and if by that hour the United Nations had not established any effective legal title, the administration set up by the Jewish inhabitants in their sector of Palestine would hold the arena alone.

Jewish representatives now strove desperately in the lobbies for postponement of any decision by the General Assembly. They knew that if the United Nations voted for a trusteeship or any other form of successor régime, the prospect of American recognition for an Israeli government would recede. A group of delegations, led by Australia, New Zealand, Uruguay, Guatemala and the whole Soviet bloc, fought tenaciously against any step which might prejudice the establishment of a Jewish State. Thus the trusteeship plan, strongly assailed and weakly defended, fell away into the air, and the discussion became narrowed to two issues. The first was the appointment of a mediator to 'promote a peaceful adjustment' of whatever situation the United Nations might encounter when the Mandate expired. The second was an attempt to save the Holy City for international control.

Jerusalem was in torment and chaos. It had had a Jewish majority for a hundred years, but its conquest by the Arab Legion seemed imminent. The Jews were still prepared to accept the international régime by which the United Nations in November 1947 had promised to give Jerusalem 'security, peace and order'. But the Arabs fought against anything short of total Arab control. The General Assembly had accepted the view of the United States that it would have to act before the expiration of the Mandate at 6 p.m. that day if it wished to establish a legal basis for United Nations authority in Jerusalem. For the Charter empowers the United Nations to establish trusteeships over territories only at the request of those holding current jurisdiction in them. Thus the submission of the Palestine question to the United Nations by Great Britain was the sole authority for United Nations action in Jerusalem; and this autho-

The original Scroll of Independence of the State of Israel

...ישראל‬ ‫תהא מוכנה לשתף...
...המאוחדות בהגשמת החלטת העצרת מ...
...ואים לאומות המאוחדת ליתן יד לעם היהודי ב...
...לקבל את מדינת ישראל לתוך משפחת העמים...
...ראים — גם בתוך התקפת-הדמים הנערכת עלינו זה...
— לבני העם הערבי תושבי מדינת ישראל לשמור על השלום...
...חלקם בבנין המדינה על יסוד אזרחות מלאה ושווה ועל יסוד...
נ מתאימה בכל מוסדותיה, הזמניים והקבועים.
מושיטים‬ ‫יד שלום ושכנות טובה לכל המדינות השכנות...
הן. וקוראים להם לשיתוף פעולה ועזרה הדדית עם העם העברי...
...מאי בארצו. מדינת ישראל מוכנה לתרום חלקה במאמץ משותף...
...דמת המזרח התיכון כולו.

קוראים‬ ‫אל העם היהודי...
...שוב בעליה ובבנין ולעמוד לימינו בכל התפוצות...
...איפת הדורות לגאות ישראל.

...נתוך בטחון בצור ישראל...
...לעדות על הכרזה זו, במושב מועצת המדינה הזמנית...
על אדמת המולדת, בעיר תל-אביב, היום הזה, ערב שבת
ה' אייר תש"ח, 14 במאי 1948.

rity would become void the moment that Great Britain herself abandoned control.

Beyond the legal niceties lay the deeper issue of responsibility. An international authority which could not offer protection to Jerusalem was not likely to receive its obedience. The emptiness of the internationalization formula now came into the open. The General Assembly took one look at Jerusalem's agony and washed its hands of all responsibility for the city's fate. After a discussion under specially expedited procedure, it rejected first a Guatemalan proposal that an international régime be ratified in the same terms as those proposed in 1947; second, an American-French proposal seeking to establish an interim 'Government of Jerusalem consisting of a United Nations Commissioner and such officers as may be appointed by him or by the Trusteeship Council'; and third, an Australian proposal described by its author as a last attempt to 'establish a link of any kind between the United Nations and Jerusalem'. This plan would have empowered a UN Municipal Commissioner to undertake executive responsibilities in the city. Even this amount of resistance to the expected Arab conquest was too much for the United Nations to bear.

By its rejection of every plan for the international defence or administration of Jerusalem, the General Assembly thus repudiated its previous intention in the most emphatic way. Its effective policy was to let Jerusalem fall under Arab control. Knowing that a British Act of Parliament ending the Mandate would take effect in a matter of minutes, the General Assembly refused to step into the breach and to interpose even a theoretical barrier against Arab invasion. The result in law was that Jerusalem lost its Mandatory Government on 14 May at 6 p.m. and the General Assembly decided not to give it an international régime or to offer it any protection. It was an active relinquishment of responsibility in face of danger. At six o'clock, when the Mandate expired, the Iraqi representative ran exultantly to the podium and cried: 'The game is up!' The General Assembly, repudiating its own claim of succession, had abandoned the Holy City to its fate; it had, in effect, decided to leave its destiny to the fortunes of war. Later, when things were quiet, the United Nations would claim its 'rights' in the city where it had shirked its responsibilities.

The Jews of Jerusalem, engulfed in death and famine and fighting against odds for survival itself, had little time to reflect on the deliberations of those who had promised them 'security, peace and order' only five months before. Their choice was now clear. They must either sit back, paralyzed and inert, while violence, anarchy and starvation engulfed their homes; or they must

David Ben Gurion, one of the major forces behind the creation of the state and its first Prime Minister, at the age of 86. Retired now at Kibbutz Sdeh Boker, he devotes his time to writing

call up their energies to avert a conquest no less destructive than those of
ancient Babylon and Rome. Any idea that they could have peace or survival
except in total union with Israel was banished forever from their minds.

While the General Assembly thus refused to establish a successor régime
either in Palestine as a whole, or in Jerusalem alone, its indecision was redeemed
by action beyond its walls. When the American representative, who had been
urging the establishment of a trusteeship, startled his audience – and himself –
by announcing United States recognition of Israel, the Arab confusion was
immeasurable. Here was the threat of 'Mongol massacre' being defied not
only by little Israel, but by the greatest of the Powers. Within a short time,
the Soviet Union, and then Guatemala, were to announce their recognition.
'We have been duped', roared Dr Charles Malik of Lebanon in an assault of
fury upon the American delegates. By now it was 6.15 p.m., and the Mandate
had ended. The successor régime of Israel had arisen and had snatched the
prize of American and Soviet recognition, while the United Nations had
failed to interpose any bar against the legality of Israel's proclamation. The
attack by Arab armies would now be made against a recognized state, and
the aggression would thus stand rebuked by the central law of the Charter.

As the delegates gathered up their papers at United Nations headquarters in
New York, the British High Commissioner aboard the *H.M.S. Euryalus*,
six thousand miles away, was being greeted by the aircraft carrier *H.M.S.
Ocean* just outside Palestinian territorial waters. As he stood on deck, the
ship's band could think of no better valediction than: 'Should auld acquaintance be forgot and never brought to mind?' But in Israel the acquaintance
with the mandatory epoch was quickly being lost both from mind and memory
in the throng of new dangers. Now that British authority had been annulled,
the Foreign Minister of Egypt dispatched a note to the United Nations
Security Council announcing that his government proposed to send its
forces beyond its own frontiers 'to restore order' in a neighbouring country.
It was midnight at the United Nations and dawn in Israel when Egyptian
aircraft dropped their first bombs on Tel Aviv.

History has preserved the text inscribed on an arch of the Forum in Rome
to the glory of 'Titus Caesar Vespasian, Father of His Country, who subdued
the race of the Jews and destroyed their City of Jerusalem, a city which all
kings, commanders and nations before him have either attacked in vain or
left wholly unassailed'. This victory of the Roman Legions took place in the

opposite The Jewish Quarter of the Old City of Jerusalem
far right The 'Davidka', a relatively ineffective but very noisy field
mortar, helped to correct the arms imbalance in 1948

year AD 70. Nearly nineteen centuries had passed between the loss of Israel's independence and its restoration on 14 May 1948.

The emotion of the world on the day of this renewal was partly clouded by the tensions of the war. But it was also enlarged by vistas of memory. Nothing in history was comparable to the resurgence of a people in a land from which so many centuries had kept it apart. The people had been scattered – its original union corroded by distance, time and variety of tongues. A tenacious link between the Jewish people and the land had been preserved by small Jewish settlements in Galilee, while the major streams of Jewish history had flowed far away in other continents. But stronger than any physical connection were the memories and longings which tied the spiritual life of this people to its first anchorage. The land had given birth to no other single nation; and the people had achieved a collective identity in no other land. The bond between the people and the distant land, long preserved in dreams and prayers, was now becoming a part of the world's tangible reality.

For many millions in the world, this was a unique and noble mystery. Israel's rebirth resembled neither of the conventional forms of national liberation. Here was neither an indigenous uprising against an occupying power nor a colonial migration to an unknown land, but a reunion between a people and a land which had been separated for nineteen hundred years. Yet, for all the length of the separation, the restored nation still uttered the speech and upheld the faith which that same land had nourished three thousand years before. A world which had seen the birth and death of many nations

now, for the first and only time in its history, beheld a resurrection.

Hundreds and thousands of Jews in Israel, and millions across the world, went to bed that night with a sense of being larger and prouder than they had at dawn. Many things that had been uncertain in the morning had been answered, for good or ill, by the afternoon. Would the British administration really depart? On the surface, there had seemed no room for doubt. After all, the mandatory régime had been liquidating itself for several months, with Arab or Jewish forces moving into every vacuum of territory or administrative function that Britain left behind. Yet many people suspected that the intensive preparation to depart concealed a subtle determination to remain. In the mythology of many peoples, and especially of Jews, British ·diplomacy had built a reputation for intense subtlety; it was thought that British intentions must always be the exact opposite of British declarations. The popular belief was that Britain had deliberately created chaos so that either the Jews or the Arabs or the United Nations – or all of them together – would implore her to prolong her rule. This view ignored the immense fatigue of a British people exhausted by war and economic decline. In London that winter, most citizens had been thinking more about how to keep warm in coal shortages than about how to retain imperial assets abroad. In fact, the desire to see an end to the mandatory régime in Palestine was the only thing that Jews, Arabs and the United Nations held in common with each other and with the British people. Yet it was not until the High Commissioner actually set sail that everyone believed that he would really go, and many Israelis would not have been surprised if he had found reason to come back the next morning.

Similarly, many in the world still harboured a doubt about the Jewish intention to proclaim independence. The decision to do so had been adopted by the Actions Committee of the World Zionist Organization on 6 April by 40 votes to 18. Ten of the negative votes were cast by the left-wing Mapam, which did not want to foreclose a possible truce; the other eight opponents were Revisionists, who understood that to proclaim statehood in part of the country could be thought to mean the renunciation of statehood in the rest. The successive truce proposals, which would have postponed independence, had only been rejected by Jewish authorities after agonizing debate. On 13 May, the actual text of the Proclamation had been adopted in the Provisional State Council by 16 votes, with 8 abstentions. Most abstainers had reservations about the text, not about the establishment of the state itself. But the fact nonetheless remained that in the debate on the Proclamation Jewish decisions had not been unanimous; and until the last moment there was always a possibility that some new stratagem would be evolved in Washington, New York or elsewhere which would induce some Jewish leaders, at least, to think again. On the morning of 14 May, when the Proclamation came to the vote, it was unanimously adopted, and one could almost hear the relief which comes in hard decisions from the very termination of suspense.

Thus between one dawn and another, all the obscurities had been resolved. British rule had ended; Israel had proclaimed her rebirth; America had moved to Israel's side; the Arab states had launched their invasion; and the United Nations, by its own default, had enabled these streams of history to rush together in a single torrent. Between dawn and nightfall, Israel, Britain, America, the Arabs and the United Nations had each, by action or omission, performed something of great consequence.

And yet, amid the popular joy there was still a sensation that nothing was yet fully secure. That night the settlers of the Etzion Bloc, near Hebron, were captured by the Arab Legion, after their womenfolk had been sent to Jerusalem. At five o'clock the next morning, while Ben Gurion was making a broadcast in Tel Aviv, the city was bombed in an effort to put its airfield out of use; two Egyptian aircraft were brought down and their pilots captured. Newspapers across the world were divided between emotion at Israel's birth and speculation about her ability to survive. Most foreign correspondents were pessimistic on the second score; in the British press the Proclamation was treated as a moving but futile gesture, soon to be shattered by military defeat. In the Arab world not a single voice suggested that Israel would exist a month after its birth.

The Jewish communities across the world were in a torment of divided feeling. They knew that the Proclamation had not reduced Israel's dangers; some thought that it might even have sharpened them. But all understood that the conditions in which peril would be faced had been transformed. After all, the central fact in Jewish political life had been passivity: Jewish history had consisted of what Jews suffered, endured, resisted or survived, not what they themselves initiated or resolved. The point of reference had always been the attitudes and policies of others. Now, for a change, the world had been waiting many days to see what Palestinian Jewry said or did. There was, for the first time, an exhilarating sense of being able to have some control over the flow of events. Within a territory, however small, Jewish decisions could now move armies, levy taxes, create institutions, receive kinsmen, reanimate a culture and compel the reaction of others, near and far. The national history had entered a phase of autonomy. It was a day that would linger and shine in the national memory forever – a moment of truth that would move Israel to its ultimate generations.

2
The Long Road Back

*The secret of success lies in knowing
how long it takes to succeed.*

Montesquieu

In the history of Zionism, two strands come together in a single thread. The first is the insistence of Jews on preserving their identity, which is strongly linked to memories of the land in which they had known their brief but radiant spell of freedom thousands of years ago. The other is the rise of European nationalism, which infected persecuted and humiliated Jews with the same kind of dream as that which was then bringing many other nations to freedom and self-assertion.

The national idea had to undergo a special transmutation if it was to be effective in Jewish experience. In no other case had any people maintained its identity and distinctiveness in exile for thousands of years with sufficient vitality to ensure its ultimate rebirth. The singularity of Israel lay in an extraordinary power to flourish in the Diaspora. The sense of common destiny was not always, or everywhere, held firm against erosion; but the main nucleus of Jewry always remained intact and separate. The first and primary motive of national consciousness was the biblical literature. Jews never ceased to brood on their ancient writings, not only in a spirit of religious ecstasy, but also in search of distinctive national roots. What arose in their minds were not only the ideas of Judaism, but the images and recollections of the land in which it was born: 'If I forget thee O Jerusalem, may my right hand forget its cunning'; 'I will bring your seed from the east and gather you from the west. I will say to the north, give up, and to the south, keep not back. Bring my sons from far, and my daughters from the ends of the earth'.

The effect of these myriad repetitions day by day over the centuries was to infuse Jewish life with a peculiar nostalgia, strong enough to prevent any sentiment of finality or permanence in any other land. But it was not only a matter of constant prayer and hope. The physical link was never broken. A thin but crucial line of continuity had been maintained by small Jewish settlements and by the academies in Jerusalem, Acre, Haifa, Jaffa and Ramle,

The 'Street of the Jews' in the Frankfurt Ghetto shown in a
19th-century engraving. Even when restricted to closed ghettos,
the Jews retained their dream of a return to their own land

later to be reinforced by a stream of pious immigrants who established academies in Jerusalem, Safed and Hebron. The land itself passed under many conquerors – Byzantium (395), Arabs (636), Seljuks (1072), Crusaders (1099), Mamelukes (1291), Ottoman Turks (1517), and Britain (1917). The Jewish foothold was sometimes challenged, most strongly by the Crusaders, but it was never overrun. And throughout the centuries Palestine was always the province of an empire which had its centre somewhere else; it never became the cradle of another independent nation. Every one of its conquerors had his original home or centre of his faith elsewhere. Thus, the association of the land with Jewish history was never obscured or superseded.

The total result was that multitudes of Jews, wherever they lived, saw their spiritual home as rooted in a remote land which none of them had ever seen and which few ever expected to behold with their eyes. They lived in a permanent nostalgia, sustained by ways of life which, though often poor and sometimes squalid, nevertheless had the dignity of self-knowledge and self-assertion. This talent for corporate existence was especially conspicuous in the *shtetl*, the Jewish village within the Pale of Settlement of the Russian Empire. The lives of Jews, however miserable, went forward there in an atmosphere of autonomy. Most of the Jews in Russia and Poland lived under oppression, but they did not feel rootless. Their lives were bound up with religious observance, and their minds and hearts were filled with the images of Jewish history and faith. Even when they bowed their heads in secular subservience to gentile empires, they secretly saw themselves as the descendants of prophets and kings temporarily cut off from their own inheritance.

Zionism is both a documented ideology and a career of action and experience. It has many different facets, but they all reflect the same light. Rabbi Zvi Hirsch Kalischer brought the biblical messianic promise into modern expression to conclude that the divine promise of restoring the Jewish people to its ancestral home should be ratified in organized action. In a more secular vein, Moses Hess in *Rome and Jerusalem* (1862), demanded the establishment of a Jewish State based on ethical principles as a radical solution to Jewish distress and social discrimination. Leon Pinsker in his *Auto-Emancipation* (1882) sub-titled as an 'Admonition to His Brethren from a Russian Jew', declared it vain to protest against anti-Semitism when all energy should be given over to seeking Jewish emancipation from physical vulnerability and moral inferiority. Inspired by these visions, small groups of Jews actually set out for the Holy Land in the 1880's under the slogan 'Bilu' (Beit Israel Lechou Ve'nelecha – House of Israel let us return). In a few years a number of agricultural villages were established at Rishon le-Zion, Gederah, and Petach

left Moses Hess (1812–1875), whose *Rome and Jerusalem* (1862) was
a precursor of Zionist thought
centre Leon Pinsker (1820–1891), author of *Auto-Emancipation*,
which called for a return to Jewish national consciousness
right Theodor Herzl (1860–1904), founder of the World Zionist
Organization

Tikvah. They fell into deep penury, but they would survive and endure
into better days.

Jews who were apathetic to the trappings of sovereignty but profoundly
concerned for the survival of the Jewish spirit, like Asher Ginsburg (Ahad
Ha'am), were drawn to the movement for giving Jewish nationhood a territorial expression. Ahad Ha'am believed that a Jewish society should be based
on intensive cultural activity and draw its values from qualitative rather than
quantitative ideas. But this vision, too, was based on the assumption of a
Jewish society in the land of Israel itself.

All this spiritual agitation, however moving, might have subsided without
much trace had it not been incorporated in an organized movement in the
ebbing years of the nineteenth century. Moved by the scandalous anti-Semitism
revealed in the Dreyfus Trial, Theodor Herzl, a Viennese Jewish journalist
hitherto remote from all Jewish solidarities, was moved to reflect on Jewish
history and destiny. The result was a fervid messianic document published in
1896 under the heading *The Jewish State*.

This pamphlet had an electrifying effect both on Jews looking for a solution
to grievous distress and on those for whom the restoration had always been
a pillar of faith. Herzl's genius was not only to give the idea a galvanizing
expression, but also to understand the immense role of institutions in trans-

forming ideas into reality. Thus modern Israel's secular history rightfully begins with the First Zionist Congress, convened by Herzl in Basle in 1897.

The Congress was a grand affair, full of pomp and dignity. It was inspired by Herzl's own majesty of speech and bearing. His tall figure, large burning eyes and dominant temper appealed to a longing in the Jewish masses for a dignity and grace which the rabbis in their bleak ghettos had been unable to provide. But anybody who turned his eyes away from the utopian dreams of the Congress to the reality of Palestine itself soon became aware of what was long to remain a characteristic of Zionism: an enormous disparity between the means available and the end desired. For Palestine itself was a backward and desolate place. The word 'stagnant' best describes its natural state and its human condition. Nothing seemed to flow. It had no political or administrative identity. Parts were subject to the provinces of Beirut and Damascus; others to the district of Jerusalem; all were within the corrupt and inefficient Ottoman Empire. There were scarcely any roads, no industry, little profitable commerce and none but the most primitive agriculture, constantly ravished by malaria and pestilence. In this squalor, some 25,000 Jews lived within a total population of 450,000. And it was into this unpromising, almost repellent environment that the first groups of Zionist pioneers came in the decade before and after Herzl's initiative.

By the end of the century, the number of Jews had grown to some 50,000, more than half of them in Jerusalem. The pogroms in Russia and the expulsion from Moscow had brought on unexpected reinforcement, although far greater numbers of Jews were streaming to America, where they were to found the largest and most powerful community in Jewish history. Even with the infusion of thousands of immigrants into Palestine, the battle against nature seemed so unequal that everything would have collapsed but for the tutelage of Baron Edmond de Rothschild, who took some of the first villages under his care and invested nearly £6 million to acquire 125,000 acres of land for the first compact and serious Jewish settlements. But even this benevolence turned sour. The Baron's representatives were guided by a mood of philanthropy and condescension which did not make their beneficiaries particularly grateful. By 1900, the small Jewish community settled in the Land of Israel was divided into three. Pious orthodox Jews living on charity from abroad; struggling farmers subservient to the autocratic, sometimes corrupt officials of the Baron; and a few men of idealistic mind and ardent temper who sought escape both from Rothschild's philanthropy and from religious obscurantism by creating collective villages (which later developed into *kevutzot* and kibbutzim) in the Upper Jordan Valley.

Herzl had set his sights far above any level that this struggling Jewish community in Palestine seemed able to achieve. Within seven years of the First Zionist Congress he was dead. The meteoric rhythm of his rise and fall is part of his legend. He was only forty-four years old at his death in 1904, but his decade of leadership had exhausted him as surely as it had infused new energies into his people.

Herzl's vision and personality were the greater part of his legacy. The rest of it consisted of the Congress, the organization, its financial agencies, its network of societies across the world, its vigorous democratic life – animated by the religious (Mizrachi), labour (Poalei Zion), and General Zionist parties – and the supreme asset of emergence from anonymity. Zionism was not a 'crank' idea. It was now on the map of world politics.

Yet the next decade was a doldrum period. Herzl's immediate successors were almost invisible in the blinding aftermath of his radiance. The Congresses continued; the societies debated and gathered funds; the idea of a Hebrew University was born; the Jewish National Fund painfully redeemed acres of land with the pennies of masses across the world; and a Palestine office was established in Jaffa, under Dr Arthur Ruppin, to organize settlement on the land. In the main, however, Zionism was engaged in a holding action, waiting for some turn in the wheel of history to carry it forward.

But if the political fortunes of Zionism were static, there was progress in the practical tasks. In 1904 a wave of immigration (the Second Aliyah) began to reinforce the fragile community in Palestine. In the decade before the outbreak of the First World War, some 40,000 Jews went to Palestine, mostly from pogrom-ridden Russia. Many returned or moved on to other destinations. But by 1914 the Jewish community of Palestine was about 80,000, which was about one-eighth of the total population. The urban centres of Tel Aviv and Haifa had been founded; collective and cooperative villages dotted the landscape; and the organized labour movement was taking form. It was becoming a Hebrew society, adorned with the first secondary school (Herzliyah Gymnasium, 1905), a Technical Institute at Haifa (1912), an art museum (Bezalel, 1906); and several leading Hebrew writers.

Forty thousand newcomers in ten years has a modest ring about it in the dimensions of our time. Yet the Second Aliyah brought to Palestine's shores people of such sharp individuality and intense spiritual power that it may justly be called the generation of Israel's founding fathers. The ideas which they generated, the standards which they upheld, the ways of life that they followed became the normative values of the Yishuv (pre-State Jewish community) and thereafter of Israel. In particular, it was by their example that pioneering became the central ethic in Palestinian Jewish life.

Life was lived in a general atmosphere of suffering. The immigrants lacked money and medical facilities and were even short of food. In their outlying settlements they felt a sharp cultural isolation, as well as a pervasive physical danger. The new society was marked by a deep sense of moral preoccupation. The settlers tormented themselves with endless debates about the meaning of their lives, the purpose of their actions and the shape of the nation they were struggling to build. Rigorous ideals of equality were pursued in the socialized communities which they founded. They were driven by a fierce and constant sense of mission. They had little training for their new pursuits and, for the most part, could only learn from experiment and failure. They were seeking an inner rebuilding of their souls, a total reconstruction of the national will. They were building an avowedly élite society, animated by a puritanical zeal. They had little place for some of the gentler attributes, such as relaxation, humour, tolerance, diversity, style or a concern with aesthetic values. They were almost ferociously solemn and contemptuous of any order or convention in dress, habits or amenities. But they knew how to unite ideas with action and to translate freedom into creative growth.

At first it seemed to the Zionists that the world war in 1914 was more likely to liquidate their dream than give it new energy. Zionism was a voluntary movement dependent on widely scattered communities. It could only breathe freely in a world of open communications. Yet now the various sections of the movement in Europe were cut off from each other, and all of them were sundered from Palestine.

In the event, it was the war that carried the idea of a Jewish State into the life and law of the international community. In a brilliant exercise of sustained persuasion and influence, a small group of Zionists in England, led by Chaim Weizmann, induced the British Government in 1917 to publish a declaration 'viewing with favour the establishment in Palestine of a National Home for the Jewish people'. This declaration, issued by the Foreign Secretary, Arthur James Balfour, had the support of the United States and would later be endorsed by the other Powers. On the first day of Hannuka 1917, when British troops, under Field Marshal Allenby, entered Jerusalem, his armies included three Jewish battalions of the Jewish Legion, formed by volunteers from British, American, Canadian and Palestinian Jewry. At the San Remo Conference in 1920, the Balfour Declaration was ratified by the Allied Powers. Prime Minister Lloyd George sent Weizmann on his way with the words:

above Members of the Poalei Zion movement in Pinsk, 1900
below, left Jewish pioneers working in the vineyards of Rishon
le-Zion (1910), one of the first settlements founded with the aid of
Baron Edmond de Rothschild
below, right Eliezer Ben Yehuda (1858–1922), who devoted his life
to the renascence of the Hebrew language

'Now you have your State. It is up to you to win the race.' Two years later the Balfour Declaration was embodied in a Mandate of the League of Nations entrusting Britain with the government of the country.

In later years, when many complex problems crowded in, it became the fashion to say that Zionists in the early Weizmann era suffered from two illusions: they convinced themselves, without reason, that a 'National Home' inevitably meant a sovereign state; and they failed to grasp the ominous consequences of Arab opposition. In each case the judgment is too harsh. When the British tutelage began, Zionists had a very clear conception of what it was meant to achieve. The authors of the Balfour Declaration and the Mandate envisaged that an autonomous, distinctive Jewish society would evolve until it was strong enough to establish an independent government. It was also believed, not unreasonably, that since Arab nationalism was going to win lavish gains in the main centres of Arabism, it would accommodate itself to an independent Jewish neighbour. The British Royal Commission in 1937, having examined the documents, stated clearly that the plan was for the Mandate to be succeeded by Jewish statehood, and that if the Arabs 'secured their big Arab State outside Palestine, they would concede little Palestine to the Jews'.

The slogan was 'Arabia for the Arabs, Judea for the Jews'. This was not mere wishful thinking. It seemed very real when, in June 1918, Weizmann met the acknowledged leader of Arab nationalism, the Emir Feisal, later to be King of Iraq, and in 1919 drew up with him an agreement on Arab-Jewish co-operation. It was destined never to be carried out, but it embodied the central morality on the basis of which Zionists constructed their vision of Arab-Israeli relations.

It should be remembered that the main objective of Arab nationalism was to secure a promise of independence over a very large area, which then embraced Syria, Iraq and the Arabian Peninsula. Palestine had fallen to the Arabs in 634–6 and remained under the rule of the caliphs for four centuries, before being conquered by the Crusaders and, in the sixteenth century, by the Ottoman Turks. Thus, ever since the sixteenth century it had been under non-Arab rule. That Palestine was not like other Middle Eastern territories in its relationship to Arab history was implicit in the attitude of Arab leaders after the First World War. The Arabs of Syria and Iraq demanded full independence. About Palestine, the Arab leaders were, for a time, open to compromise. Their main task was to secure the promise of independence in those territories whose Arab character and connections were unreserved. Feisal, son of Hussein, King of the Hejaz, who led the Arab cause at the Peace Conference, was uncompromising in his demand for independence in purely Arab lands. When he looked at Palestine he seemed to grasp the historic forces which had shaped its destiny. His meeting with Weizmann near Aqaba in 1918 led to the first and only understanding ever recorded between leaders of the two national movements. Later, after talks with Jewish leaders in London, Feisal issued a statement which was published in *The Times* of 12 December 1918:

> The two main branches of the semitic family, Arabs and Jews, understand one another and I hope that as a result of the interchange of ideas at the Peace Conference each nation will make definite progress towards the realization of its aspirations. Arabs are not jealous of Zionist Jews and intend to give them fair play, but the Zionist Jews have assured the nationalist Arabs of their intention to see that they too have fair play in their respective areas.

Thus the British Royal Commission was not exaggerating when it said: 'If King Hussein and Emir Feisal secured their big Arab State . . . they would concede little Palestine to the Jews.'

The hour of grace was poignantly short. The Arabs did not 'secure their big Arab State'. They therefore declined to 'concede little Palestine to the Jews'. Britain dominated Iraq, and France expelled Feisal from Damascus. Savage disappointment gripped the Arab national movement. It now made its unequivocal claim for the complete liberation of Syria, its union with Palestine and opposition to the Jewish National Home, and Feisal's vision was allowed to perish. Arab nationalism and Zionism were henceforth locked in mortal combat.

Nor was Arab opposition the only challenge to harass the Zionists after the war. Their relations with the British mandatory power deteriorated sharply. The British authorities in Palestine rapidly pushed the Balfour Declaration and Mandate into the background of their concern. For a time, the policy of the Jewish leadership in Palestine and of the Zionist movement was one of unrequited goodwill towards the mandatory power. It was still hoped that Britain, nudged and prodded by world opinion, could be persuaded to fulfil its obligations. This conviction became steadily undermined. Relations between Britain and the Zionists became increasingly tense. They were to reach a breaking point with the White Paper of 1939, which drastically limited Jewish immigration and land settlement and proposed, in effect, to hand the country over after ten years to the 'mercies' of an Arab Government.

The White Paper of 1939 was not a sudden enactment. It was the climax

of a long series of political and administrative acts whereby Britain first cut
down the area in which the Jewish National Home could develop; then
limited the right of Jews to purchase land; thereafter subjected immigration
to cruel restrictions, even in times of Jewish agony in Europe; and ultimately
developed ideas of self-government which would make the Jews a minority
under Arab rule. A brief and exceptional act of vision came in 1937 with the
Royal Commission's report proposing the partition of Palestine into Jewish
and Arab States. The commission had understood the central fact: Jews and
Arabs in Palestine were not pursuing common aims or striving for common
ends. The choice, therefore, was either to subordinate one to the other or to
create a framework of separate sovereignty for each. Official Britain recoiled
from this wisdom and courage. The partition concept was jettisoned in surrender to Arab pressures. But its central logic was inexorable; and it was to
come to life a decade later.

When all is remembered, written, appreciated or regretted, the period of
the British Mandate stands out in Israeli memory as a phase of substantive
advance towards Jewish independence. Immigration ebbed and flowed in
accordance with the vagaries of the Jewish position in Europe and in conformity with whatever could be done to overcome British obstruction. But
by the end of 1947 the Jews numbered 650,000, which was thirty per cent of the
population. The National Home was developing its economic strength. Its
main foundation was agriculture; but, especially during the Second World
War, impetus was given to industrial progress. One of the most fruitful Jewish
achievements during the Mandate years was the construction of an educational
system controlled by the Jewish community, extending from kindergarten
through secondary schools, and culminating in university institutions at a
higher level of excellence than would be normal in a society and economy
of its size.

  As the Mandate ebbed away in the late 1940's, after three decades, it could be
said that the Jews had neither wasted their opportunities nor fully used them.
They had created something which, in the relative scale of Middle Eastern
strength, was solid and had to be taken into account. What they had built was
a nation in every sense and, indeed, a state in everything but name. The leadership of this enterprise was solidly vested in the magnetic Chaim Weizmann,
whose bearing and personality also contributed to the aura of imminent
sovereignty. He insisted on other governments behaving towards him as
though he were already President of a sovereign state equal in stature to theirs.
He and they knew that this was not strictly true; but something in his presence,

Dr Chaim Weizmann, by the Israeli artist Meron Sima (1945).
The leader of the Zionist cause from the Balfour Declaration (1917)
until statehood, Weizmann was elected Israel's first President

and in their own historic imagination, forbade them to break the spell.

The British administration and forces were sometimes lukewarm about defending Jewish lives against Arab attacks. Likewise, it was not predictable that they would stay forever. In the mandatory years the Jews of Palestine developed a shield on which their lives and fortunes were to depend. The Haganah was formed in 1920 at a conference of the main wing of the labour movement which also adopted measures reorganizing the movement in conformity with new needs. The problem of defence now became a responsibility of the Jewish leadership, together with its other tasks in economic, political and cultural development. The vision was of a citizen army; the Haganah was rigidly subservient to the civil authority provided by the Jewish Agency. From a handful of guards who went out at night to watch over the fields, the new organization would grow into an important instrument in shaping Palestine's political destiny. Three major undertakings, settlement, immigration and physical protection, would have been impossible without it. The Israel Defence Forces would later spring from its loins.

The society created between the two world wars was a source of pride for the Jewish people and an arresting and original spectacle for the world. Here, and only here, the Jews faced history in their own authentic image as Jews and nothing else; they were not a marginal gloss on other societies. A people's national attributes were all reflected on a miniature scale, but in growing completeness. The driving force was the quest for identity. The ideals and priorities of Palestinian Jewry were collective, not individual. What mattered was a man's service to the growing nation, not his prowess in self-advancement. Life was earnest, austere, responsible, resolute, effervescent, somewhat irrational and – to strangers – a little self-conscious in its enthusiasm. Every first tree, road, street, settlement, school, library, orchestra, university was ecstatically celebrated. The Jewish people was living at last with the taste of creativity. But the White Paper, as the fruit of Arab hostility and British alienation, warned them that time was running out, and the ring was closing in. There was little chance of gradual evolution. The agonies of the Second World War would set the stage for the final eruption into statehood. What compelled the transition was not any constitutional impatience from within, but the danger from outside. The approaching war and holocaust would create the revolutionary hour. It was no longer possible to work and wait.

'There is darkness all around us and we cannot see through the clouds.' Chaim Weizmann's voice faltered as he closed the Twenty-first Zionist Congress at

Mementos of the period of austerity in the early 1950's, including various types of ration cards and (in lower right-hand corner) a sticker proclaiming 'I do not buy on the black market'

Geneva on 24 August 1939. Less than two weeks later the clouds had burst; but the darkness was even deeper than before. The imminent war spelled misery for many nations; for the Jewish people it threatened a vast havoc without precedent in recorded history. Nor was there any prospect of shelter from the coming storm. A few months before, the Chamberlain Government had published its White Paper on Palestine, which would turn the Jewish National Home into a ghetto with locked doors – a pale of settlement under Arab rule. But now the Jewish disaster was merged with the universal tragedy. As the Nazi columns prepared to fall on Europe and tear it limb from limb, an immense and seemingly inexorable danger menaced every Jewish home.

There was some hope that Britain, facing a danger from the same enemy as that which confronted the Jewish people, would at least modify some of the severities of the White Paper. In London and Jerusalem, the Jewish Agency offered Palestinian Jewish manpower and economic resources for the prosecution of the war. In May 1939 relations between the British Government and the Jewish population had taken an ugly turn: the publication of the White Paper was followed by a general strike and mass demonstrations in all Jewish towns and villages. It was then that the first seed of resistance was planted; the Haganah formed a special unit to attack telephone lines, railroads and other government property if the repression became too severe. The

above The Twenty-first Zionist Congress (1939) was held in the shadow of the impending world war. Here delegates receive news of the Molotov-Ribbentrop Pact

outbreak of the war halted this momentum; but the pause brought no relief to Jewish hopes. Britain still nourished illusions of Arab support in the war and was resolved to implement the White Paper in all its rigour. When the number of refugees sailing to Palestine from Nazi-occupied Europe over-reached the meagre immigration quota, the British Government decided to deport them. In November 1940 the *Patria*, with 1,700 people aboard, was about to be forced to sail for Mauritius when it was sabotaged by the Haganah to prevent its departure. In February 1942 the *Struma*, carrying refugees from Rumania, was turned back by the Turkish authorities after the British Government had made it clear that the immigrants would not be allowed to set foot in Palestine. The ship sank in the Black Sea, and 770 refugees lost their lives; there was only one survivor.

The British Government also enacted the Land Transfer Regulations forbidding Jewish settlement in the greater part of the country. Yet the war was against Hitler; and there could be only one Jewish response. In Ben Gurion's words: 'We shall fight the war as if there were no White Paper, and we shall fight the White Paper as if there were no war.' In a spectacular volun-tary mobilization, 136,000 Palestinian Jews reported for service under British command. The offer was not so much rejected as evaded; and the British Government began to harry the Haganah. Searches for arms were carried out in many Jewish settlements. Simultaneously, the Jewish Agency was negotiating vigorously in London for the establishment of a Jewish Division. This opportunity was also turned down.

In 1942, when there was danger of a German inundation of all British positions in the Middle East, there were some brief episodes of British-Jewish cooperation. But when the tide of war ebbed at the end of 1942, the conflict between the British Government and the Palestinian Jews was sharpened. For political and military convenience, the British Government had sponsored the establishment of an Arab League, in which all Arab states participated, and which, at its first conference, pledged its members to defend the rights of Palestinian Arabs. Simultaneously, Winston Churchill was promising Weizmann that when the war was won he would bring his country's policy back into conformity with the Balfour Declaration. In November 1944 a British Cabinet committee was actually discussing a plan for partition, es-tablishing a Jewish State roughly in much of the area envisaged by the Peel Report of 1937.

The possibility of a favourable turn in British policy seemed to revive again in 1944, when Winston Churchill instructed the Ministry of War to accede to Dr Weizmann's request for the establishment of a Jewish Brigade Group consisting of Jewish infantry, artillery and surface units from Palestine. Yet, with supreme paradox, the government intensified its campaign against the very Haganah from which the reservoir of Jewish fighters was being drawn.

Yet what plunged Palestinian Jewry into its most profound anguish was the horrifying news that began to reach it in 1943 of the Jewish holocaust in Europe. At first the ears refused to hear and the mind to believe the stupendous nature of the catastrophe. But there were too many witnesses coming out of Europe to allow any comforting illusion to persist. The facts were hideous, but inescapable: millions of Jews – men, women and children in the Jewish communities of Nazi-occupied Europe, all the way from Norway to Greece, and especially in the densely populated Jewish centres in Poland, Rumania and the Soviet Union – were being herded like cattle into railway trucks, shipped off to special camps and there simply destroyed like useless rubbish. In those days, to be a Jew in Europe meant that a man would be dragged out of his home, put into a cattle truck with thousands of others, deported to a distant camp, separated from his family, beaten and humiliated for a few days, weeks or months of forced labour, after which his emaciated, wrecked and shambling body would be dispatched into a gas chamber, where he would be scientifically asphyxiated, his hair shaven off to make mattresses, his bones crushed and melted down to make soap. The gold fillings from his teeth would be assembled to sustain the declining German war effort. In the meantime, his wife and children would be submitted to similar agonies, tortures and murders in specially constructed camps. Particularly unbelievable, yet patently true, was the fact that a million Jewish children were being flung into furnaces and burned to death. Years after, mountains of their little shoes would be preserved in museums to testify that the inhumanity of man had no finite limit.

Not even this convulsive and revolutionary event had any effect on the British bureaucracy in Palestine, which continued to woo an Arab world that had, for the most part, taken sides with Britain's adversaries. There was intense sympathy with the Jewish plight in London, where, in a moment unprecedented in parliamentary history, the House of Commons was brought to its feet in silent mourning for European Jews. But together with this there was a relentless assault on the Jewish National Home, which was clearly the only Jewish hope of refuge and asylum.

To make matters worse, it took only a few weeks after the end of the war for the Jewish leaders to become convinced that even victory against Nazism would not bring automatic relief to its primary victims. Great hope had been

Although six million Jews went to their death in Nazi-occupied Europe, there were pockets of brave resistance, as symbolized in Ben Shahn's representation of the Warsaw Ghetto uprising

Ben Shahn

placed in Churchill and Roosevelt, who then bestrode the world's scene with colossal power. Within a few months of the Allied victory against Germany, Roosevelt had died and Churchill was removed from power. True, the Labour Party that formed the government in Britain was strongly committed to a pro-Zionist policy; but on 13 November 1945 the Foreign Secretary, Ernest Bevin, revealed an aspect of British political nature that many believed could not exist. He announced the intention to carry out the White Paper restricting Jewish immigration to a mere trickle; and, to add insult to injury, he warned that if Jewish victims of Nazism tried 'to push themselves to the head of the queue' for salvation, they would evoke anti-Semitism. Their best mission, in his obtuse view, would be 'to contribute their talents to the reconstruction of Europe'. Now Europe had quite simply exterminated the Jews, who had no taste for 'reconstructing' their executioner. With a fine disregard of Britain's own need for American support, Bevin insultingly turned down a proposal by President Truman for the admission of 100,000 Jewish displaced persons into Palestine. 'They want to be evacuated now', President Truman's emissary, Earl Harrison, had said. 'Palestine is definitely and pre-eminently the first choice; only there will they be welcome and find peace and quiet and be given an opportunity to live and work.'

In an effort to associate the United States with his repressive policy, Bevin sponsored the appointment of an Anglo-American Committee to report on the situation in Palestine and make recommendations. To Bevin's chagrin, the committee unanimously recommended the admission of 100,000 immigrants into Palestine at once, as well as the removal of the anti-Jewish land restrictions. It proposed that, for the time being, no statehood would be granted either to Jews or Arabs. Bevin rejected even this compromise and went on with the disarming of the Jewish population. Thus the Labour Government dispelled the hopes of rescue which the Anglo-American Report had raised in the hearts of tens of thousands of Jewish refugees.

The accumulated bitterness in Jewish hearts burst at the Zionist Congress in Basle in December 1946, the last which the great Weizmann attended. Its members were torn between a deep affection for his person and a conviction that his name symbolized a policy which both they and he no longer upheld. The truth was that their resentment against Britain was as nothing compared with his. But a statesman sometimes remains a symbol of an attitude long after the attitude itself has passed away. The Zionist movement emerged without Weizmann at its head and with no successor to the presidency; and 1946 became a year of overt warfare between the British mandatory government and the Jewish resistance forces. Meanwhile, the British people was becoming increasingly impatient with a commitment of wealth and manpower in Palestine. It disliked having its soldiers killed and killing others for no evident need or cause. There was a mood of disengagement. On 2 April 1947 a historic turning-point came with Britain's submission of the Palestine question to the UN General Assembly.

The United Nations was still an unknown factor in world politics, and Jewish prospects seemed dubious. The scales were heavy against the prospect of Jewish success. The Arab League, after all, had five fully sovereign members in the General Assembly, whose membership then numbered fifty-seven. Other Moslem states would certainly rally to its cause. There was no reason to expect a departure by the Soviet Union from its traditional anti-Zionist doctrine. Britain would certainly exercise its influence on West European and Commonwealth delegations. Nevertheless, the Jews could feel that their problem had been internationalized and that their diplomacy could now be deployed in a broader arena than that in which British interests decided every issue.

At this point, Jewish political fortunes took an unexpected upward turn. The United Nations was then still conscious of its original identity as an anti-Nazi alliance. There was an innate sympathy for the Jewish leaders who gravely presented the spectacle of their people's plight and its aspiration for a

The British created heavily defended security areas to protect their major installations, such as the area in central Jerusalem nicknamed 'Bevingrad' by the Jews after British Foreign Minister Bevin

new birth of freedom. A full hearing was granted to the Jewish Agency in the
Political Committee of the General Assembly in April 1947, thus auguring a
future international recognition of Jewish nationhood. A special committee
(UNSCOP) was appointed to deal with the Palestine question. Against
strong Arab opposition, the committee decided to link its investigation with
a careful study of the situation of the displaced persons in Europe. And the
major break-through for Zionism, in April 1947, was a cautious statement
by the Soviet Union abandoning a long ideological tradition to hint at the
possibility of support for an independent Jewish State.

On 1 September 1947 an important milestone was reached: a majority
of UNSCOP suggested a partition scheme establishing a Jewish State in the
Upper Jordan and Beisan valleys, the Valley of Jezreel, the coastal plain and
the Negev. Zionism had not known a similar political victory since the days
of the Balfour Declaration itself. The scope of the proposal, and the international authority behind it, even eclipsed the Royal Commission Report
of 1937 as a decisive verdict in favour of Jewish national independence in
Palestine.

It was an important turning-point, for the time being, no more. It was
clear that if the committee had rejected the case for Jewish statehood, the
United Nations would never adopt a favourable recommendation. Now
that the committee advocated the establishment of a Jewish State, there was
a chance – but no more than a chance – that the General Assembly would add
its endorsement. Political activity on behalf of a Jewish State now shifted to
the General Assembly in New York. By mid-October it was clear that both
American and Soviet support for the majority report could be expected.
On 29 November 1947 the General Assembly adopted its Resolution for the
Partition of Palestine. The vote was 33 to 13, with 10 abstentions. The majority
included the United States, the Soviet Union, many European countries,
most of the Latin American countries and the four members of the British
Commonwealth. Britain, on whose initiative the United Nations had taken
up the Palestine question, abstained.

A wave of joy swept through Palestinian Jewry when the news came. But
the jubilation was short-lived. The Palestinian Arabs and the Arab states had
threatened that they would set the resolution aside by violence. Their action
was true to their words. The morning after the General Assembly voted on
the partition resolution, the Arab Higher Committee announced a general
strike, and Arab mobs burned and looted in Jerusalem. It was clear that the
UN resolution was all very well, but that Jewish independence, if it was to be
secured at all, would be bought with a heavy price of blood.

As Jewish leaders in Palestine and abroad surveyed the scene, their future decision seemed almost to be compelled by events. Dark in their recent memory were the ashes of millions of their kinsmen; the uncomprehending screams of Jewish children in Nazi torture chambers; the knowledge that Jews beyond number had been slaughtered with a brutality that, in most civilized countries, would not have been shown even to the lowest animals. And on another plane of recollection was Palestinian Jewry's own ordeal and the knowledge that the toil and dreams and sacrifices that had gone into its making must now either be lost from history or be ratified by larger sacrifice and higher dreams. There were many cautious voices above the din of surrounding violence, counselling them to hold back and put their dwindling trust in something beyond themselves. The cold fear that a declaration of Jewish statehood would invite a massacre that might otherwise be avoided had gripped some men and governments favourable to the Jewish cause; and within the Jewish camp there were those who feared the result of liberating the outside world from all responsibility for the Jewish fate. Restraining voices were even heard in the Jewish labour movement, which then, and thereafter, had the central voice. But the majority, rallied by Ben Gurion and spurred on from afar with unwonted impatience by the aging, but indomitable, Weizmann, was convinced that if the sun set on 15 May without the renewal of Jewish independence, it would never rise again.

What a long, weary and blood-drenched Jewish journey it had been across the infinities of space and time since the nation had first been born under that very sky! There had been the generations in which kings and prophets flourished, and then the seemingly final end, when Jerusalem crumbled before the legions of Titus Vespasian. And across all the intervening centuries the beat of Jewish hearts had everywhere been quickened by the prospect of the return! Now the hour of choice had come, imminent and implacable. And, no matter how it fell, something of great moment would be enacted of which future Jewish generations would never cease to speak and dream.

So 14 May 1948, dawned, bright and clear, with opportunity shimmering in the spring air. It had been a long road back; but now the old journey had ended and a new one would begin. No wonder that a silence, full of awe, sat heavy on the museum hall until the last words of the proclamation died away:

> With trust in Almighty God, we set our hands to this Declaration . . . in the City of Tel Aviv, on this the Fifth Day of Iyar . . . the Fourteenth Day of May, One Thousand Nine Hundred and Forty-Eight . . .

3

The War of Independence

*This is not the first time that
the Arab States, which organized
the invasion of Palestine, have
ignored a decision of the Security
Council or of the General Assembly.*

Mr Andrei Gromyko Head
of the Delegation of the USSR
in the Security Council,
29 May 1948

'Any line drawn by the United Nations will be nothing but a line of blood and fire.' The Arab representative who made this declaration in November 1947 knew what he was saying. Within a few days the partition resolution had been adopted; and a week later scores of Jews had been killed. It was brutally clear that the Jews would not have their State 'awarded' to them or 'established' by international decree. The United Nations resolution had stark limitations. It had contributed decisively to the British departure. It had exalted Jewish morale. It had given advance legitimacy to a Jewish State that would arise by its own responsibility and sacrifice. But it gave no assurance of survival.

So Israel would not owe the debt of its existence to the outside world. This fact was to shape the national mentality for years to come. The memory of having won birth and survival by a lonely decision would work on Israel's life and policy in many ways. The War of Independence would be invoked in the future both as a summons to national unity and as a warning against giving inflated importance to pressures or restraints from outside. This applied, in particular, to the United Nations, which appeared to Israelis very much like the alligator, which, according to the zoologists, gives birth to its young with great tenderness and then devours them with calm apathy. Self-reliance

During the early hours of 22 February 1948, Arab terrorists,
together with two British Army deserters, blew up several
buildings on Ben Yehuda Street, Jerusalem, killing 54 people

became the inevitable posture for a people for whom nobody outside would risk any blood, even when destruction stared it in the face. The loneliness of the ordeal enhanced Israel's sense of sovereignty and rescued it from the atmosphere of tutelage surrounding its political struggle in early days.

What became known as Israel's War of Independence was, in fact, more than five months old when independence was declared. Its first phase had begun on 2 December 1947, with the murder of Jews in Jerusalem, and took its course to the end of the British Mandate and the establishment of the state on 14 May 1948. The second phase came with the invasion of Palestine by the armies of neighbouring Arab countries on 15 May and reached its military end with the Egyptian acceptance of armistice negotiations on 7 January 1949.

In the first phase, the assault had been waged by the Arabs of Palestine, reinforced by volunteers from neighbouring Arab countries under the command of Fawzi el-Kawakji and the direction of the Arab League. The volunteers called themselves the Army of Liberation, but they liberated nobody and would leave the Palestine Arabs with no reason to call them blessed. Arrayed against them were Jewish units consisting mainly of the Haganah, whose striking force was the four battalions of the Palmach Commando Units, with about 2,100 members and 1,000 reservists. In addition, there was the Chel Sadeh (field army), consisting of about 1,800 full-time members and 10,000 reservists. The Haganah could also count on the Chel Hamishmar (garrison army) with 32,000 members, many of whom were tied down to the defence of their areas of abode in villages and cities. Finally, there was the Gadna, made up of youngsters being trained for auxiliary tasks with the ambition of joining the Palmach. Apart from the Haganah, and not always acting in concert with it, were two smaller resistance groups: the Irgun Zvai Leumi, composed of 5,000 men; and the Lochamei Herut Israel (Lechi), with about 1,000 men. The IZL and Lechi functioned as independent military organizations. It was only in the later stages of the war that they merged their membership with the Haganah into the broad stream of the Israel Defence Forces.

Jewish manpower was meagre and the weaponry pathetically inadequate. It consisted at first of rifles and light and medium machine-guns, with no artillery or air support. In the beginning there was a primitive structure of command and organization which only evolved into an orderly pattern towards the end of the war.

As Jewish dead piled up in December, it seemed that the threshold of statehood would never be crossed. The Jews were on the defensive. Arab forces surged around them with impressive vigour, attacking their isolated settlements, as well as the Jewish sectors of the cities with mixed populations. There was no particular territorial ambition in the Arab assault; the aim was simply to shed a great deal of blood and thus illustrate the vulnerability of Jewish lives and population centres and mock the idea that a Jewish State could arise against the Arab will. Moreover, geography was not neutral. The Arabs inhabited and controlled most of the high ground and arteries of communication. They were in a good position to inflict casualties on Jewish civilians and cut Jewish population areas off from contact with each other.

The war was certainly not going to respect the frontiers recommended by the General Assembly. Indeed, it was in the area allotted to the Jews that the Arab assault was most fierce. The first effort of Jewish forces was to retain thirty-three settlements which, under the partition map, would have been included in the Arab State. For each of these villages the Arab forces made a desperate bid; they were defended with equal desperation.

A major target of the Arab attack was the Etzion Bloc, south-east of Jerusalem. The assault was repelled; but the population of Etzion, cut off from any sustaining proximity of their fellow Jews, was in constant need of arms and supplies. On 17 January 1948 thirty-five young men of the Palmach and the Chel Sadeh on their way to reinforce the Etzion settlements were ambushed and killed by Arab forces in the area. Their bodies were savagely mutilated; the Arabs would not even give the Jews the decent dignities of death.

Yet despite their numerical advantage, the Arab forces were not able to capture a single Jewish settlement in the first phase of the war. They turned in frustration to attacks on Jewish quarters in the cities, especially in Haifa and Jerusalem. Soon outlying quarters in Jerusalem were isolated from the centre of the city, and orderly traffic to and within the city came to a halt. The major successes of Arab forces in this phase lay in their ability to isolate suburbs and villages by occupying main arteries of traffic. By the end of March their strategy seemed to be succeeding. The Negev was cut off from the centre of the country; Jerusalem was isolated from the coast; and the villages of western Galilee had no contact with other areas of Jewish population.

No wonder that military strategists and political observers across the world grew sceptical of Jewish prospects; and their appraisal found immediate reflection in the political climate. It was now that the original supporters of partition began to waver, and the search for alternative solutions began. All of these would have meant an indefinite postponement of Israel's statehood. Israeli leaders could have no doubt that their political fortunes would remain bleak unless they could reverse the military tide.

April was the month of counter-attack. The Haganah rallied its forces and

took the initiative with the aim of consolidating its hold on all the areas assigned
to the Jewish State by the partition resolution. Another objective was to prepare
the defence against a probable invasion by neighbouring Arab armies, and,
especially, to unite the fragmented Jewish community by establishing continuous lines of communication.

All this time the main accent was placed heavily on Jerusalem. It was vital
to open the road joining the city to the coast. To this end 'Operation Nachshon'
was conceived. The aim was to secure a corridor to Jerusalem which would
enable free movement in and out of the city. This, in turn, necessitated the
capture of several Arab villages lying along the corridor. Some of the battles,
such as that at Kastel, took a heavy toll of blood. To this day, the traveller on the
road between Jerusalem and Tel Aviv can see the charred remains of half-tracks
and armoured vehicles lying along the roadside in mute but eloquent testimony
to the cost of Jerusalem's lifeline. Young men by the scores were shrivelled and
lacerated to death within these burning infernos.

'Operation Nachshon' came to successful fulfilment on 6 April, when
the first convoy of vehicles bearing supplies entered Jerusalem. It was an
achievement which went far towards allaying the grief of a bereaved community and the toll of a sorely pressed army.

The Haganah was emerging from a fortress mentality. It was learning to
do more than merely rebuff Arab attacks. The Jews no longer waited for the
enemy to come and put his fingers on their throat. Operations using complex
technical methods and sweeping waves of movement were now attempted in
areas outside Jerusalem. Tiberias was captured on 18 April, and a rapid encir-
cling operation caused Haifa to fall on 24 April. Most of Haifa's seventy
thousand Arabs fled to Lebanon on the encouragement of their leaders in
Beirut, who were confident that they would return when the Arab armies
captured the whole of Palestine. It was incontestably in Haifa that Jewish
leaders made their most strenuous efforts to preserve the hope of coexistence
by keeping the Arab population intact. But the flight went on. At first sight
it seemed an advantage for the Arabs to have somewhere to go. In a deeper
sense, the possibility of escape became the source of their weakness. Those who
have nowhere to flee cling most tenaciously to their ground. This was the
Jewish strength.

With Tiberias and Haifa in their hands, the Haganah leaders were now able
to reinforce the Jewish units in Upper Galilee, especially in Safed and Rosh
Pinah, and to take Arab villages in that area. Tel Aviv, the centre of Israel's
strength, had been under constant harassment from neighbouring Jaffa, which
would have surrendered to the Haganah in mid-April had not the British forces

The Haifa oil refineries ablaze in March 1947. During the war
all but 3,000 of the Arab inhabitants of Haifa left, believing the
Mufti's promise that they would return in a few days

intervened. It had since become a thorn in Tel Aviv's vulnerable flesh. The
battle for supremacy went on from 26 April to 13 May, when the British
forces left and the Arabs in Jaffa laid down their arms.

But the priority of Jewish concern returned again and again to Jerusalem.
It was always to be Israel's most sensitive nerve. It was plain that when the
British Army moved out it would be hard to ensure physical security within
the city. So the Harel Brigade was transferred from the Jerusalem corridor to
the city's centre. This move encouraged the Arabs to seek control of the city's
western approaches and force Jewish Jerusalem into isolation again. The
Haganah fought desperately to restore communications with outlying
settlements. Some of these strongholds were taken and held, but access to
Jerusalem remained fragile and sporadic.

It had been a strange war so far, with no fronts and few demarcations between
armies and civilians. Scores of Jews, mostly civilians, had been murdered
in the week after the partition resolution. The tide of blood never seemed
to stop. On 31 December thirty Jews at the Haifa oil refineries were murdered by Arab workers. On 22 February 1948 more than fifty Jews were
killed when a car on Jerusalem's Ben Yehuda Street, laden with dynamite,
exploded in mid-morning. On 11 March thirteen Jews were killed and forty
injured by a bomb in the courtyard of the Jewish Agency. In March international pessimism about Jewish fortunes came mainly from this exposure of
ordinary citizens to death and mutilation. Some weeks later, the Arab civilian
population began to suffer from the mounting virulence of the combat. On
9 April a combined IZL and Lechi force captured the village of Dir Yassin

and killed over 250 men, women and children. The Jewish Agency as well as several other official bodies expressed their execration of a deed which, in their view, went beyond the intrinsic savagery of war and cast a needless cloud on the honour of the military struggle. On 13 April Arab forces attacked a convoy of doctors, nurses and medical teachers on their way to the Hadassah Medical Centre on Mount Scopus, leaving seventy-seven dead behind. This was plain vandalism. The feeling that the war to prevent the rise of Israel would be a war of populations, not of armies, had its part in stimulating the flight from Arab centres, in some cases without the refugees having heard a single shot.

On Independence Day the Jewish condition, though still fragile, had a more robust look than could have been imagined six weeks before. Haifa, Safed, Tiberias and Acre had been secured. About a hundred Arab villages had fallen. Jewish Jerusalem had survived and was not completely severed from neighbouring settlements. The Arab Liberation Army and Kawakji's forces had been routed in the north. All Galilee, both east and west, was under Jewish control. The Jewish position was less stable in the Negev, but at least the roads were open; and the Jewish forces everywhere had been strengthened by the mobilization of manpower and by shipments of Czech rifles. There were now 50,000 armed men in the field, with IZL and Lechi under Haganah command everywhere and maintaining independence of action only in Jerusalem. A rough-and-ready artillery unit had been built up around veterans of the Second World War. Palestinian Jewish manpower was being replenished and encouraged by the arrival of Jewish volunteers (Machal) from abroad. These were especially crucial in training pilots for the minuscule air force. Even a small navy had been put together and manned mostly by Jewish volunteers from abroad. Thus the Jewish leaders could well celebrate their wisdom in not having been tempted to cut their losses by defeatist solutions when military fortunes had temporarily been at a low point in March.

If the issue were now to be drawn between Israel and Palestinian Arabs with their 'Liberation Armies', the prospects of Jewish victory would have seemed high. But, of course, everybody knew that this was not the issue. The context of the war was now going to change. Compared with the improvised Jewish forces and Arab bands in Palestine, the Arab armies poised to sweep down on Israel had a professional and formidable look. If they had not marched off the parade ground onto the battlefield, they would have preserved an impressive military reputation.

Indeed, the second phase of the war, which opened with the invasion by Arab armies, seemed at first to bode ill for Israel's cause. The first danger

Degania, the first kibbutz (est. 1909), preserves parts of its proud history. During the War of Independence, Syrian tanks broke through the kibbutz perimeter, where their advance was halted

came from the north, where Syrian, Lebanese, Iraqi and Jordanian armies planned to move on Haifa and capture its port and refineries. Meanwhile, the Egyptians attacked along the coast, while the remnants of the Arab Liberation Army harassed Jerusalem and carried out assaults on Jewish settlements in the rest of the country.

The struggle would have had a different outcome if all this Arab activity, much of it intense and all of it sustained by superior numbers, had been better organized. The disruptive elements in Arab life and politics prevented any unified command from coming into existence. An Arab tendency of individualism and dispersal of energies was to stand Israel in good stead in many future ordeals.

The Syrian attack on the north began in real gravity on 16 May. By 20 May Syrian forces had captured several settlements and had reached the gates of Kibbutz Degania. Another Syrian column was advancing in eastern Galilee towards Mishmar Hayarden. Degania has a symbolic as well as a physical significance for the Israeli farming communities in the north. It is the 'flagship' of the kibbutz movement, and dire results to morale would have ensued from its fall. With the aid of a few light field guns, which had hardly been unpacked the day before, the kibbutz members repelled the Syrian attack.

But there was other cause for worry in the northern and central sectors. The Iraqi army entered Palestine in the area of Kibbutz Gesher, at Kaukab el-Hawa. Having failed to capture this area, it concentrated its efforts on seizing the Arab triangle: Nablus, Jenin, Tulkarem. A success for the Transjordan Arab Legion was achieved by the capture of installations of the Palestine Electric Corporation on 14 May. It was now evident that the Arab war against Israel had a latent level of inter-Arab rivalry. There was a jockeying for positions about who would capture what and how the corpse of the Jewish National Home would be carved up. The frank hope of the Iraqi and Transjordanian forces was to secure the triangle area and then advance into the coastal plain so as to get there before the Egyptians. But from mid-May the chief brunt of the Israeli danger came in Jerusalem. On 19 May the Arab Legion isolated Mount Scopus and entered the Old City.

It was a dark moment in Jewish history. There were approximately 2,500 Jews within the walls, and the general fear was that all would be massacred, as Jewish captives had been at the Etzion Bloc. Desperate attempts were made by the Haganah and the IZL to retake the Jewish Quarter. Although an Israeli breakthrough was made at the Zion Gate, the position soon had to be relinquished. In the end, the Old City fell entirely to the Arab Legion, with the Israeli forces holding out in peripheral areas such as Ramat Rachel and the

Tel Aviv, founded in the same year as Degania, has grown
into the country's largest city and Israel's industrial, commercial
and cultural centre

areas around Mandelbaum Gate and Notre Dame. But the future of the city
would be decided not so much by the fighting within it as by the attempt
to cut it off from outside. The gains of 'Operation Nachshon' had by now
largely been annulled and would have to be redeemed by new sacrifice. For
the Arab Legion commanded the coastal road, cutting Jerusalem off from the
rest of the Jewish population and preventing Jewish convoys from bringing
supplies and ammunition to the city. By the end of May it became a serious
possiblity that even the western part of Jerusalem, with its Jewish majority,
would not be able to hold out unless ways were found of opening a lifeline.
While maintaining full pressure on the main coastal route, Jewish forces
attempted to open an alternative line. Working in secrecy, the Haganah
transformed a sandy path winding around the south of Latrun into what was
to be known as the 'Burma Road', and later Kvish Hagevurah – the 'Road
of Heroism'. Jerusalem was almost down to its last gallons of water and loaves
of bread when the first convoys, circumventing the main route, burst triumphantly into the city. On the advance trucks of the convoys were inscribed
in large letters the words: 'If I forget thee, O Jerusalem, may my right hand
forget its cunning'. The Jews of Jerusalem were not forgotten or alone.

New dangers erupted in the south. At first the Egyptian forces achieved no
results even remotely commensurate with their numbers or equipment.
They became more formidable when they tried a dual movement, one
column advancing northwards hugging the coast, the other making for south-

above The advancing Egyptian forces were stopped by a handful of
Negev kibbutzim. Although some were temporarily overcome, in
most places the farmers managed to repulse the attacks

ern Jerusalem, through Beersheba and Hebron. The resistance of the Jewish communal villages, Yad Mordechai, Kfar Darom and Nitzanim, slowed the Egyptian advance. But it had ominously reached Isdud (Ashdod), within 25 miles of Tel Aviv. Indeed, the easterly Egyptian column likewise had little success in capturing Jewish villages; but by seizing some of the cross-roads it was able to prevent the Negev, with its twenty-nine Jewish villages, from maintaining secure connections with the rest of the Jewish territory.

The main battles had been on land, but the outline of a full military structure was now beginning to emerge. The Israeli Air Force was using its reconstructed Messerschmidts in the last days of May and early June to carry out operations in support of the army, as well as to bombard Damascus and Amman and to attack Egyptian troop-carrying ships. And obsolete guns, tied ingenuously onto 'illegal' immigrant boats, were harassing the Egyptians, who would otherwise have had complete command of the coastal seas.

All this time, the Powers and the United Nations had been impotent to prevent the war or influence its course. Indeed, the Arab governments had launched their invasion in direct defiance of a joint American-Soviet position. The notion that small nations always tremble and surrender when Washington and Moscow stand together now suffered its first blow. Washington and Moscow, which at that time agreed about little else in the world, were together in condemning the Arab assault as an act of aggression. Yet the aggression went forward. As the war took its toll, the possibility that both belligerents might soon have an interest in calling a halt stimulated the Security Council to a new effort to affirm its presence. On 20 May Count Folke Bernadotte had been appointed as Mediator for Palestine 'to ensure the maintenance of essential services and the protection of the Holy Places and to promote a peaceful solution to the conflict'. On 24 May the Security Council renewed its call for a cease-fire, which was accepted by Israel but rejected by the Arab states, who still believed that their superior numbers and equipment were only now beginning to have effect. Their position was that they would stop their attack only if its aim was achieved by Israel's consent. If Israel would cancel its independence, the Arabs would stop fighting. The Israeli answer in the Security Council on 16 May had been brief: 'If the Arab states want peace with Israel, they can have it. If they want war – they can have that too. But whether they want peace or war, they can have it only with the State of Israel.'

The reply of the Arab states was contemptuous. But by the second week in June they were having different thoughts. The stark fact was that they had

above The water tower of Kibbutz Be'erot Yitzhak retains the scars of the 1948 war for survival begun with immense advantages, but they had not managed to translate them into effective military success. In the first phase of the war, their only territorial success was the victory of the Arab Legion at the Etzion Bloc. Elsewhere Jewish villages were intact, the 'mixed' towns had been secured by Jewish forces and communications had been weakened but not shattered. In the three weeks since the invasion by Arab armies, the Arab advances had, for the most part, been restricted to areas which Israel did not regard as part of its territory. Arab forces had taken the Old City of Jerusalem and a small area around Sheikh Jarrah. Egyptian forces had only captured three settlements in the Negev, although their presence as far north as Isdud was a source of deep Israeli concern. There had been a slight Syrian advance into Jewish territory, and the Arab Legion had frustrated Israel's attempt to break through at Latrun. But these successes did not add up to the 'Mongol massacre' which the Arabs had planned. Ghengis Khan would certainly not have been satisfied with such meagre results.

The truce negotiated by Count Bernadotte for the Security Council came into effect on 11 June 1948 at 10 a.m. It was to endure for a month. The thirty days that followed were merciful in the absence of blood, but full of alarms for Israel in other fields. The Security Council had laid down the fatuous provision that 'no military advantage should be gained' by either side. Why two belligerents should accept a truce unless each hopes to improve its position seems incomprehensible to ordinary minds. But United Nations rhetoric has a life and style of its own, with little relation to real events outside.

For Israel, the weeks of truce were well used for regrouping and organization. The army had lost its amateur status. Its commanders, drawn mainly from the leaders of the Haganah, with additions from IZL and Lechi, had sworn their allegiance late in May and had emerged from their previous anonymity into a somewhat bashful, uniformed prominence. The Israel Defence Forces were officially constituted by an order of the Provisional Government on 26 May 1948. Ranks were established and all other military organizations became illegal. But the actual situation did not yet reflect the legal monopoly of the Israel Defence Forces. The IZL had denounced the truce and would continue to exist in Jerusalem until that city was ruled by Jews.

The anomaly of a divided military jurisdiction came to a head on 22 June, when the IZL brought a 5,000-ton ship, called the *Altalena* to the coast north of Tel Aviv. On board were 800 immigrants, 250 light machine-guns, 5,000 rifles and much ammunition. The government demanded that the ship be placed under its authority. The IZL refused to comply and insisted on an agreement which would leave a substantial part of the arms in its own possession. In one of his most agonizing decisions, Ben Gurion ordered that force be used by the Palmach Brigade of the Israel Defence Forces to secure the *Altalena's* compliance with governmental orders. There was resistance by IZL units, and fifteen lives were lost on both sides. The *Altalena* went down under heavy mortar fire.

Ben Gurion's action was sustained in the Provisional State Council by a vote of 24 to 4. It is certain that a legacy of bitterness was left behind, and some valuable arms were lost. But in the larger perspective, it may be said that Israeli sovereignty was born that day. There were two issues involved: could the government exercise the effective monopoly of force, which is the primary test of whether a government is a government at all? And was there any reality in international obligations assumed by the Israeli Government, which was then seeking recognition from the world community? Ben Gurion understood that the declaration of 14 May would be a worthless scrap of paper unless a positive answer were given to both these questions.

Another disturbance to Israel's tranquillity came with the publication on 1 July of a report submitted by Count Bernadotte to Israeli and Arab representatives at his headquarters on the island of Rhodes. The report was based on the assumption that a sovereign State of Israel did not yet exist and that the boundaries between a Jewish State and its neighbours could be redrawn by the United Nations. Bernadotte proposed that the areas originally allotted to an Arab State in Palestine be joined to Transjordan, together with the whole of Jerusalem and the Negev. Haifa and Lydda were to be free ports, and the 'Jewish State' would have western Galilee. The Jewish State and Greater Transjordan would have a unified fiscal, military and foreign policy, so that neither would be completely independent. Jewish immigration after two years would be subject to approval by the Economic and Social Council of the United Nations; but Arab refugees would be repatriated and have their property restored.

The plan was rejected by Israel because it gave the Jews too little, and by the Arabs because it gave the Jews too much. After all, it did allow a Jewish State of some sort to exist. Most of the Arab governments also resented the attempt to inflate Transjordan into a state of greater international and regional importance than was objectively warranted or subjectively acceptable. On the other hand, the plan was espoused with suspicious enthusiasm by Britain and, less fervently, by the United States Department of State. Since Transjordan was still a sort of British semi-colony, the plan was open to the suspicion of having been dictated by British strategic interests, to which many Europeans of Bernadotte's generation were traditionally deferential. It was also marked by disrespect towards those governments who had voted for the Partition Plan of 1947 out of authentic conviction. Under this combined acrimony it was destined to fall. But for many years afterwards, 'Bernadottism' lingered on, meaning a tendency to regard Israel's sovereignty as optional and subject to a greater measure of tutelage and external interference than is ever suggested for other states. Israel was no longer prepared to regard itself in any measure as an international ward. Perhaps if the United Nations had done something effective to save Jewish lives and protect Jewish interests after November 1947, its offer of advice might have been more respectfully understood. As things were, the United Nations was bound to appear in the intolerable posture of claiming jurisdiction without accepting either responsibility or sacrifice.

Would the truce be prolonged or terminated when the allotted month came to an end? On 7 July the Security Council called for a renewal. The Arab refusal was adamant. It was inspired by the intuition that if the war were at an end, Israel's independent existence was sufficiently established to become permanent. All that the Arabs could then hope to do would be to restrict its development by the exercise of political and economic pressure. They were not ready to cut their losses. Their aim was 'all or nothing'. Israel was to owe much at every stage of its history to Arab insatiability.

Egypt renewed the fighting on 8 July, the day before the official expiry of the truce. It was the first of many disastrous and suicidal decisions that the Arab leadership was to take in Israel's first quarter century of independence. The Arabs were now to suffer resounding defeats in what was to become known as the 'Ten Day Offensive', and they had put themselves in the wrong with world opinion. They had managed to manoeuvre themselves into the unusual position of an unpopular underdog. Bernadotte himself had said that

The police station of Iraq el-Suweidan was a major stronghold of the Egyptian Army until it was captured by the Palmach, thus restoring communication with the Negev settlements

'a decision to resume fighting would be universally condemned and a party taking such a decision would be assuming a responsibility which will be viewed by the world with the utmost gravity'.

In the next ten days, the Egyptian assault was finally and decisively shattered. Egypt lost over 700 killed, 1,000 wounded and hundreds of prisoners. Israeli forces under Colonel Moshe Dayan swept forward to capture Lydda and Ramle on 11–12 July and to repel a Transjordanian counter-attack inflicting 600 fatal losses. In the north, Colonel Moshe Carmel, long freed from any pressure in Haifa, drove Kawakji's forces back across the Lebanese frontier and captured Nazareth. Near Jerusalem, Colonel David Shaltiel's troops dislodged Egyptian forces south of the city and took Ein Karem in the west. Israel had by now even acquired some offensive air strength in the form of venerable and slow-moving Flying Fortresses, which attacked Cairo and Damascus with more damage to Arab morale than to the bombed cities. When the Security Council met on 15 July, both the Soviet and American delegates turned their fury on the Arab governments. A resolution was adopted which not only 'ordered' a cease-fire, but determined the existence of 'a threat to the peace' and menaced the Arab governments with sanctions under Chapter VII of the Charter if they declined to cease fire. Moreover, the truce was not to be limited by a new date of expiry; it was to continue until 'a peaceful adjustment' was reached.

This was strong language. But if the Arabs now accepted the truce, their response was probably dictated more by the disintegration of their military resistance than by the strength of international pressure. On 18 July the truce came into effective force.

There would be more fighting in the autumn and winter months of 1948 and in January 1949, when Israel struck out to break an Egyptian blockade of their settlements in the Negev and to banish some pockets of Arab forces in

Galilee. The first of these operations brought Beersheba under Israeli control and enabled Israeli forces under General Yigal Allon to take over the Negev and, eventually, to occupy Eilat peacefully in March 1949.

There had been some sixty days of fighting in three separate spurts between December 1947 and January 1949. Israel's losses – 4,000 soldiers and 2,000 civilians killed – sound limited in comparison with the enormity of the change which had come about in the nature and direction of Jewish history. But we should recall that the Jewish community which paid this price had only 650,000 citizens. It was as if the United States had lost a million and a half killed in 1947–9. And there were other burdens and anxieties. There was a salient cutting into Israel's farming area in Upper Galilee. Mount Scopus was cut off. Jerusalem was divided. The Latrun salient was still in Arab hands. At a rough estimate, Israel, whose export earnings then amounted to less than

above Count Folke Bernadotte, seen here with Dr Ralph Bunche and Moshe Sharett, was assassinated four months after he was appointed UN Mediator for Palestine in 1948

$50 million, had spent $500 million on the prosecution of the war.

But all these defects were little more than blemishes on the glowing coun-
tenance of Israel's triumph. The new state was solidly entrenched. In the words
of Ralph Bunche, Count Bernadotte's deputy and successor, Israel was 'a
vibrant reality' by the autumn of 1948. Its rule now extended over the whole
of Galilee; the entire coastal strip, except for the 27-mile Gaza salient in
Egyptian hands; the whole of the Negev; and west Jerusalem, with a sizable
corridor to the coast. Its area of effective jurisdiction was over 8,000 square
miles. The Arabs had prevented the establishment of a separate Arab State
west of the Jordan and had also obstructed the internationalization of Jerusalem.
The parts of western Palestine outside Israel's jurisdiction were under Transjordanian or Egyptian control. Above all, the gates were open and masses of
Jewish immigrants were flowing in. Israel was free to build its future; and it
had carved its freedom out of adversity, unaided and alone.

Whatever happened, the image of this war would live on, unfading in the
nation's memory. It had told the infant nation some unexpected things about
itself. It had brought to the surface a whole range of qualities which would
have further tests in other ordeals. Clearly, there was an underlying coherence
beneath the diversities and separations which marked the Israeli population.
There was a capacity for organized action, a talent for making the most of
small resources and a unifying energy which could be evoked in times of
stress. Above all, there was a conviction that the central national aims were
worthy of sacrifice and that individual advantage must, if necessary, be qualified
by the general need. All these attributes had been enlarged by a sense of history.
For the most part, the fighters knew the dark background out of which Israel
had emerged and into which it would again subside if its defence or resolution
faltered. Without victory there would be no survival.

When the clang of arms was silenced, the nation looked back with pride
and rectitude on what it had accomplished in those sixty days. The graves
that had been dug, the tears that had been shed because of them, the griefs
that had been suffered, the perils that had been surmounted, the inexpressible
hopes that had been kindled would all live on, deep in the mind and heart of
Israel, so long as any memory of the past endured. There were some who had
gained particular renown in action or death. But in the deeper sense, it was the
people's victory, won by countless unknown men and women caught up
together in unbearable alternations of suffering and hope, of courage and
despair. When the war ended it was everyone's possession; and from its dust and
havoc a new tomorrow was waiting to be born.

4

Years of Consolidation, 1948–1951

Each day we witness the creation of a new heaven and a new earth.

Thomas Paine

We can take 18 July, 1948 as the point at which Israel's mind began to shift from mere survival towards the tasks for which it had survived. The Arab states had laid down their arms in exhaustion and defeat, but there was no disarmament of their spirit or emotion. They would strain every nerve to defeat Israel by political and economic pressure. They could still hope to prevent the world from getting too accustomed to the idea of Israel as a sovereign state; and they watched avidly for any sign that Israel's social structure might break down under the strain of mass immigration and economic tension.

The Provisional Government moved swiftly to consolidate Israel's position in the world. Military success had given momentum to the political struggle. But Israel was still not a member of the United Nations or of its specialized agencies; and only a minority of the world's governments maintained relations with it. Membership in the United Nations would clearly have a dual effect: it would crushingly refute the Arab doctrine of Israel's illegitimacy; and it would cause most governments to regard Israel as a natural subject for their recognition and cooperation.

In the way of these prospects, like a massive roadblock, stood the Bernadotte Report. Little had been heard of it since July; but it would now become the focus of an international debate about the peace settlement. There was no chance that Israel would accept it; but there was always the possibility that if she stood alone in rejecting it, Israel would be in conflict with the United Nations before establishing an alternative system of bilateral relations on anything like a universal scale. Early in September 1948, the Israeli Government launched a political offensive with two aims in view: the defeat of the Bernadotte proposals, and the admission of Israel to membership in the United Nations.

A reeling blow was struck against these efforts on the eve of the UN General Assembly session in Paris. On 17 September Count Bernadotte and his

Foreign Minister Moshe Sharett, with Abba Eban, Israel's
Permanent Delegate, and other members of the delegation, raises
the Israeli flag outside the UN headquarters on 12 May 1949

assistant, Colonel Sarrault, were assassinated in Jerusalem. The credit for
this act, if it can be so called, was claimed by an underground organization
called the Fatherland Front, consisting of former members of Lechi. For
the Israeli Government this was another warning of the danger to its sovereignty if dissident armed organizations were to exist in any place where it
claimed jurisdiction. More than two hundred members of illegal organizations were arrested and the IZL was issued an ultimatum to hand over its
arms and to liquidate its separate formations in Jerusalem. Count Bernadotte's
murderers were not traced; Israeli authority at that time was more slender
in Jerusalem than elsewhere. But the murder put an end to all traces of the
divided authority which had survived the pre-State period and which threatened to undermine Israel's domestic authority and international status.

There was reason to fear that Bernadotte's death would give his proposals
the sanctity of a testament bequeathed by an international martyr. The prospect
of his report being adopted as an international policy had therefore increased.
It was also expected that the heavy atmosphere created by the assassination
might cause Israel's application for membership in the United Nations to fail.
In the event, these fears were only partly fulfilled. Although the United
States had joined Britain in support of the Bernadotte Plan, there were many
reservations in Washington towards a proposal based, after all, on the excision
from Israel of the very Negev to which President Truman had solemnly
supported Israel's claim in a talk with Dr Weizmann in November 1947.
Moreover, the United States was on the verge of a presidential election. The
Republican nominee for Secretary of State, John Foster Dulles, did not
hide his opposition to the Bernadotte Report, which he regarded as a proposal
narrowly conceived to fit Bevin's parochial view of British interests.

    After a turbulent debate in the Political Committee of the General Assembly,
all the provisions of the Bernadotte Report were defeated. They had been
shattered by cross-fire from a strange coalition. They were opposed by Israel
because they threatened to mutilate its territory. They were rejected by the
Arabs because they provided for the existence of a Jewish State. Other
governments, not particularly moved by sympathy for Israel or the Arabs,
voted against the plan to salvage their own honour, which they had committed
only a year before to the partition resolution. It seemed presumptuous to
them for a single mediator to set aside what the entire Assembly had solemnly
confirmed. Finally, the Soviet Union, not without reason, regarded the
Bernadotte Plan as inspired by a desire to reinforce Britain's strategic position
in the Middle East by creating a base in the Negev with continuous com-

munication between Egypt and Transjordan, in each of which Britain had a special position guaranteed by treaties of alliance and defence. In the Middle Eastern conflict it is clearly possible to displease all the parties most of the time. The Bernadotte Plan, despite its author's earnestness, achieved this versatile alienation.

When Israel's application for membership in the United Nations was submitted on 29 November 1948, the anniversary of the original partition resolution, the debate ended with five votes for Israel's admission – the United States, the USSR, Ukraine, Argentina and Colombia. This fell two short of what was necessary under the Charter. But it was hoped that more votes would be added when the Security Council met under a new composition in January 1949. It was confidently believed, for example, that France and Canada could be brought around.

The General Assembly ended its meetings on 11 December 1948 with the appointment of a Palestine Conciliation Commission. Its task was to bring about a permanent peace by negotiation, either directly or through the Conciliation Commission itself. On the assumption that the peace settlement would come soon, the General Assembly recommended that refugees who wished to return to their homes should be permitted to do so on condition that they would live at peace with their neighbours. All the Arab states voted unitedly against the resolution. They were to invoke some of its provisions later on their own behalf. But at the time they saw it as a sinful ratification of Israel's sovereignty and of its status as a partner in international negotiation. The underlying assumption of the resolution was that peace could not be decreed by an international blue print; it would have to be achieved by negotiation between the states concerned. In those days the word 'negotiation' was still permissible in the UN vocabulary on peace in the Middle East.

Towards the end of 1948, there were other events bearing on Israel's future. Despite the sceptical predictions of the world press, Harry S Truman was re-elected as President of the United States. This ensured that American

Prime Minister Ben Gurion during an official visit to President Harry S Truman, the first head of state to grant recognition to Israel

policy towards Israel would be executed by the man who had taken such audacious responsibility for the partition plan and for recognizing Israel a few minutes after its establishment. Two weeks later, Israel registered another political success in the international arena when, on 16 November 1948, the Security Council, after wearily discussing whether Israeli forces should be at Beersheba and whether Israel had been justified in breaking the Egyptian attempt to throttle the Negev settlements, decided on a new phase. On Canada's initiative, it proposed that the truce be replaced by an armistice to be achieved by negotiation between Israel and the Arab states. Under this agreement armistice-demarcation lines were to be established, putting an end to the fluid positions of the truce, which did not give even a temporary legitimacy to any boundary lines.

The first Arab reaction to the idea of an armistice was hostile. But by early January 1949, after the Egyptian hold on the Israeli Negev was broken, and Israeli forces bent on opening the road in the Negev had entered north-eastern Sinai and advanced towards Rafah, British aircraft flew in support of Egypt, and six of them were brought down by Israeli guns. Egypt prudently abandoned its militance. It used the 16 November resolutions as a face-saving bridge towards the negotiating table. Thus all in all, 1948 had been Israel's wondrous year. As it ebbed away, most Israelis and Jews wondered if they would ever know such a year again.

eastern Sinai and advanced towards Rafah, British aircraft flew in support of Armistice negotiations between Egypt and Israel opened at Rhodes on 13 January 1949 under the auspices of the acting mediator, Dr Ralph Bunche. Both delegations, as well as the UN staff, were stationed at the Hôtel des Roses. On the first day, the negotiations were held separately between Dr Bunche and each delegation. But the awkwardness and absurdity of this separation became so manifest that by 15 January the delegations were facing each other across a single table under Dr Bunche's able chairmanship.

The negotiations were difficult and sometimes bitter. One deadlock after another had to be resolved. A crisis arose when the Egyptian delegation asked for an Egyptian Military Governor for Beersheba, from which Egyptian forces had very recently been expelled. Obstacles were patiently overcome until, in an atmosphere of international enthusiasm, an agreement was reached and concluded on 24 February 1949.

When the text was studied in the world capitals, it became clear that the system of relations which it described went beyond the normal concept of an armistice. There was, of course, the provision for a cessation of fire; but this was accompanied by a rigorous undertaking that the cease-fire would be permanent and would last until a final peace settlement had been achieved. Thus the agreement reflected none of the permissive indulgence to renewed belligerency which was always implicit in the classic concept of armistice.

On the contrary, the object of the agreement was defined as the promotion of 'the return of permanent peace to Palestine'. It was conceived as 'an indispensable step towards the liquidation of armed conflict and the restoration of peace'. The demarcation lines were not final. Indeed, it was laid down (Paragraph V [2]) that 'the Armistice Demarcation Line is not to be construed in any sense as a political or territorial boundary and is delineated without prejudice to rights, claims and positions of either party as regards ultimate settlement of the Palestine question'.

In bringing the agreement for confirmation by the Security Council later that year, Dr Bunche added a sentence that was to reverberate in future crises in 1956 and 1967: 'There should be free movement for legitimate shipping and no vestige of the war-time blockade should be allowed to remain, as they are inconsistent with both the letter and spirit of the Armistice Agreements'.

The agreement was subject to revision by mutual consent within a year. The signatories, as well as the UN Chairman, were convinced that they were building a temporary but solid structure which would soon be replaced by a peace treaty. A provision, rare in armistices, for the exchange of all prisoners-of-war was agreed upon; and a mechanism for fulfilling the agreement and registering complaints was established in the form of a Mixed Armistice Commission, consisting of representatives of each government and a UN Chairman.

The effect of the Israeli-Egyptian agreement was to freeze the military positions as they existed in the Negev at the time of the cease-fire on 7 January. Thus Egypt remained in occupation of the Gaza-Rafah coastal strip, about 27 miles long and 4 miles wide. The strategic area of El Auja, on the Palestine side of the demarcation line, was to be demilitarized; and an Egyptian brigade encircled in the Faluja pocket in the Negev was to be allowed to abandon its positions and return to Egypt with military honour.

Among the officers in the encircled brigade was a young graduate of the Egyptian Staff College, Major Gamal Abdul Nasser. He had fought several battles in Palestine, apparently with some valour. Six years later he was to write that he detested war; he had said to himself 'that humanity does not deserve to live if it does not work with all its strength for peace'. In his recollection of the 1948 war, Nasser added: 'When I learned that one of my friends had been killed, I swore that if one day I found myself in a responsible position I should think a thousand times before sending our soldiers to war. I should only do it if it were absolutely necessary, if the fatherland were threatened and if nothing could save it but the fire of battle.'

Before the Egyptian-Israeli armistice negotiations had ended, it was known that Lebanon and Jordan would follow Cairo's steps. On 3 April, after four weeks of negotiation, Israel and Jordan signed an Armistice Agreement establishing a tortuous boundary 330 miles long and leaving the densely populated Arab hill country of the West Bank under Jordanian occupation. The armistice also crystallized the division of Jerusalem between the two countries. The boundary ran straight down the middle of the Dead Sea to the Gulf of Aqaba, with the Jordanian port of Aqaba and the Israeli port of Eilat, a few miles apart, separated by the armistice line.

The scene now shifted to the Lebanese-Israeli boundary, where, at Rosh Hanikrah, an Armistice Agreement was signed on 23 March. The demarcation line was identical with the former international boundary; and Israeli forces withdrew from all the Lebanese villages that they had occupied. It was hoped, perhaps too innocently, that this withdrawal would have its effect when Israel came to demand Syrian withdrawal from areas west of the Syrian-Palestine boundary which had come under Syrian military domination in the 1948 fighting.

Iraq, whose troops were stationed in heavy concentrations in the West Bank of the Jordan, refused to sign an international agreement with Israel. This obduracy was evaded by the replacement of Iraqi forces by forces of the Transjordan Arab Legion.

The Syrian Government, always unpredictable except in its ferocity, was the last to enter armistice negotiations. The talks were rancorous and constantly on the verge of breakdown. By 20 July an agreement had been concluded. Under its terms the Syrians withdrew from a belt of territories west of the international boundary in return for an Israeli agreement to demilitarize it. Israel had thus secured effective control of its main water sources: the whole of the Sea of Galilee was within its jurisdiction as well as Lake Huleh. But the Syrian Government had never made a real decision to leave Israel alone. It constantly harassed Israel's development projects in the demilitarized zone and created a sense of obscurity about political sovereignty in the small evacuated area.

For eighteen years the Armistice Agreements were to be the only recognized framework of relations between Israel and its neighbours. Although the

A sculpture by Yehiel Shemi on the Mediterranean shore at Achziv commemorates the 'illegal' immigration of 1946–8

demarcation lines were defined as not permanent, the fact that they could only be changed by mutual consent gave them something very like the character of permanent boundaries. In any case, they had relegated the 1947 partition map to the past. The Arab assault had released Israel from any sense of obligation to the original map. The Arab governments had put their fate to the chance of war; they could not now escape the verdict which they had sought.

As water flows into a canal, so was Israeli life to grow and develop within the armistice lines until their quaint contours became the familiar shape of Israel. But the Arab governments, assuming that subsequent change could only be to their benefit, refused to acknowledge the permanence of the armistice map. In their rhetoric and jurisprudence, they constantly stressed its provisional character. Indeed, they denied the concept of Israeli sovereignty in any part of what was formerly Palestine, and they kept alive the hope and dream that one day the armistice lines, and Israel with them, would be swept away by successful force. From 1967 onwards, they were to regret their tenacious struggle to deny permanent validity to the armistice lines.

The 1949 agreements remain to this day the only successful example of an Arab-Israeli compromise leading to a contractual obligation. On 11 August 1949 the representative of one of the Great Powers put his finger on the main reason for the success of the armistice negotiations: 'Since experience has shown that direct negotiations between the parties have brought about such good results, namely, the cessation of military operations and the temporary settlement of affairs in Palestine, why not continue this good procedure in the future and allow the parties themselves to settle the questions between them by the method which they have used hitherto, that is, by direct negotiations without any interference in this matter by a third party?' The statement came from the head of the Soviet delegation, Ambassador S. Tsarapkin. It made strange reading a few years later.

Apart from their stabilizing regional effects, the Armistice Agreements gave a sharp stimulus to Israel's campaign for international recognition. In late summer 1948, American and Soviet embassies had been established in Tel Aviv; on one messianic occasion, the two flags flew in unison over the modest hotel on the Tel Aviv shorefront in which both Ambassadors happened to be staying at one and the same time. The American Ambassador, James G. Macdonald, and his Soviet colleague, Pavel Yershov, became conspicuous figures in Israel. They were stared at with the faintly incredulous awe whereby Israeli citizens registered the fact that great nations in the world now recognized their

After the establishment of the state, Israel was flooded by a wave of immigration from Europe and the Arab lands. These immigrants from Morocco represent one of Israel's many ethnic groups

statehood and presented their credentials to their eminent President, Chaim Weizmann. There was much of Jewish pride in the air in those days.

The wave of recognition of Israel swept over most of western Europe, the Commonwealth and all of Latin America. On 4 March 1949, the Security Council recommended Israel's admission to membership in the United Nations. France and Canada had now joined the five who had voted for this course two and a half months before. Norway and China added their votes, leaving Syria alone in opposition and the United Kingdom in embarrassed abstention.

Yet, when the General Assembly convened in New York in April 1949, it was evident that Israel's application for membership would not have clear sailing. The Arab governments had belatedly awakened to the decisive nature of this issue. The United Nations Charter is, in effect, a treaty between the member states, which then numbered fifty-eight, to recognize each other's sovereignty and to make common cause in the universal interest. If Israel were admitted, who would put any credence in the Arab concept that Israel was either nonexistent or illegitimate? What state, other than the Arabs and those most closely aligned with them, would refuse Israel official recognition? And what chance would there be of a successful boycott, if, by the very fact of its admission to the General Assembly, Israel became a member of the World Bank, the World Health Organization, the International Postal Union, the Food and Agricultural Organization and the other agencies which had begun to express the planetary spirit and draw sovereign states together in a covenant of development and peace?

So the Arab governments mounted a strong offensive against Israel's admission. They succeeded in obstructing it at early procedural stages. They even organized a spectacle without precedent or subsequent parallel: the Israeli representative was publicly interrogated by a committee of the whole Assembly about what Israel's policy and attitudes were to be. The Israeli Government refused to buy its membership by any undertaking to return to the November 1947 lines that had been shattered by Arab violence. It offered to contribute to the solution of the refugee problem, but not to assume its total burden; and it proposed that in Jerusalem the international principle should apply not to the administration of the entire city, but only to the Holy Places and to religious rights and immunities.

Despite these reservations, Israel scored a triumph on 11 May 1949. It was less spectacular, but internationally more effective than that of 29 November 1947. The partition resolution had merely recommended that a Jewish State be established. It did not, by that recommendation, give any

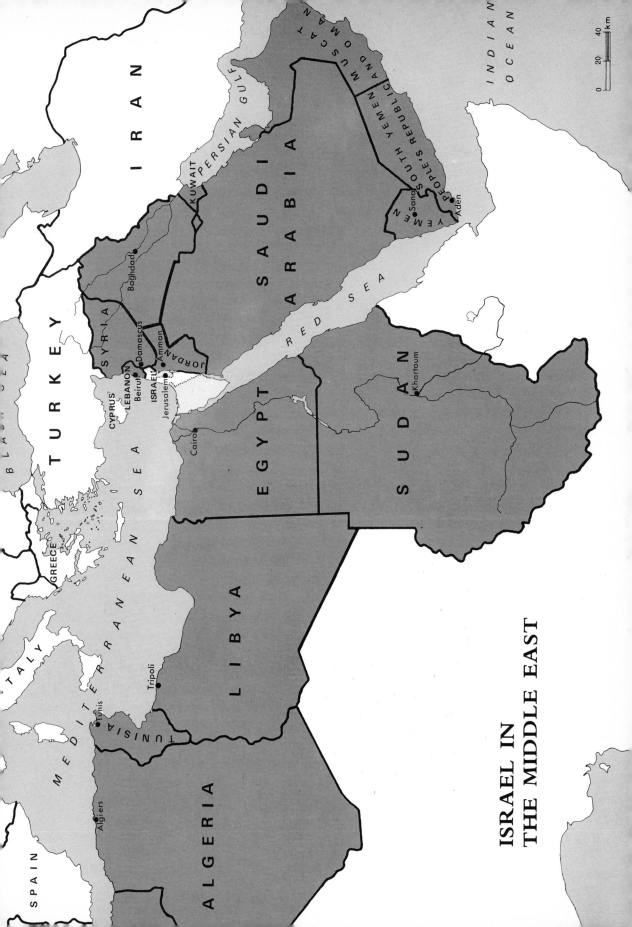

ISRAEL IN
THE MIDDLE EAST

international status to the state nor ensure its integration into the international community. But on 11 May 1949, when Israel took its seat as the fifty-ninth member of the United Nations, it had secured its place in the international community as a partner equal in rights to the Arab states – and all others. On 12 May photographs of an Israeli delegation sitting behind a desk boldly marked ISRAEL, and later hoisting Israel's flag on its mast in the courtyard of the UN headquarters, electrified the Israeli people with a new sense of recaptured dignity. 'A waking dream', said Foreign Minister Sharett in reporting to the Knesset, 'Israel amongst the nations! A sovereign Jewish State secure within the international family. Words are inadequate to express the enormity of this transition.' In later years, Israel was to have much frustration and grief from some of the actions of the United Nations; but it would never cease to draw dignity and political assurance from the simple fact of its membership.

We must now return to the end of the fighting in July 1948 and trace Israel's steps in the consolidation of its own society and economy. The war and the political struggle had delayed these tasks. After all, if Israel was not going to survive in its sovereign identity, it would have little chance of constructing its social order. With its immediate political and military aims assured, the nation's main business could now begin. There was no doubt where the priority lay. The task was to open Israel's gates, to heal the wounds and dispel the haunting memories of whatever remained of European Jewry. Israel could also respond to a surge of exaltation in other parts of the Jewish world, where the rise of a Jewish State was like the sound of a trumpet calling Jews to change the purpose and direction of their lives and to join with sovereign Israel in the construction of a Jewish society. This, at any rate, was how the Jews in Arab lands, nurtured on the old prophecies, saw Israel's rebirth. Nothing new had happened in their conditions of life; what was new was their freedom to escape them.

In the first four months of Israel's independence, when the country's fate was still in the balance, some fifty thousand immigrants reached her shores. By September 1948 the stream had become a flood. It was to pour copiously into Israel until October 1951. Within three years, between May 1948 and December 1951, 687,000 newcomers had landed in Israel: 101,828 in 1948; 239,576 in 1949; 170,249 in 1950; 175,095 in 1951. It had taken thirty years under British mandatory rule for the Jewish population to increase by 600,000. This had now been accomplished and even surpassed by the sovereign State of Israel in a period of less than three years.

up the struggle, and the Jews of Yemen were convinced that prophecy had been fulfilled and that Israel's 'captivity had been turned'. Their suffering in Yemen was familiar. Their opportunity to escape it was new.

Since Egypt had closed the Suez Canal to Israeli traffic, Yemenite immigrants could not be brought across the Red Sea. The only alternative was an air-lift to Israel. The Jewish Agency and the American Jewish Joint Distribution Committee, under contract with the American Alaska Airlines and the Near-East Air Transport Company, organized an air-shuttle to bring Yemenite immigrants to Israel. Since the hostilities between Israel and the Arab states had its effects in the air, these flights often had to take circuitous routes. In the first phase of 'Operation Magic Carpet' (December 1948 to March 1949) fifty-five flights were carried out; each plane carried from 90 to 150 passengers.

The second and larger phase of 'Magic Carpet' began in May 1949. The Imam of Yemen had by now rescinded the ban on Jewish emigration. Many Jews intended to make the journey to Israel on foot or by donkey. With the permission of Arab principalities through whose territories the Jews had to pass, and now with British cooperation in Aden, it was possible to intensify the air-lift. Most remaining Jews in Yemen and Aden were borne by air to Israel in the final month of 1949. Nine thousand were evacuated in the first nine months of 1950. 'Operation Magic Carpet' officially came to an end on 24 September 1950, when the last transport of 177 arrived at Lydda airport.

The Jews of Yemen had lived for centuries in a condition of statutory inferiority. They could not own land or walk on the pavement if a Moslem passed by. Sometimes, the Imams would tolerate them in a spirit of feudal paternalism. They had pursued a life of religious piety, drowning their present adversities in recollections of ancient glory. In Yemen they had been limited to small shop-keeping and primitive crafts, such as the working of

ar left 'Illegal' immigrants interned n detention camps on Cyprus leave or Israel early in 1949
eft Virtually the entire Jewish population of Yemen was transferred o Israel in the winter of 1949/50 in a mammoth air-lift called 'Operation Magic Carpet'
ight Thousands of youngsters were brought to Israel from post-war Europe and the Arab countries by Youth Aliyah. Many of them began a new life at camps, like this one at Naharia in 1948

silver and copper. When they embarked on aircraft for Israel, they had never even travelled in a land-bound vehicle. Therefore, as the trucks and buses took them along the road from Lydda to the villages in which they were to be settled, they felt a sense of surprise and alarm because the vehicles did not take off into the air. Their simple imaginations took them back to the prophecy in Exodus: 'I will bear them on eagles' wings and bring them unto Me.' Like the Yemenite Jews who had preceded them in the nineteenth and early twentieth centuries, their assimilation to Israeli society was rapid and complete. The Hebrew language positively sang on their lips, and their old pieties were now deployed under congenial skies.

At the same time, the Jews of Iraq were coming to Israel in even greater numbers. 'Operation Ezra and Nehemiah' was the name given to the air-lift of the Iraqi Jews to Israel in the period between May 1950 and December 1951. Conditions were less propitious than in Yemen. Since 1948, and until 1950, the emigration of Jews from Iraq to Israel had been regarded as a capital offence. In May 1950, however, the Iraqi Parliament passed a law permitting Jewish emigration to Palestine, although it deprived Jewish emigrants of their Iraqi citizenship, froze their assets and seriously limited the personal property that they could take with them. The Near-East Air Transport Company, which had been involved in 'Operation Magic Carpet', carried out the new air-lift. The Iraqi Government had demanded that the planes fly not directly to Israel, but to some 'neutral country'. In deference to this fiction, an intermediary landing was made in Nicosia, Cyprus, where immigrants were transferred to Israel-bound planes. March 1951 had been fixed by the Iraqi authorities as the deadline for filing applications to emigrate. By that time over 100,000 Jews had registered to emigrate to Israel as against some 25,000 who chose, disastrously, to remain in Iraq.

By now all Jews living under Moslem or Arab rule were in a state of ecstatic ferment. A flow of immigration came in from the Jewish communities of North Africa, Morocco, Algeria, Tunisia and Libya. Here, the driving force was not only a love of Zion inculcated by a religious upbringing, but also the cold wind coming from Arab nationalism. In less than a decade the Jewish communities of Libya, Tunisia, Algeria and Morocco were drained of most of their Jews, with relatively small numbers remaining behind.

The European exodus was concentrated mainly in the years 1948 and 1949. The years 1949 and 1950 saw the return of Oriental Jewry. On 15 May 1948 there had been 650,000 Jews in Palestine. By the end of 1953, the Jewish population of Israel was 1,484,000.

Plunged in physical combat and uncertain of its physical survival, the nation

Vast transit camps were established to cope with the immigration of 1948–54, like this sea of tents at Beit Lid during the winter rains of January 1950

could not give its full attention to the absorption of immigrants during 1948. Just as a refusal of Jewish masses to come to Israel would have discredited the national enterprise, so would failure have ensued from natural disasters in absorption, such as famine, plague, homelessness. There was every objective reason for these fears. To imagine that a small community could receive a population equal to itself without any of the newcomers sleeping in the street, or suffering starvation or having their children bereft of school for a single week seemed at first too much to ask. Yet no less than this was achieved.

First among the problems was that of housing. At first the immigrants were settled in suburbs and villages left by the Arabs in their flight. When this possibility had been exhausted, there was no choice but to prepare temporary transit camps for the immigrants until more permanent housing could be built. Former British military camps in various stages of ruin and neglect were also used. Tents and barracks by the thousands were hastily erected in and around the camps. Although it was difficult to cope with the inflow, the number of immigrants was so vast that at times thousands arrived at the camp even before the most primitive housing could be improvised.

Still, Israel in those years was overflowing with hardship. The transit camps were frequently situated in areas far from the main cities. Their occupants were, for the most part, unemployed. Their basic needs were supplied by the public authorities; but neither the government nor the Jewish Agency had the resources necessary to settle them permanently and absorb them in productive work. By the end of 1949, more than 100,000 were living in transit camps. The existence of these camps was in itself a triumph of organization. But they resulted in enforced idleness and retarded the integration of the

immigrants. They were also uneconomic and placed a strain on Israel's meagre financial means. The most rapid solution was also the most expensive. New and better answers had to be found.

In mid-1950, under Levi Eshkol's imaginative direction, a new system of absorption and settlement was devised. The *ma'abarah* (transition centre) was a unique Israeli experiment. It was designed to speed up absorption by encouraging immigrants to become independent as soon as they arrived. First, they were taken to a clearance camp; soon after they were transferred to the *ma'abarot* established near existing towns or settlements where they could be employed or in places where public works were being carried out. Gradually, two types of *ma'abarot* evolved. Some were to become permanent settlements; others were to be dispersed as soon as their occupants found employment. The immigrants in *ma'abarot* were placed in tents or huts of wood and tin; but each family was independent in providing for itself. Public services such as clinics, dispensaries, schools, labour exchanges and other social services were provided by the government or the Jewish Agency. By the end of 1952, 113 *ma'abarot* were founded with almost 250,000 inhabitants. Life in the *ma'abarot* was less stringent than in the earlier camps, but conditions were still harsh. The *ma'abarot* were primitive and crowded. They were flooded by winter rains, exposed to the asperity of the summer heat and cut off from the main cities and villages. In the winter of 1950 the situation in some of the *ma'abarot* was so critical that the army was called in to bring food and salvage tents and huts that had been swept away by the unceasing torrential rains.

If the dislocations and resentments of the camps and the *ma'abarot* never exploded into hostile demonstration or in a movement for emigration, it is because there was something unique in the Israeli air during those early years. Physical adversity was mitigated by emotional solidarity. The immigrants might be poor and committed to long suffering, but they had a sense of being wanted. They knew that the entire nation regarded their absorption and integration as the central purpose of its existence. The sense of collective adventure that had been so prominent in the pioneering years now came to Israel's rescue. Vast sources of voluntary service were revealed in every section of the community. In the rhetoric of those times, the immigrants were often referred to as 'brands plucked from the burning', or as 'the returning remnant'. Behind each one redeemed was the memory of hundreds whose lives had been extinguished. The reception and support of immigrants was a national mystique. Everything in Israel was subordinate to this task. Not for a moment was there any serious suggestion that the existing community should restrict the inflow in order to protect some of its own standards and institutions against the disruptive effects of the incoming torrent. The Jewish communities in the Diaspora, especially in the United States, harnessed themselves ardently to this cause. Massive institutions of financial aid grew up in voluntary movements, such as the United Jewish Appeal, whose participants were not only animated by financial generosity, but were also drawn each to the other in a spirit of concern and responsibility for Israel that carried over into the political and public domains as well. Most of the enlightened world looked with respect on this attempt of a nation to rebuild itself from its own debris.

The tide was bound to ebb sooner or later. By mid-1952 there was a sharp decline in immigration. In 1953 no more than 10,000 came to Israel. There were only 50,000 immigrants during the years 1952–4. The decline in these numbers had depressive effects which, together with other developments, made the period 1952–6 a doldrum era in Israel's first quarter century. The only compensation was that the slowdown enabled the government and the Jewish Agency to rearrange their work and to plan better systems of settlement and absorption in the future.

During these extraordinary forty months of mass-immigration, Israel was a vast, noisy workshop filled with the clatter of countless tools knocking houses, roads and schools together at headlong rate. Seventy-eight thousand dwellings with 165,000 rooms had been completed; 345 new villages, kibbutzim, moshavim, and moshavot were established in 1948–51, which was fifty more than had been founded in the previous seventy years. The map of Jewish habitation, which had been full of gaps in 1948, was now dotted comfortingly with new and living place-names. Only in western Galilee, the Negev, and the Judean hills did the population pattern remain sparse.

The immigrants would eventually become Israel's main economic resource. In the first phase of their arrival, however, professional economists saw them as a mass of non-producing consumers. The government had inherited from the mandatory régime a high cost of living, rising prices and inflationary tendencies across the length and breadth of the economy. The need to finance the war aggravated all these trends. Above all, mass-immigration meant that the number of consumers had grown spectacularly, while, as a result of mobilization, the providers had become fewer. Little had been allowed into the country by way of consumer goods, so that there was an exorbitant rise in the prices of whatever the shops contained. Israel had been established as a welfare state from its inception, with the government constantly

above A new neighbourhood is constructed near Rishon le-Zion. The strained finances of the new state were burdened even more by the necessity to embark upon a vast building programme for housing new immigrants

left During the early years of the state, improvisation was the order of the day. An enterprising immigrant has created a 'shop' out of a packing crate at the Athlit camp

obliged to make social services available to the population. This led to the
rapid expansion of the bureaucracy. When the immigrants were added to the
soldiers and government servants, the residual labour force available for
actual production was seen to be pathetically small. On the small army
of workers fell the burden of the new roads to be built and of agricultural
land to be reclaimed, irrigated and cultivated. The housing programme strained
the budget to the breaking point and the labour force to exhaustion. By the
middle of 1949, wages and prices were climbing high, and Israel's fragile
economy was threatened with collapse. It was absolutely essential that
resolute governmental intervention come into play immediately.

The first step was to impose strict austerity on the country. The ungrateful but necessary task was entrusted to Dr Dov Joseph, whose work as Military Governor of Jerusalem during the siege had made him a kind of expert in the infliction of salutary hardship. The aim of the Finance Ministry, under Eliezer Kaplan, and of Joseph's Ministry was threefold: first, it was necessary to reduce prices; second, foreign currency resources had to be husbanded by reducing foreign imports to a minimum; and third, as a corollary, it was necessary to increase local production in industry and in agriculture.

The austerity programme came under political fire from various directions. Commercial and industrial interests chafed at a controlled economy based on scarcity. They were right, of course, in saying that this was no way to build a dynamic economy. But the architects and exponents of austerity never held it as a dogma to be sustained in all conditions. Their contention was that they had no other course under the impact of mass-immigration. From the left-wing of the labour movement came expressions of grievance about the fact that the workers were automatically the victims of rationing programmes, while others were able to profit from the black market and other evasions. All in all, however, Israelis considered that economic stringency was not too heavy a price to pay for the relief of military victory and the exaltation of seeing the refugee camps in Europe emptied and oppressed Jews from Moslem lands streaming into the gates. Moreover, the policy of economic restraint was manifestly successful: within 1949, the cost-of-living index fell from 493 points to 378.

The Israeli economy had undertaken tasks far beyond its unaided power. In 1951, Prime Minister Ben Gurion summoned a conference of Israeli leaders with the leaders of American and world Jewry. Targets which seemed astronomical in those days were laid down as a challenge to Jewish solidarity and enterprise. The revenues of the United Jewish Appeal would be expanded. A State of Israel Bond issue would be launched in the United States and elsewhere, and the proceeds would be applied to development, immigrant housing and agricultural expansion. In addition to Jewish sources, an effort would be made to secure grant and loan assistance from the American Government. It was also decided, despite a stormy and bitter debate in Israel, to call on the German Federal Republic to make a payment to the State of Israel in partial compensation for the material losses suffered by the Jews. The sum requested was DM 3,000,000,000 ($750,000,000). Another DM 450,000,000 ($110,000,000) was requested by the Conference on Jewish Material Claims representing Diaspora Jewry and Jews outside Israel who had suffered under the Nazis and who were to receive personal restitution. By September 1952, the Compensation Agreement with the Federal Republic had been concluded; the United Jewish Appeal had reached magnified targets; the Bond Drive had succeeded, to the confusion of the sceptics; and the United States Government had secured from the Congress an authorization for $65,000,000 to assist Israel in receiving and absorbing immigrant refugees. Together with the buttressing of Israel's credits and the receipt of long-term loans, these measures gave Israel's financial condition a healthier look in 1952 than would have seemed possible a year before. Indeed, the relief was so profound that a new policy was decreed with the aim of stimulating the economy. With the removal of rigid controls, prices were allowed to seek their own level and the index rose by fifty per cent. It was clear that one of Israel's most difficult struggles would be for economic consolidation, and the difficulties of planning would be increased by the fact that many factors governing economic life were outside the national control. The Israeli arms budget was dictated by Arab hostility and rearmament; immigration, and therefore housing, education and social services, would be determined by the pressures exerted upon Jews abroad, as well as by the intensity of their desire to seek reunion with Israel. In any case, the state was committed by its very first law, adopted on Independence Day, to keep its gates unconditionally open to any Jew who was seeking a home within them.

When Israel's third Independence Day celebrations came around in 1951, the country could look back on three crucial achievements. It had won a war against Arab armies superior in manpower and weapons; it had fought its way into the international community, a majority of whose members now gave it full recognition; and it had taken on a vast burden of Jewish misery and longing by absorbing hundreds of thousands of kinsmen driven or attracted to its shores. When these achievements were compared with the impotence which marked the Jewish condition at the end of the war, the first forty months of statehood could fairly be described as a revolutionary transition.

The whole of Jewish history is an eternal celebration of resilience. It teaches that there are no situations from which recuperation is totally impossible. This quality had rarely come to finer expression than in the manner whereby Israel seized and created its opportunities between 1948 and 1951. There was an unusual sense of command over the flow of events and the direction of history. In a short span of time we had passed from a world in which the existence of a Jewish State had seemed inconceivable to a world which would have seemed inconceivable without its existence.

5

The Peace That Failed

War can protect; it cannot create.
Whitehead

After four such years it seemed to many Israelis that everything was possible if only enough energy of spirit were devoted to its attainment. For this very reason they felt sharp disappointment at not winning the most cherished prize of all. Peace had seemed a tangible prospect when the Armistice Agreements were signed in 1949; it soon receded into horizons of doubt and failure.

International bodies and the major Powers failed to grasp the Armistice Agreements in their full potentiality as a springboard towards permanent peace. There was something in the international behaviour after the signature of the 1949 agreements that led the Arab governments to expect indulgence for controlled belligerency. Close on the heels of Dr Bunche's success in the armistice negotiations came the fiasco of the Palestine Conciliation Commission. That body had been established by the resolution of the General Assembly in December 1948. It was composed of delegates from the United States, France and Turkey. The American representative was Mark Etheridge, the editor of a newspaper in Louisville, Kentucky. France was represented by a diplomat of good nature and graceful manners, whom nobody in Paris claimed to be the most incisive figure in French diplomacy. The Turkish representative, Mr Yalcin, was a benevolent and subtle journalist of advanced age. From the first day of its work until it faded away, as United Nations committees often do, in silent and progressive atrophy, the commission was grappling with problems beyond its scope. It lacked the zest and drive with which Bunche had responded to his opportunities. The truth is that triumvirates throughout history have never been famous for unity of thought and purpose.

The commission made its first error in convening all the Arab states together – and separately from Israel. Dr Bunche's achievement had owed much to the fact that Israel and each Arab state negotiated separately and directly on matters of bilateral concern. Israel's 'non-existence' and 'illegitimacy' had been articles of Arab faith for more than a generation. It followed that even if the interests of a single Arab state pointed towards a peaceful settlement, the common de-

Israel has consistently expressed its readiness to help find a solution
to the problem of the Arab refugees, but the Arab countries have
preferred to use their plight as a political weapon

nominator of all of them together could only be found in the traditional hatred. Soon we found Arab governments watching each other with hawk-like vigilance to see who would be first to violate the sacred principles of anti-Zionism.

The Arab delegations began unpromisingly by refusing to meet the Israeli representatives. They then insisted on a return of all the refugees as a condition of negotiation. When the commission invited all participating governments to give their views on a boundary settlement by comparison with the 1947 map, the Arabs clearly understood the implication that the armistice lines were already being down-graded; they were not even suggested as the starting point for the territorial discussion. The Arab governments proposed that Israel be confined to the 1947 partition area minus the whole of Galilee and the whole of the Negev! Their proposal would have left Israel nothing but a small strip on the coastal plain. It would have been a draconian settlement even if Israel had been totally defeated in the 1948 war. Why a victor should cooperate in his own mutilation was something that Arab governments never troubled to explain.

Israel proposed, as she was constantly to do for the next eighteen years, that the armistice lines be converted into permanent boundaries. All that the Conciliation Commission could do was to diagnose the existence of a wide gap in the positions of the parties. It went on to make a crucial error when Israel offered to receive 100,000 Arab refugees within the framework of a peace settlement. We must remember that at that time the Arab refugee population did not exceed 650,000. If Israel's offer had been followed by other Middle Eastern states in proportion to their objective capacity, the problem would have been brought out of deadlock and placed into movement on a long but promising road. The response of the Palestine Conciliation Commission was to describe Israel's gesture as insignificant and thus to incite the Arab governments to reject it. Israelis had the impression that it would be easier to reach agreements with their Arab adversaries directly than with the UN diplomats who were supposed to help them reach that agreement. By 1950, the Palestine Conciliation Commission had virtually acknowledged its own failure. It was to do nothing for the next two decades except report annually on lack of progress in efforts that it was not even making. The momentum established by Bunche had been frittered away.

A similar story of missed opportunities unfolded in the General Assembly at the end of 1949, when the question of Jerusalem was discussed. The Armistice Agreements had established Israeli and Jordanian jurisdiction in the two parts of the city. In each case, the populations concerned were inseparably loyal to the nations of which they formed a part. The situation seemed positively to cry out for a compromise which would have enabled an international authority to assume responsibility for the Holy Places while leaving the secular evolution of Jerusalem to be determined by the relations between the states concerned. Instead, the General Assembly, which had abandoned Jerusalem and its population to their fate when the war raged, now proposed the establishment of an international régime, which by this time would have disenfranchised both Israelis and Arabs and exchanged their independence for tutelage. The UN Charter has a great deal to say about developing subject communities towards independence. It makes no provision for a contrary process of transferring populations from national independence to an untested form of international colonialism.

The proposal for internationalization was rejected more vehemently by Jordan than by Israel, for the Jordanians were opposed even to the establishment of an international authority to look after the Holy Places. Israel supported international supervision of the Holy Places, which gave Jerusalem its special universal interest, but without prejudice to secular sovereignty over the city.

It soon became clear that the General Assembly adopted its resolution for internationalization without any serious intention of fulfilment. The fact that the United States, Britain and the non-Catholic countries of Europe opposed it indicated that there was not even a Christian consensus in its favour. The only lasting effect was to bring about a resolute Israeli reaction. The Knesset and government ministries had been established in Tel Aviv, both for physical security and because Israel had been willing in 1947–8 to give the internationalization formula a fair chance. The General Assembly resolution of 1949, however, was so contemptuous of Jewish historic sensitivity, and of Israel's sacrifice that the government, on Ben Gurion's motion, decided to move the capital to Jerusalem. On 11 December 1949 the Knesset convened in Jerusalem and took a solemn oath never to leave the capital again. At the same time, it reiterated Israel's willingness to cooperate with reasonable solutions for expressing universal interests in the Holy Places.

The fact remained that by the end of 1951 Israel's achievements at home and political successes abroad had not been crowned by peace. It has become conventional to speak as if peace depends on the multiplicity and skill of diplomatic initiatives. A more rational analysis reveals that before 1967 there was no powerful incentive for the Arab states to make peace. They were not suffering in any major respect from the absence of peace. Israel had proved its strength in war; but it had neither the will nor the ability to impose its own terms on defeated Arab states. The pressures of the Great Powers and the United Nations, as well as Israel's own preoccupations with development, made it obvious to the Arab states that they were in no danger of an Israeli attempt to erupt beyond the armistice lines. Even the refugee problem was not acutely felt; the Arab governments had shifted the whole burden of refugee maintenance off their own shoulders to those of the international community. Egypt had no such problem; the refugees under its juris-diction were simply excluded from the Egyptian society and economy and segregated miserably in the Gaza Strip, separated from Egypt's population centres by the empty Sinai desert. Syria had accepted only 70–80,000 refugees, which it had ample capacity to absorb or to reject according to its political calculation. Lebanon was faced with a more difficult problem as its population had been swollen by 80,000 refugees, most of whom were Moslems. But Lebanon, with its precarious balance between Christians and Moslems and its constant zeal to allay suspicion about its lack of nationalist fervour, had little to say in the Arab world on the general issue of peace and war. Jordan alone was to enfranchise the refugees as citizens and to use its increased population as a symbol of its growing importance in the Arab family. Jordan alone had something to gain by an early peace, and this interest was to express itself with dramatic results.

In general, however, the fact remained that the Arab governments saw the transition to peace as something which involved immense risks. The Arabs were in a crisis of wounded pride. They had gone to war in boastful con-fidence of swift and easy victory. They regarded themselves as inherently superior to their despised foe. However the outside world might regard them, they saw themselves as authoritative governments performing a respectable task of 'restoring order' in a neighbouring territory suffering from turbulence created by 'Zionist gangs'. Once they had committed themselves to the absurd-ity that the Jewish nation in Palestine was little more than a well-organized crime syndicate, the rest of their logic became impressively consistent. They had portrayed their adversary as subhuman creatures, devoid of valour, nobility, or authentic national feeling. In caricatures, Israel was drawn in the stereotyped figure of a verminous, hook-nosed, bearded, oily creature, sometimes with horns sprouting from the forehead. The impression was of something falling outside the human context and worthy only of extermina-tion. It followed that to be defeated by so contemptible a creature dealt a traumatic blow to Arab self-esteem. It was only in order to avoid greater humiliation that the Arabs had accepted the Armistice Agreements. On the

above Jews are believed
to have lived in
Kurdistan since the days
of Ezra. Virtually the
entire Jewish population
of the area emigrated
to Israel under the
auspices of 'Operation
Ezra and Nehemiah' in
1951

left Living conditions
during the early years of
the state were
characterized by
unrelenting hardship.
The immigrant camp in
Talpiot (January 1950)
was characteristic of
the general condition

morrow of their signature, the Arab states began to ignore those provisions which committed them to permanent peace. After all, they had not signed peace treaties; therefore they had not lost the game. The war was interrupted, not concluded. There would be another round, and then another, and in the long run they would be victorious. Here, the arithmetic of demographic and territorial strength seemed to be on their side. Azzam Pasha, the Secretary-General of the Arab League, said:

> We have a secret weapon which we can use better than guns, and this is time. As long as we don't make peace with the Zionists the war is not over. And as long as the war is not over there is neither victor nor vanquished. As soon as we recognize the existence of Israel, we admit, by this act, that we are vanquished.

The internal politics of Arab states also worked against peace. Here the dominant theme was Arab unity. This had never been expressed in real habits of cooperation; there was more rivalry than fraternity in the relations between Arab capitals. But they could all come together on the plane of rhetoric and ideology. If Arab unity was not strong enough to bring about affirmative cooperation, it did have enough power to justify each state trespassing on the affairs of others. If Jordan was suspected of making explorations for peace, there would be an outcry in Egypt, Syria and Saudi Arabia. If Lebanon gave indications of peaceful intent, Jordan would join the other Arab states in verbal assaults upon her. To make peace, therefore, would have involved an Arab leader in the fear of physical violence against him. At the very least, he would be assailed by the organizations which held Arab unity to be superior to the interests of individual Arab states. He would be guilty if not of treachery, at least of 'particularism', which ranked high in the Arab hierarchy of sin.

Above everything else, the Arab mind was haunted after the failures of 1948 by an irrational but authentic fear. There has always been a sharp ambivalence in the Arab vision of Israel. Sometimes the tendency is to portray Israel as beneath any standards of honour or respect; a figure to be derided and contemptuously liquidated. At other times, Israel's qualities are magnified until they come close to omnipotence. Israelis and Zionists, according to this portrayal, are unlimited in their capacity, cleverness, strength, skill, malevolence and international power. They have a lordly imperial dimension and their existing state is only a stepping-stone to a domain that would ultimately extend from the Nile to the Euphrates. Intelligent and responsible Arabs, including Nasser himself, have spoken as if they really believe that a map showing this Israeli empire is suspended on the Knesset walls. Seen in this light, Israel's very existence was deemed a threat to Arab security. The least that could be done was to abstain from making peace with something that would one day disappear. The audacity and sacrifice involved in making peace seemed disproportionate to any substantive gain. The plain fact is that the peace effort lacked incentive and motivation on the Arab side.

The refusal to make peace with Israel found its most dramatic expression in the attitude of the Arab governments to the refugees. The refugee problem was the direct result of the war. Once it is established that Arab governments, by an act of policy, created an acute human problem, it would seem natural for them to assume a large measure of responsibility in its solution. There were moments of candour when Arab leaders themselves gave expression to this principle. On 15 September 1948 Mr Emil Ghoury, Secretary of the Arab Higher Committee, said:

> I do not want to impugn anyone but only to help the refugees. The fact that there are refugees is the direct consequence of the action of the Arab states in opposing partition and the Jewish State. The Arab States agreed upon this policy unanimously and they must share in the solution of the problem.

There is a surprising similarity between this lucid statement and that of Ralph Bunche:

> The Arab States had forcefully opposed the existence of a Jewish State in Palestine in direct opposition to the wishes of two-thirds of the members of the Assembly. Nevertheless, their armed intervention had proved useless. The [Mediator's] report was based solely on the fact that the Arab States had no right to resort to force and that the United Nations should exert its authority to prevent such a use of force.

These are among the documentary monuments of the Arab invasion of 1948. It also left behind the testimony of Israel's graveyards; and the misery of Arab refugees was its living memorial. Yet for the next two decades the world was to observe the unique spectacle of governments whose policies helped to create the refugee problem rejecting all possibilities for its solution.

The flight had not been spontaneous in its first phase. In the early months of 1948, political and military leaders believed that their chances of overwhelming Israel would be greater if Arab civilians were removed from the line of fire. Many of the larger movements of refugees came from areas, such as Haifa, in which hardly a shot had been fired. In its later phases, the flight was nourished by additional causes. After the Arab assault on Jewish civilians, Arab civilian populations found themselves caught up in areas of conflict. Panic and uncertainty spread through the Palestinian Arab community when it became apparent that Arab armies were not delivering the victory they had promised. The possibility that many Arab communities would come under Israeli rule had become tangible. Since Arab propaganda had portrayed Israel as composed of powerful and inhuman savages, it was hardly reasonable for Arab leaders to expect Arab populations to accept such unspeakable domination or to return willingly to areas which it controlled. There were towns, such as Lydda and Ramle, whence the flight arose from Israeli armed actions and desire of civilians not to be in the range of shells, which were falling on the ground. The fact that Arabs – unlike the Israelis – had kindred countries in which they could find shelter without any sentiment of danger or exile contributed to the ease of the exodus. Moreover, Arab cities and villages are very close-knit in their allegiances. They have a strong sense of hierarchy. It was natural for them to follow their leaders' examples. Since all the leaders of Palestine Arab nationalism saw their duty or interest to lie in movement to Beirut or elsewhere, the masses were without responsible direction. They argued, not unreasonably, that if people like Jamal el-Husseini, Emil Ghoury and others found good cause for not remaining in Palestine, the reasons for flight must be overwhelming.

In the coming years the misery of refugee camps, deliberately perpetuated by Arab governments, was the primary card in the strategy of hostility to Israel. It was said that this human misery was the result of Israel's establishment. There was more truth in Bunche's statement that it was the result not of Israel's birth but of a violent attempt to prevent it from being born.

The suffering itself was grave and often poignant; yet most of the Palestine refugees had fled not to foreign climes but to other parts of Palestine itself. When an Arab moves from Jaffa to Nablus or Tulkarem he does not suffer great national or cultural alienation any more than a man forced to move, for example, from Hampshire to Cornwall, or from Massachusetts to New York. The Arab refugee had lost his physical home but not his national environment. Above all, unlike Jewish victims of persecution in Europe, he was assured of life. He was physically secure, breathing Arab air under Arab skies and living on soil which was a part of his national patrimony. He was not like a Hungarian refugee fleeing to Venezuela, or Jewish refugees from Russian pogroms seeking shelter in alien societies. The Arab governments, with international aid and Israeli cooperation, could have integrated the refugees into the economies and societies of the Middle East. This had been the answer to all the refugee problems created by modern wars; in no case had there been a mass return. The rule had been for refugees to be resettled in countries to which they were akin in language, faith, social habits and national sentiment.

Since the sense of national belongingness is powerful in Arab hearts, there is no doubt that the desire not to be under non-Arab rule played its full part in the exodus from what was evidently going to be non-Arab territory.

If the problem had been faced in concert by Middle Eastern governments as a human issue to be jointly resolved, a remedy could have been found. Massive international aid was available for the resettlement and economic integration of refugees in the countries to which they had fled. Many of these countries, especially Jordan and Syria, would find economic, social and human reinforcement in this influx, just as Israel would be rewarded in the long-term for the strain involved in absorbing hundreds of thousands of Jewish refugees from Arab lands. Yet for the next two decades and beyond, the Arab governments were to refuse to accept as equal citizens the kinsmen whose plight had been the direct result of their policies. They often kept them herded and segregated in camps. They threw full responsibility for their maintenance on the shoulders of other nations. They educated refugee children towards violent and passionate hatred of Israel. They indoctrinated them with the mission of becoming the spearhead of a war more destructive than that which had brought about their flight. In 1968 the Director General of UNESCO may well have been startled to receive from the Syrian Minister of Education, Suleyman al-Khash, a letter stating that: 'The hatred we indoctrinate into the minds of our children from their birth is sacred.' (UNESCO is an international agency for the eradication of hatred.)

In December 1948 the General Assembly had recommended that 'refugees wishing to return to their homes and live at peace with their neighbours should be permitted to do so at the earliest practicable date, and that compensation should be paid for property of those choosing not to return, and for loss or damage of property which under principles of international law or equity should be made good by the governments concerned'. It was soon forgotten, however, that the same resolution urged the negotiation of a peace settlement and called on the Palestine Conciliation Commission to 'facilitate the repatriation, resettlement and economic and social rehabilitation of the refugees and the payment of compensation'. Thus the General Assembly was not doing anything so quixotic as to recommend that the refugees be returned except in the context of a final peace to be negotiated between Israel and the Arab states. All other refugee problems in Europe and Asia had found their solution after the Second World War within a framework of political conciliation. There was no precedent for maintaining a state of war while calling on one belligerent to receive masses of hostile people from the territory of another.

The knowledge that Arab governments would continue to practice war against Israel, while pressing Israel to absorb hundreds of thousands of people dedicated to its own destruction, had a profound effect on the Israeli attitude to the refugee problem. There was no indifference to the human misery itself. But Israel, alone among the nations, had converted such misery into creative optimism amid masses of people in a short time. Israelis could not understand why an Arab government would not absorb and rehabilitate an Arab refugee with the same sense of duty and pride as that which inspired Israelis to take Jewish refugees into their society. The failure of Arab kinship was beyond Israeli understanding. Israelis were certain that the return of Arab refugees beyond a certain number would threaten the nation's security and national identity. Arab leaders supported this fear with their own candid affirmations: 'The return of the refugees means the destruction of Israel', was Gamal Abdul Nasser's compact definition.

This did not mean that Israel felt itself exempt from any responsibility. In any regional and international project Israel would make its due contribution. In 1949 the Israeli Government, despite sharp dissension at home, agreed to accept 100,000 refugees; and thousands of Arab refugees already in camps on Israeli soil were resettled. There was also a policy of reunion of families, and $11 million in refugee's blocked accounts were transferred by Israel to the banks of countries at war with her and practising economic warfare against her. When the Palestine Conciliation Commission and the United States Government advised the Arab states not to accept Israel's 1949 proposal, they virtually presented Israel with an 'all or nothing' dilemma. In such a choice Israel could only look at the savage assaults on its security by blockade, boycott and political incitement and ask itself what chance of survival it would have if it took a seething mass of hostility into its midst. In the General Assembly in November 1952, the Israel representative asked:

Can governments really create a vast human problem by their aggression; possess the full capacity to solve it; receive bountiful international aid towards its solution; and then refuse to join in the acceptance of any permanent responsibility for the fate of their kith and kin?

The plain fact was that Arab governments could do all of these things. Once they denied the humanitarian character of the issue and placed it squarely in the context of their belligerent policies, the Arab governments linked the fate of the refugees with the conflict itself. Now and again an attempt would be made to find an orderly and balanced solution through projects of economic development in the Middle East. It was in this spirit that an Economic Survey Mission, appointed in 1949, suggested constructive schemes to employ refugees in new locations all over the region. The proposal was rejected by the Arabs, with the result that the United Nations could only confine itself to relief work through the Relief and Works Agency (UNRWA), appointed in 1949. In 1952, the General Assembly allocated a sum of $200 million for resettlement and rehabilitation, as distinct from mere relief. The allocation remained unused because the Arab governments refused to cooperate. At various times the United States and others tried to counter-balance the call for repatriation by an equal stimulus for vocational training, which would make refugees self-supporting. These proposals, too, were frustrated by the Arab governments. Attempts to shift the accent of United Nations activities in refugee camps towards anything which would enable young Arabs to be absorbed in the expanding labour market of the Arab world were systematically obstructed by Arab governments. The truth is that it was impossible to solve a problem of this magnitude against the resolve of Arab governments to prevent its solution. As the years went on, the refugees found themselves in better econom-

left An entire generation of refugee children have grown up nurtured on hatred and on a hope for a country they never knew. Children at a refugee camp in Lebanon collect their meal as part of an UNRWA programme
right An aged immigrant and her grandchild attempt to keep warm in a camp in Jerusalem during the cold winter of January 1950 before resettlement in permanent housing

ic and social conditions than many of them had been in poorer Arab villages before their flight. They were also assured of services not available in many Arab villages in sovereign Arab countries. But their deep nostalgia and ardent militancy remained intact.

In 1951 Mr Galloway, a former representative of UNRWA in Jordan, said in Amman:

> It is perfectly clear that the Arab nations do not want to solve the Arab refugee problem. They want to keep it as an open sore, as an affront against the United Nations and as a weapon against Israel. Arab leaders don't give a damn whether the refugees live or die.

This is probably the most concise and comprehensive description of the reality that has ever been formulated. Yet the proximity and coexistence of Israel with the Arab refugee problem created in many minds an impression of cause and effect. It was argued that the refugees were an effect of Israel's emergence; therefore Israel should endanger its existence in order to absorb the refugees. In Israel itself there was no general sentiment of guilt, but the public conscience was ill at ease. There was a sentiment of regional responsibility, and, above all, an attitude of grievance towards Arab governments, which saw political hostility as a higher aim than human salvation.

By the beginning of 1950, the hopes kindled by the Armistice Agreements had declined. The conflict was dormant, but not dead. The Arab governments were still dedicated to Israel's downfall. A virulent swell of hate propaganda was let loose on Israel from every direction. The Palestine Conciliation Commission had failed. The problems of boundaries, Jerusalem and refugees were annually discussed in the General Assembly; the debates were not meant to be a method of solution, but a substitute for it. Public rhetoric held the field, and private conciliation was eclipsed.

The best that Israeli policy could hope to achieve was the stabilization of the arms balance, the prevention of a hot war and the exploration of peace beyond the uncongenial searchlights of UN debates. In May 1950 the United States, Britain and France signed a tri-partite declaration committing them to resist any change of the armistice lines by force and to ensure that imbalances of arms were not created. For many years this was the nearest that Israel was to get to anything like an international guarantee. In later years the declaration would be down-graded by one or more of its signatories whenever its fulfil-ment entailed any risk or complication. At the time it did seem to convey a hint of international recognition for Israel's right to security within the armistice lines. But it did not have the psychological effect which might have come from a formal treaty; and the quest for a negotiated peace went on beyond the framework of the United Nations and away from the Great Power arena.

The most promising attempt to reach a direct settlement ended on 20 July 1951, when Abdullah, King of the Hashemite Kingdom of Jordan, was shot dead while attending prayers in the Mosque of El-Aqsa in Jerusalem.

Abdullah's death did not only thwart a serious attempt to reach a peace agreement between Israel and an Arab state, it was to have a deterrent effect for many years afterwards on any Arab who was gripped by the 'heresy' of moderation. In the sequel to the Armistice Agreements, the Hashemite Kingdom of Jordan had annexed the West Bank and the Old City of Jerusalem without asking or obtaining international or even Arab recognition for this step. It had thus become the only Arab state to benefit from the 1948 Arab-Israeli war. It seemed to have a strong interest in consolidating its gains by moving to a peace treaty under which its tenure of the territories west of the Jordan would become internationally recognized. Abdullah was thus acting not so much in altruistic moderation as in a spirit of lucid Arab self-interest.

Between November 1949 and March 1950, Abdullah participated in many meetings with Israeli representatives. These culminated in a draft agreement between the two countries which was initialled, but never signed. The document was held in abeyance while the King sought means of overcoming resistance to himself and his policies from Arab extremists in Cairo, Damascus, Baghdad and elsewhere. Many meetings took place without the King being able to append his signature to the agreement. By this time he had been traduced as a 'traitor' to the Arab cause.

The result was that Israel entered its fifth year endowed with much international recognition, but without the crowning achievement of regional peace. All the world's governments, except the Arab states and their closest Moslem allies, had established relations with Israel. These assets of trust and friendship were an important compensation for neighbouring hostility. But the task of replacing Arab hostility by a new order of peaceful relations in the Middle East remained the only one of Israel's ambitions towards which no progress had been made in the first half decade of independence. Israel's qualities would have to be tested in siege and rancour. Its narrow land, its scanty water, its capital city, its right to security and development, its commerce with other countries, its maritime outlet to half the world – gifts which other nations inherited at their birth – would, for Israel, be the fruit of bitter contest.

6

A State Is Fashioned: Israel At Home

The bulwark of a city is its men.
Pericles

Israelis could have been forgiven if, in those first hectic years, they had come to believe that a state was something to be fought for and argued about rather than something to be built and developed. The urgencies of battle and diplomacy were so intense that the institutional problem was eclipsed. There was nothing like the brilliant and protracted constitutional exercise that preceded the American Declaration of Independence. Nor could Israel's hastily written Proclamation compare in eloquence with Thomas Jefferson's sonorous text. For any purpose except survival, Israel's founding fathers were quite simply short of time.

Yet they had some elements of consensus about the kind of society they wished to build. It would obviously have to be rigorously democratic, for was not Jewish history a constant rebellion against tyranny? It would have to be a parliamentary system, for the state had, in a sense, been born out of a parliament. The Zionist Congresses never had power to levy a single tax or exercise any degree of coercion on anybody, but they had wielded large authority in Jewish life, and a varied pattern of loyalties and beliefs had been woven around them. Zionists had no choice but to be great talkers – both to each other and to anyone outside who was willing or compelled to listen to them. In addition, it was accepted that an Israeli society would have to be egalitarian and socialist; these were the basic ideals of the immigrants who had fixed the Jewish community's values and goals. Beyond these signposts there was a special predicament to be faced in the conflict between tradition and modernism.

All this work was not to be done on a clean slate, for Palestinian Jewry had several decades of constitutional experience behind it. But four separate and difficult adaptations were now required. First, there were many autonomous bodies, voluntary associations and social movements which had already functioned as political units but would now have to be enlarged to include the duties of a sovereign organism. Secondly, services which had previously

Children in the Mea Shearim Quarter of Jerusalem throw election slips in the air. Certain ultra-orthodox circles do not recognize the state and instruct their supporters to boycott the elections

been allocated on a sectarian basis would henceforth have to be provided universally to all citizens. Then there would also have to be institutions and procedures for regulating the newly won political power among many contestants competing for it. And the fourth problem was to integrate diverse ethnic elements into a new Israeli identity.

The transition to sovereignty was not particularly complex in the institutional sense. Some of the tools were ready to hand. The Jewish Agency had been dealing with political problems, such as land settlement, defence and immigration. It had also developed an active diplomatic role. Then, there was the the Vaad Leumi (National Council), an indigenous organization representing the Jewish sector of the Palestinian population in its relations with the British. Above it was a representative body called the Asefat Hanivcharim (Elected Assembly). In addition, local government bodies had developed in the Jewish sector. Several voluntary associations formed in the pre-State period operated in areas usually covered by national ministries and social services. Many of these were, in essence, functions of state. With the transition to sovereign status it was natural for the Jewish Agency and Vaad Leumi leaders to assume the titles and capacities of government leaders.

While the cohesive nature of Palestinian Jewry was well known, some of its sharp sectarian tendencies were underestimated abroad. Some institutions, such as the Vaad Leumi, had represented the whole Jewish population; but many services had been provided by movements and associations on an exclusive basis to their own adherents alone. There was thus a plethora of state services in a condition of fragmentation. They would now have to be arranged by the government on a comprehensive basis for all citizens.

To regulate political power among those competing for it, a democratic structure had to be formed. It consisted of an executive, a legislative and a judicial branch. The roots of the executive and legislative parts of government went back to Palestinian Jewry's own institutions. There was no such existing basis for the Israeli judicial system, since this role had, in the nature of things, been monopolized by the central government during the Turkish period and the British Mandate.

The Israeli judicial system was not based on a written constitution. After 1949 several attempts to reach an agreement on a constitution were to fail through inability to agree on whether it should be based on secular or religious law. The judicial process was to be governed by a set of basic laws which proclaimed the human rights of all citizens, together with a series of *orders nisi*. In some spheres legal remnants of Turkish and British rule in Palestine remained in effect. Personal matters, such as marriage, divorce and inheritance, continued to fall under the jurisdiction of religious law and of the Rabbinical Courts with a possibility of appeal to the secular Supreme Court even on matters under religious jurisdiction.

The legislative branch of government was the Knesset, a one-chamber house of 120 members elected every four years by rigidly proportional representation through party lists. The votes cast throughout the country were counted, and seats were allocated to each party in exact accordance with whatever percentage it had gathered of the total vote. The Knesset was to elect the President of the State and to supervise the government (Cabinet) through its power to declare no-confidence and thereby dissolve the government. It was given the power of investigating government functions, and it determined the annual budget of the ministries. The Knesset could only be dissolved by its own decision. It was thus a powerful centralized authority, and no executive could be effective without constant parliamentary support. The dynamic of parliamentary life in Israel arose from the fact that no party was ever destined to enjoy a clear-cut majority in any election. All governments from 1949 onwards were to be coalitions of several parties which were committed to vote in the Knesset for government proposals. This meant that the opposition parties would also have to form a coalition in order to win a vote of no-confidence. Forming a government or an effective opposition was never to be easy in face of so many differing ideologies. The major party divisions were partly along economic lines (socialist-capitalist), and partly along religious lines (religious–secular).

Mapai (Mifleget Poalei Eretz Israel – Palestine Workers' Party) was the leading political party in the pre-State period and was to maintain a strong position in every election. It never won a clear majority in any national election, but it always won the largest number of votes and, therefore, was the party around which government coalitions were built. While Mapai began as a strictly socialist party, it soon developed a pluralistic base and drew support from many groups outside the organized labour movement.

Achdut Ha'avodah, another socialist labour party, was a shade left of Mapai. It had once been a part of Mapai, split off in 1944 for ideological reasons which were sometimes obscure, as well as for motives of personal rivalry which were always clear. Its main support came from the kibbutz movement. When independence came, Achdut Ha'avodah, together with a more leftist movement dominated by the kibbutzim of Hashomer Hatzair, formed a single parliamentary party called Mapam (Mifleget Poalim Meuchedet – United

THE PARTIES AND HOW THEY FARED

Knesset	First (25 Jan. 1949)		Second (30 July 1951)		Third (26 July 1955)		Fourth (3 Nov. 1959)		Fifth (15 Aug. 1961)		Sixth (2 Nov. 1965)		Seventh (28 Oct. 1969)	
Electorate	506,567		924,885		1,067,795		1,218,483		1,274,280		1,449,709		1,758,685	
Valid votes cast	434,684		787,492		853,219		969,337		1,006,964		1,206,728		1,367,743	
Party	*%*	*Seats*	*%*	*Seats*	*%*	*Seats*	*%*	*Seats*	*%*	*Seats*	*%*	*Seats*	*%*	*Seats*
Mapai	35.7	**46**	37.3	**45**	32.2	**40**	38.2	**47**	34.7	**42**	36.7[5]	**45**	46.22	**56**
Achdut Ha'avodah	—	—	—	—	8.2	**10**	6.0	**7**	6.6	**8**	6.6	**8**		
Mapam	14.7[1]	**19**	12.5[1]	**15**	7.3	**9**	7.2	**9**	7.5	**9**	6.6	**8**		
Rafi	—	—	—	—	—	—	—	—	—	—	7.9	**10**		
Herut	11.5	**14**	6.6	**8**	12.6	**15**	13.5	**17**	13.8	**17**				
Liberals[2]	5.2	**7**	16.2	**20**	10.2	**13**	6.2	**8**	13.6	**17**	21.3[6]	**26**	21.67	**26**
	4.1	**5**	3.2	**4**	4.4	**5**	4.6	**6**			3.87	**5**	3.21	**4**
National Religious Party	12.2[3]	**16**	8.3	**10**	9.1	**11**	9.9	**12**	9.8	**12**	9.9	**11**	9.74	**12**
Agudat Israel			3.7[4]	**5**	4.7	**6**	4.7	**6**	3.7	**4**	3.3	**4**	3.22	**4**
Poalei Agudat Israel									1.9	**2**	1.8	**2**	1.83	**2**
Communists	3.5	**4**	4.0	**5**	4.5	**6**	2.8	**3**	4.2	**5**	3.4	**4**[8]	3.99	**4**
Arabs (associated with Mapai)	3.0	**2**	4.7	**5**	4.9	**5**	3.5	**5**	3.5	**4**	3.3	**4**	3.51	**4**
Others	10.1	**7**	0.8	—	1.9	—	3.6	—	0.7	—	2.9	—	6.61	**8**

[1] In 1949 and 1951 Mapam included Achdut Ha'avodah.
[2] Figures for the first four Knessets refer respectively to General Zionists and Progressives, who merged in 1961 to form the Liberal Party. See also notes 6 and 7.
[3] In 1949 these parties constituted the United Religious Front.
[4] In 1951, 1955, and 1959, these two parties constituted the Torah Religious Front.
[5] Alignment (Mapai and Achdut Ha'avodah).
[6] Herut-Liberal Bloc (Gahal).
[7] Independent Liberals.
[8] Three New Communist List (Rakach) and one Israel Communist Party (Maki).

Workers' Party). For a few rhapsodic years most of its leaders believed that the USSR could do no wrong and the West no right. Later, in 1954, the leftist group split off to form a separate party; Mapam was now the name of a part, not the whole, of the left wing of the labour movement, and Achdut Ha'avodah reverted to its former name. Mapam became the only major non-Communist party to make the causes of Israel's Arab minority a major platform of its general policy. The three labour parties, Mapai, Achdut Ha'avodah and Mapam, were to go their separate ways until 1969, when they faced the electorate together in an alignment and came close to winning a majority of the votes and seats.

The Communist Party was the only non-Zionist group competing for votes. Before the establishment of Israel it favoured the establishment of a bi-national Arab-Jewish State. But it was converted to support of Israel's independence by the favourable shift in Soviet policy in 1947. The party's main support came from the urban slums and from Israeli Arabs. At its height, the party never received more than five per cent of the vote, and in 1965 it split into two, the one radical but patriotic (Maki), the other virulently identified with the Arab-Soviet critique of Israel (Rakach).

Herut was the main opposition party when the state was founded. It was the outgrowth of the Revisionist Party, which left the World Zionist Organization in 1935 because it favoured a more militant policy towards Britain and the Arabs. It had also formed its own military organization. In economic policy, Herut opposed the socialist measures of the government led by Mapai. It was the party of nationalist militance and of social protest, and it attracted those dissatisfied with government policies, with international moderation and with social democracy. From 1951 to 1961, Herut was usually Israel's second largest party, as large as Mapam and Achdut Ha'avodah together. In 1965 it was to form an alliance, called Gahal, with the more moderate centre Liberal Party, with whom it won twenty-one per cent of the vote in the Knesset elections. The Liberal Party had been founded in 1961 by a merger of the Progressive and General Zionist parties; but when it joined with Herut to form Gahal, the Progressive wing broke away to form the Independent Liberal Party. The Liberals' greatest support came from the middle class, the citrus growers and the free-enterprise sector in industry. The Progressives (Independent Liberals) were composed mostly of professionals, academicians and a small kibbutz movement.

When the state was founded, the major religious parties were Mizrachi; Hapoel Hamizrachi, based on the religious labour movement; Agudat Israel, the ultra-orthodox party; and Poalei Agudat Israel, its labour counterpart. In 1955 Mizrachi and Hapoel Hamizrachi combined to form the National Religious Party.

When this list of parties is written down for foreign eyes it sounds hopelessly complex. But to the Israeli voters who went to elect their Parliament in January 1949, there was something intimately familiar in the party landscape. Most voters had grown up with these organizations, either in Zionist Congresses or in elections to the Vaad Leumi, and some of the party names were animated in the popular consciousness by a vivid gallery of leaders. Thus, Mapai was the party of David Ben Gurion and his associates in the first Provisional Government – Moshe Sharett, Eliezer Kaplan, David Remez, Zalman Rubashow (Shazar). There were well-known Histadrut (National Labour Federation) leaders, like Golda Meir, Levi Eshkol, Mordechai Namir and Pinchas Lavon, who would join later administrations. Achdut Ha'avodah had its ideological oracle, Itzhak Tabenkin, who brooded in his kibbutz remote from ambitions of office. And Mapam's patriarchs, Meir Ya'ari and Ya'akov Hazan, in similar fashion, guided a succession of Mapam ministers in governments which the two leaders themselves never joined. The leading Herut figure was Menachem Begin, who had commanded the small, but intensely militant underground IZL movement in the pre-State era. He had worked in hiding, much sought by the British Government, which wanted him dead or alive. With the departure of the British administration, he emerged into parliamentary life, where his skilful and vehement oratory scourged the compromises which Ben Gurion deemed necessary for Israel's early development. The religious parties were naturally inclined to hierarchical structures. The Mizrachi and Hapoel Hamizrachi were led by the venerable Rabbi Yehudah Fishman (Maimon) and the gentle, pragmatic Moshe Shapira. Agudat Israel was symbolized by the sad eyes and flowing beard of Rabbi Itzhak Meir Levin, a survivor of the piety and learning of Polish Jewry. The Progressives were headed by Pinchas Rosen, a pillar of German Zionism and an exemplar of its finest virtues, including an unvarying moderation and a cool scepticism which offered relief from the more extreme passions of his East European colleagues. The Israeli voters in 1949, and thereafter, knew quite clearly what and whom they were voting for – or against.

The Israeli political party was an intensely important element in the life of its adherents. Most of the major parties had evolved from social movements in the pre-State period. The range of their control over their members' lives and activities was far-reaching. Each movement instilled in its members the

Israel's electoral system incorporates a plethora of political parties.
This Jerusalem billboard during the Knesset elections of 1965
bears posters of nine of the parties that contested for seats

belief that it represented a way of life, and not merely a collection of interests. Ideologies aroused deep emotions and strong loyalties. Attempts at merger among several parties in an effort to decrease their total number were difficult. Each party to a merger would have to compromise on its concept of the right way of life. In joining coalition governments small parties asked themselves suspiciously if they were not sacrificing principles for expediency. In the end parties would join the government coalitions on the grounds that political power would enable them to support legislation and policies favourable to their ideology. In the Israeli political vocabulary, 'power' was an invidious term, and ideological purity much admired. The convention was for politicians to represent the assumption of office as a hardship which they had reluctantly assumed in order to promote their higher values.

In the first twenty years of statehood there were to be six changes of government between elections. Only two of them led to a new composition of the coalition. Coalition partners from the earliest period included the Mapai, Mapam and the Religious parties. Mapai invariably won the largest number of votes, though never a total majority. As a result, it retained the portfolios of Prime Minister and Ministries of Defence, Foreign Affairs, Finance, Education and Culture, Agriculture and Police.

Israeli society was so diverse in its origins that many people wondered if it could hold together at all. One of the basic assumptions was that a common Jewish denominator would make for social cohesion. It was also assumed that positions of power would be allocated by standards of achievement, and not on the basis of communal or ethnic origins. Yet the ethnic problem was to become increasingly important in municipal institutions, in the new development towns throughout the country and, eventually, in the composition of the Knesset itself. Soon, all the national political parties decided to include deputies of Oriental background in their lists for the Knesset. On the national level, this in turn enabled the policies of major parties to be more sensitive to the needs of immigrant groups and thereby weakened the appeal of ethnic-based political parties. The success of Israel's political institutions in bringing about social integration through the democratic process is a crucial issue. Unless the national parties can achieve this, ethnic groups will come to function as political parties, with disruptive effects on the nation's unity.

One of the centres of political power in Israel from its earliest days was, theoretically, not a political institution at all. The Histadrut (National Federation of Labour) had great political importance. Its leaders are chosen in national elections by proportional representation, and the lists are drawn up

by the same parties as those which vie for political power in the national and municipal elections. Thus the Histadrut is an additional framework in which political parties can compete, on a national scale, especially in their economic and social policies.

The Israeli state was constituted mainly by immigrants, many of whom had a sentimental link to the number indicating their wave of immigration (*aliyah*). There was the First Aliyah, which lasted from 1882 to 1903 – the *aliyah* of the Biluim, composed of about 20,000 young Zionists from Russia. They had begun as hardy pioneers; but having been rescued by Baron de Rothschild from their immense penury, they had evolved into a plantation-like society grown distant from their youthful hopes. By 1948 most of them had passed away, but their sons were now voting in their own sovereign state. After them, decisive in their influence and incomparable in tenacity of purpose had come the Second Aliyah (1904–14), comprising some 35–40,000 Russian Jews disillusioned with the Russian Revolution of 1905. Their system of values included personal asceticism, the dignity of manual labour, self-defence, self-reliance and cultural dynamism. Among the most ambitious of their dreams was the rejuvenation of the Hebrew language. In their personal life they eschewed

above Leaders of the Hapoel Hamizrachi Party drink a toast with
the Prime Minister following their joining the coalition in 1952

material ambition and found individual satisfaction in the growth of a collective enterprise. They were authentic revolutionaries in full revolt against
Diaspora life, clericalism, bourgeois convention, the traditional urbanism
of Jewish life in Europe, the separation of Jewish youth from nature, their
parents and teachers – in fact, against everything that had typified Jewish
life for generations. They were a small leaven, but they gave the Israeli
loaf its characteristic taste and smell. The Second Aliyah immigrants wanted
to be a predominantly rural community, but in 1909 they had founded the
city of Tel Aviv, as well as the kibbutz and moshav system. Next had come the
Third Aliyah (1919–23), which included about 35,000 people, also Socialist
Zionists, who expanded the agricultural and urban base and helped to establish
the Histadrut in 1920. During this period the British Mandate was in power;
and with all its imperfections, it gave wider scope for Jewish development
than the corrupt Ottoman régime. Palestinian Jewry was able to flower
into its variety of autonomous institutions and social movements. The Fourth
Aliyah (1924–31) had brought 82,000 immigrants to the country, mostly
from Poland. Many of these were of lower-middle-class origin; unlike the
previous *aliyot*, they had mostly gravitated to the towns. The Fifth Aliyah
(1932–48) had been the largest of the immigrant waves, composed mostly of
refugees from Nazi Germany, many of whom had entered Palestine 'illegally'

Dr Chaim Weizmann takes the oath of
office as first President of the State of
Israel on 17 February 1949. The oath is
administered by the Speaker of the
Knesset, Yosef Sprinzak, a leading
personality in the labour movement

in the enterprise of human rescue accomplished by the Haganah. They had brought capital, skills, an intuition for Western techniques and an element of precision and formality which Palestinian Jewish society had hitherto lacked.

To the community of over 650,000 fashioned by these five immigrant streams, there had now converged the massive immigration of 1948. The population whose representatives were to be selected by popular suffrage on 24 January 1949 amounted to 782,000. Of these, more than 500,000 were eligible voters. Eighty-seven per cent of them went to the polls that day – 440,000 strong. When the votes were counted, Mapai had won 46 of the 120 seats: Mapam, including Achdut Ha'avodah, 19 seats; the United Religious Front, 16 seats; Herut, 14 seats; the General Zionists, 7 seats; the Progressives, 5 seats; the Sephardim, 4 seats; the Communists, 4 seats; the Arabs of Nazareth, 2 seats; with one seat each to the Fighters' List (Lechi), WIZO and the Yemenite Association. The remarkable fact is that for the next twenty years there would be no more than marginal changes in these electoral results. For a party to gain or lose five seats was almost a landslide.

On 10 February, the Provisional State Council held its last meeting, and four days later the elected Constituent Assembly convened in Jerusalem to hear a moving address by its President, Chaim Weizmann:

All my life I have striven to make science and research the foundation stone of our national enterprise. But I have always realized that there were values more sublime than those of science, values essential to healing the ills of mankind – I speak of justice and integrity, peace and brotherhood.

Zion shall be redeemed with justice and they that return to her – with righteousness.

Yosef Sprinzak, a veteran labour leader, was chosen as Speaker. On 16 February the Knesset elected Weizmann as the first President of Israel. The following day, accompanied by the plaintive notes of the *shofar*, Weizmann entered the chamber to take the oath of office. The Speaker closed the meeting with the words: 'We have taken the first step towards building our lives. Israel's salvation is at hand.'

Israel's international prestige had been elevated by the choice of Weizmann to inaugurate the Presidency. He had led his people for forty years through a wilderness of martyrdom and oppression, of high aspirations and frustrated hope; and now, near the end of his days, he had come upon his due inheritance of honour – the embodiment in modern times of the kingly and prophetic tradition that had once flourished in Israel and had sent a message of redemption and freedom to successive generations of mankind. He had fought the major battles of Zionism, from the Balfour Declaration in 1917 to the recognition of Israel by the United States in 1948. He had been buffeted by many storms from outside and within, and the years had taken a heavy toll. His bearing was still erect, with a tall, sad dignity, but his voice was frail and his eyes close to blindness.

His last years were not happy. He felt resentment and surprise at the rigid limitations of his office. He found himself confined to those ceremonial functions in which he had never had the slightest interest. The Israeli Government also showed a lack of imagination and a failure of historic deference, for Weizmann's name was not included amongst those who had signed the Declaration of Independence and even his request to receive the Cabinet minutes regularly was not fully answered.

His final months were spent in sharp ambivalence of feeling. On the one hand, he had, unlike Moses, passed into the Promised Land. His historic imagination could not fail to be stirred by the thought that he had come full circle, from Motol, near Pinsk, in the Russian Pale of Settlement, to the Presidency of an independent Jewish State which, to less sensitive minds, had seemed a chimerical dream. The Weizmann Institute of Science, which was inaugurated on 2 November 1949, already showed promise, which was later amply fulfilled, of placing Israel high in the universal enterprise of scientific research. On the other hand, he chafed at his inability to impress the new society with his own vision of intellectual integrity, aesthetic refinement, and manifest dedication to peace. Israel had been born in the teeth of lawless violence; it continued to live an embattled existence.

There were times when Weizmann was seized by a poignant concern for Israel's inner quality; but whenever he fell into doubt or regret he looked through his window at Rehovot, upon the verdant rolling plains and rich orange groves surrounding the scientific institute established under his inspiration and leadership. On a clear day his gaze would go as far as the Judean hills. The landscape in between was dotted with villages and townships reflecting the new impetus given to Jewish vitality. Then a deep contentment would come upon him and his mind would become serene, as befitted a man who to a degree unshared by any figure in contemporary history had seen an improbable vision translated, largely through his own effort, into vibrant and solid reality. After a long illness, he died on 9 November 1952. His grave was situated at his own wish in the garden of his home at Rehovot.

The President's first formal duty in 1949 had been easy. The electoral verdict clearly required him to entrust Ben Gurion to form a Cabinet. Thus began a chapter of dramatic personal leadership that was to take Israel through victories and ordeals for thirteen of the next fifteen years. After three weeks of negotiation, Ben Gurion formed a Cabinet based on the support of Mapai, the United Religious Front, the Progressive Party and the Sephardic Party.

When the Knesset assembled, the new government promised to seek an Arab-Israeli alliance, friendship with the United States and the Soviet Union, economic recovery through austerity, the doubling of immigration, and a vigorous educational programme. Menachem Begin attacked the armistice agreement with Egypt. Nathan Friedman-Yellin of the Freedom Fighters' Party called for the conquest of the whole of Palestine by armed force. (After 1967, when this conquest had taken place, he was to urge that all the occupied territory be promptly given back.) Ya'akov Hazan for Mapam proclaimed the Soviet Union to be 'the bastion of world socialism, our second socialist homeland'. Twenty years later he could not find words hard enough for the Soviet Union. It was clear from the beginning that life in Israel's Knesset was not going to be dull. For the first year of Israel's independent life, the Knesset met in the Opera House on the Tel Aviv seashore. It captured the popular interest more than the opera ever had; and its forensic battles were keenly followed and minutely reported. A parliamentary tradition of some maturity grew up with unusual speed.

7

The Ebbing Tide, 1953–1956

Fire is the test of gold; adversity of strong men.   Seneca

The mood of societies, as of individuals, has a cyclical rhythm. After periods of sustained effort, there comes an interval of lassitude in which vitality declines and the zest for creation seems lost. Nations seem to need a periodic renewal of conviction, a new sense of collective purpose. Such changes of mood are not always the result of adversity; indeed, perils, if they are sharp enough, often bring societies to the highest expression of their powers. The time of danger is when objective difficulties increase without a simultaneous rise in the spirit necessary to surmount them. Israel underwent such a period between 1953 and 1956. For five years nothing important had gone wrong; there were now four years in which nothing at home or abroad seemed to go right.

Ben Gurion's temporary retirement was both the cause and the effect of this ebbing mood. In his letter to President Izhak Ben-Zvi, Weizmann's successor, he adduced 'supreme mental tension' as the reason for his departure.

He had every right to be tired. He was a buoyant, vigorous man who sent out sparks of energy in all directions. But ever since 1933 he had borne heavy responsibilities; and since Weizmann's resignation from the Zionist Organization Executive in 1946, he had carried a central and solitary burden. Although he was sixty-six years old, physical strain did not seem to be the main factor in his exhaustion. His personality and career had reached their highest development relatively late in life, as was the case with Churchill, Adenauer, de Gaulle and others before and after him. Behind his ritual words of parting one could sense a deep dissatisfaction with some elements of Israeli life. The intensity of parliamentary warfare, the fragmentation arising from the electoral system, the need to be perpetually conciliating small groups in order to maintain a coalition – all these were repellent to his active and dominating nature.

And now there were clouds on the international horizon as well. The Soviet Union had abandoned its support of Israel. The cooling-off had first come

Chief of Staff Moshe Dayan receives the French Legion of Honour, an act which symbolized the zenith of cordial relations between France and Israel during the 1950's

into evidence during the early 1950's, when the Soviet Union joined the Arab states at the United Nations in defeating a proposal for a negotiated settlement for which Israel had mustered impressive support in the committee stage. In November 1952 the Communist government in Czechoslovakia organized the trial and execution of party leaders, including Rudolf Slansky, Secretary of the Party, a Jew but a rabid anti-Zionist, and Clementis, the Foreign Minister. An Israeli Mapam leader, Mordechai Oren, had also been implausibly accused of subverting Czechoslovak security (he was later released). The trial had served as an occasion for rabid propaganda against Zionism and Israel. And in January 1953 a worse blow fell. The Soviet Union had arrested a number of Jewish doctors and accused them of diabolically seeking to murder Soviet leaders and other patients. The ugliest form of anti-Semitic agitation accompanied this judicial farce, which turned out to be one of the death throes of Stalinism. There had been demonstrations in all countries where there were Jewish communities, including Israel. The Soviet Legation in Tel Aviv had been damaged by an explosion in the yard of its chancery. Israel's official apology was swift and patently sincere: nothing in the world could have served its interest less. But the expression of regret was rejected and the Soviet Union broke diplomatic relations. In other countries where its missions were damaged, without a Jewish context, the USSR was more indulgent.

The greater likelihood is that the Soviet change of policy reflected an intensified desire to pursue the Cold War and a shrewd understanding that there were more votes and alliances to be obtained in the far-flung Arab world than in solitary Israel. In the early months of 1953, the Egyptian monarchy had been overthrown and a 'revolutionary' régime under General Neguib, and later Colonel Nasser, had been instituted. The time seemed ripe for the Soviets to detach Arab states from their traditional Western connections.

The winds that blew on Israel from the West were less harsh, but far from consoling. The Eisenhower administration in the United States, which had taken over from Truman in January 1953, did not drastically change anything in American-Israeli relations. The economic support which was then the main element of United States-Israel cooperation continued to flow. But Washington announced a 'new look', which consisted of avoiding the traditional emphasis on friendship with Israel in an effort to win Arab smiles. In October 1953, when Israel was agonizingly harassed by Arab assaults on frontier villages and by interference with Israel's irrigation projects in the north, the United States joined in heavy condemnation of Israel's reprisals, especially after the

Kibya raid, which most of Israeli opinion also regarded as excessive. In the very same month, when Israel refused to halt its development work at Bnot Ya'akov in the northern demilitarized zone, the United States suspended its grants in aid – only to renew them a few weeks later under indignant public pressure in America itself. The Secretary of State, John Foster Dulles, had visited Israel and Arab states in the summer of 1953. While his conclusions were not all adverse to Israel, he strongly hinted that Israel should offer boundary concessions to Egypt and Jordan as the price of a peace settlement, which these two governments showed no signs of desiring.

By the middle of 1953, the Soviet Union, after Stalin's death, had resumed diplomatic relations with Israel; and the American approaches to the Arab world had merely increased Israel's nervousness without fundamentally damaging its interests or arousing much appreciation in Arab countries. Yet after such tremors in Washington and Moscow, the Israeli people had less confidence than before about its place in the world. Moreover, immigration had dwindled. It had amounted to 174,000 in 1951. By 1952 it had sunk to 24,000 and in 1953 to 11,000. The number of Jews leaving Israel that year was greater than the number of immigrants.

All in all, it could not be said that Ben Gurion was handing the country over to his successor in a condition of vigour or prosperity. Sharett was inheriting a beehive without much honey; and his difficulties were also compounded by a visible lack of authority. Ben Gurion had spoken of retirement 'for a year or two'. Even during his residence in the Negev kibbutz of Sdeh Boker, he exercised strong influence on his party, many ministers and leading army officers; and, in the manner of strong leaders, he generated

John Foster Dulles, US Secretary of State from 1953 until his death in 1959, played a decisive role in developments concerning the Middle East, especially in the outcome of the Suez–Sinai Campaign of 1956

Lieutenant-General William E. Riley, who served as Chief of Staff of the UN Truce Supervision Organization from October 1948 to June 1953

a subtle atmosphere of scepticism around his successors in office. Thus an air of transience pervaded the Sharett government from the first day to the last. There was also, for the first time, a division between the Premiership and the Ministry of Defence. Sharett retained the Foreign Ministry, while Defence went to Pinchas Lavon. He was energetic and strong minded, but of contentious disposition. He gave little deference to the Premier and lived in permanent tension with leading staff officers and officials of his ministry. The country incurred all the defects of a Prime Minister's resignation without the balancing advantages of a new, stable and clear-cut leadership.

The year 1954 opened with a Soviet veto in the United Nations Security Council of a resolution which would have enabled irrigation work to proceed in the demilitarized zone at Bnot Ya'akov. The ingenuity and goodwill of the Acting United Nations Chief-of-Staff, General William Riley, soon enabled the finding of a way to evade the Soviet obstruction and go on with the work. But the veto had an ominous significance beyond its particular context. From that day on, the Security Council was closed to Israel as a court of appeal or redress. Arabs would kill Israeli citizens across the border, blockade Israel's Red Sea port of Eilat, close the Suez Canal to Israeli shipping, send armed groups into Israel for murder and havoc and decline to carry out crucial clauses of the Armistice Agreements in the complete certainty that the Security Council would not adopt even the mildest resolution of criticism or appeal. Sometimes the veto was actually used by the Soviet Union against majority resolutions; at other times the anticipation of it prevented the majority from submitting any texts which gave support to Israel's interests. On the other hand, there was no such inhibition to resolutions criticizing Israel for retaliating against provocations. The jurisprudence of the United Nations thus came to imply that Arab governments could conduct warfare and maintain belligerency against Israel, while Israel could offer no response.

On 27 January 1954 Israel tested the Security Council by submitting a complaint about an intensification of Egypt's blockade in the Suez Canal. Three years before, on 1 September 1951, Israel had won a diplomatic victory by persuading the Security Council to rule against all maritime interference or claims of active belligerency against Israel as being 'inconsistent with the letter and spirit of the Egyptian-Israeli armistice agreement'. The Soviet Union had not obstructed that judgment; its abstention was almost its last gesture of relative goodwill towards Israel. Egypt had refused to take any notice of the Security Council's Resolution of 1951. By now, the Arab doctrine was that all resolutions of international agencies were binding on Israel and optional for themselves. It was a picturesque jurisprudence and did not lack originality. What is more remarkable is the degree to which the rest of the world resigned itself to its perpetuation. The general theme was that Arabs were 'irrational' and therefore could not be held responsible for the results of their passion.

The 1954 discussion ended in futility. The Soviet Union vetoed a New Zealand resolution calling for the 1951 anti-blockade decision to be respected. The Arab governments could now reasonably believe that their warfare against Israel could be conducted behind a water-tight international defence.

It was not only a question of political discrimination. There were practical effects of the most tragic kind. The Arab governments had resolved, without risking total war, to drive Israel out of its mind by a constant torment of piecemeal violence. The crisis over the Bnot Ya'akov project had only arisen because Syria opened fire to stop Israeli development work – and it was easier for the United Nations and the Powers to order the suspension of the work than to order the cessation of the fire. The Kibya raid on 15 October was full of erroneous Israeli judgments on a number of levels; but, in itself, it was a response, not an initiative. The village had served for years as a base for terrorists across the border. In March 1954 infiltrators from Jordan attacked a bus on its way back from Eilat, killing eleven passengers and wounding several more. Neither the Mixed Armistice Commission nor the Security Council would say a word against Jordan, from whose territory the infiltrators had come and in which they obviously had easy shelter. The UN Chairman of the Mixed Armistice Commission abstained from voting, professing that he did not know where the terrorists came from and whither they had fled. The Israeli public was hot with anger, and the Israeli delegation left the Armistice Commission.

In his report to the Security Council on 7 September 1954, General Burns predicted that incidents on the Jordan-Israel border could spread 'like brush fire'. Marauding into Israel by armed gangs was serious, but 'Israeli retaliation by armed raids was a dangerous remedy'. After an Israeli raid at Beit Liqya, in response to assaults in Jerusalem, the United States used a similar formula. Infiltration from Jordan constituted a serious problem, but Israel's 'apparent policy of armed retaliation had increased rather than diminished tension along the armistice lines'.

Whether there would really have been less tension if Israel had fatalistically sat back and let its citizens be killed without 'armed retaliation' is moot. Since no such bizarre experiment in national masochism has ever been tried in any country, we shall never know the answer. The crux of the matter was that an urgent problem existed and no solution was at hand. After the Kibya raid in October 1953, Israel had proposed a thorough review of the Armistice Agreement with Jordan in accordance with Article XII. This laid down that if after a year (from March 1949) either signatory asked the Secretary-General to convene a conference with the other party to review or revise the agreement, attendance was mandatory. Secretary-General Dag Hammerskjold turned to Amman, received a refusal to attend the 'mandatory' conference – and there

the matter ended. So the Security Council was blocked by veto, the Mixed Armistice Commissions were sterile and a review of the agreement was illegally refused. Israel seemed to have nothing left open to her but the deterrence of armed response.

This was tried with little effect. The most drastic Israeli action was at Gaza in February 1955. In the previous six months, there had been forty armed clashes, twenty-seven Egyptian raids into Israeli territory, with seven Israeli deaths and twenty-four wounded. There had been no incursions by Israel into Egyptian territory; and Egypt had been condemned by the Mixed Armistice Commission twenty-six times. The Israeli riposte at Gaza left thirty-eight Egyptian and eight Israeli dead. While the Security Council was debating its routine resolution condemning the Israeli response and ignoring the prior Egyptian assaults, armed infiltrators threw grenades and opened fire at a village called Patish, 10 miles inside Israeli territory, where a wedding was taking place. A woman was killed and eighteen guests were wounded. The Mixed Armistice Commission denounced this as a brutal and murderous act of aggression and attributed the responsibility to Egypt. But the assaults went on at an unbearable rate. On 4 April, Israel asked the Security Council to convene on 6 April. Thirteen days later it decided that no new action on its part was required, since the 30 March decision condemning Israel for the Gaza raid already covered the existing border situation! The Israeli Government vehemently criticized this 'manifest instance of partiality' and added that 'the Powers, which determined the outcome of the Security Council debate, have assumed a heavy responsibility for its baneful results'.

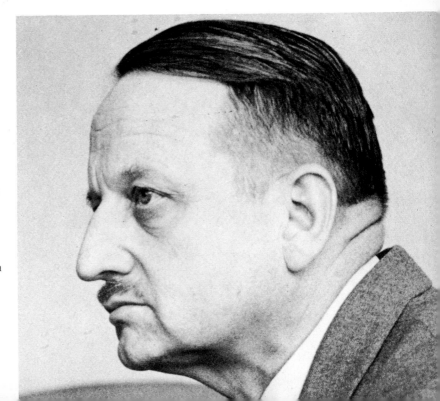

left Dag Hammarskjold, Secretary-General of the United Nations from 1953 until his death in an air crash in 1961, 'dines' with Ben Gurion at Sdeh Boker
right Major-General E.L.M. Burns became second Chief of Staff of the UN Truce Supervision Organization in 1954

October and November 1954 were sanguinary months, with raids and counter-attacks mounting in crescendo. The Egyptians were trying to make the Negev uninhabitable; and the Syrians now attempted to drive Israeli fishing boats and patrol vessels out of the Sea of Galilee. An Israeli counter-attack in December 1955 left forty-nine Syrians and six Israelis dead. It was criticized in Israel itself because of the unexpectedly heavy toll of Syrian casualties, and also because the Foreign Minister, Moshe Sharett, was in Washington at the time awaiting a response to his request for permission to buy jet aircraft. The counter-attack was followed by a deferment of the American response.

At the end of January, Hammarskjold visited the Middle East and secured agreement for some limited measures for reducing frontier tension in the Egyptian-Israeli sector. These were ratified by the Security Council in March, and another visit to the area by Hammarskjold in April promised to consolidate a relative calm. Hammarskjold was back in the area in July, again producing a lull. But it was deceptive. Raids from Jordan mounted in July and August, with Israeli civilians and soldiers being blown to pieces or mutilated at Beer-sheba, on the road to Eilat and at El Auja, and with Israeli actions of vigorous reprisal being more strongly condemned than the murders which had pro-voked them. With all respect to the tactical and technical measures constantly being proposed by the Secretary-General, it was obvious that the rate of clashes depended ultimately on political decisions and attitudes in Cairo, Damascus and Amman. These decisions evidently included a determination not to let Israel alone for too long in any one place.

The armistice system was obviously approaching a dead end. It had been founded on a basic contradiction between the intentions of its signatories. Israel had regarded it as the end of the war and as a virtual peace settlement in embryo. It therefore stressed those provisions in the agreement which gave a hint of stabilization and finality. The Arab governments saw the armistice as a temporary phase in a continuing war which had never been renounced. They therefore placed their accent on the provisional and non-committal atmosphere of some formulations, especially on the boundary question. The Major Powers and the United Nations began with strong support of the Israeli interpretation of the agreements as stable international situations; but as a result of Arab pressure and their own divisions they began to tamper with the armistice lines as though they had no durable legitimacy. Thus the political force of the Armistice Agreements was undermined at the very time that their security provisions were being disrupted by daily violence. By February 1956 Ben Gurion was calling for volunteers to build air-raid shelters and reinforce the defence of border settlements. On 9 May Hammar-skjold stated that 'the parties interpreted the armistice to mean that any one infringement of the provisions of the agreement by one party justifies reactions by the other party which, in their terms, are breaches of the Armistice Agreements, without any limitations as to the field within which reciprocity is considered to prevail'. There was no reason for him to be surprised. Israel really felt that it was normal in contractual law to assume that a breach of an agreement by one party released the other party from its obligations. But the main criticism of the Secretary-General's statement is that, like all other UN actions in the area, it confined itself to diagnosis and was almost totally deficient in remedy.

Israel's anguish in the three nightmare years, 1954–6, was not confined to the inflamed borders alone. The dispute with the Arab states, and especially with Egypt, steadily lost its localized character and became caught up in the tangle of global rivalry. The measures that the Powers took in prosecution of the Cold War with each other were surely not designed to weaken Israel's strength or spirit. But this was the result of their actions – and none of the Powers made any compensating move on Israel's behalf. This was clearly predictable in the case of the Soviet Union, which changed the situation of the Middle East in 1955 by a massive arms transaction with Egypt through Czechoslovakia. Weapons of a destructive capacity hitherto unknown in the region poured into Egypt at a rate beyond all previous experience. Israel saw itself faced with possible dangers far greater even than those involved in the daily border attacks. The bottom had clearly been knocked out of its long-term security.

The indictment of Western policy is not that it failed to prevent the Soviet penetration, but that it neglected the measures by which the effects of that penetration might have been counter-acted. What was needed was a show of Western strength to demonstrate to excited Arabs that the Middle East was not going to become a uniquely Soviet preserve; and in relation to Israel, there was a possibility of maintaining relative stability by a modest reinforcement of Israel's armaments and a stronger support of the armistice lines as de facto boundaries. Neither of these courses was taken.

The first link in the chain of events leading towards explosion was the Baghdad Pact of 24 February 1955. This was a defence treaty (Pact of Mutual Cooperation) between Iraq and Turkey, linked to an earlier treaty between Turkey and Pakistan. Britain and Iran joined in 1955. The United States did not formally adhere to the pact, but its spiritual father was John Foster Dulles and the main support in arms and money came from the United States. This was part of Dulles' policy of containing Soviet expansion by clear contractual deterrents that would prevent Soviet penetration of the Middle East. The aim was plausible, but the means did not serve the end. Nasser was violently offended by what he interpreted as an effort by Washington and London to divide the Arab world into rival blocs corresponding to the East-West division. His position as the leader of the Arab world was being challenged, and he responded by a vehement anti-Westernism, by exercising more pressure for the overthrow of pro-Western régimes in Baghdad, Amman and elsewhere and, above all, by strengthening his links with Moscow.

The arms deal of September was, above all, Nasser's response to the Baghdad Pact. His discomfiture in frontier clashes with Israel at Gaza and elsewhere were, at most, a subsidiary motive. He could have solved that dilemma simply by not attacking Israel. He might also have been able to receive arms from less compromising sources than Soviet Russia. But he could not forgive the West for 'taking over' the leadership of Arab international policy.

While the Baghdad Pact alienated Egypt, it did not win over Iraq or Jordan. In 1958, after the downfall of the Iraqi monarchy, Iraq formally withdrew from the treaty to which it had given its name. There were riots in Jordan in 1955 because of Britain's rumoured intention to work for Hussein's adherence to the pact. The British Commander of Jordan's Arab Legion, General Glubb, was summarily dismissed (March 1956), and Jordan kept away from new treaty engagements with the West.

All that now remained was the negative effect of the Baghdad Pact on Israel. Dulles' explanation was that by involving Arab states in a 'northern tier' defence against Soviet expansion together with non-Arab states, like Iran and Turkey, he would be substituting Communism for Zionism as the major foe of the Arabs and would create a sphere of Arab international preoccupation remote from the Israeli issue.

Nothing of this came about. Israel found itself alone in the Middle East. Arab states were being rearmed under defence pacts with the Major Powers, while Israel had neither an assured source of arms nor a guarantee of its security and integrity. There was a treaty between Britain and Egypt; a treaty between Britain and Iraq; a treaty between Britain and Libya; an arms-supply agreement between the United States and Iraq; an arms agreement between the United States and Pakistan; agreements between the United States, Libya and Saudi Arabia; and a treaty between Turkey and Iraq. A great structure linking the states of the Middle East with the Western world in mutual assistance was growing up, based on the exclusion of one state alone – precisely the most vulnerable state in the region. A man would have to be lost to reason to expect

Israel not to be alarmed by the sudden increase of its regional isolation. Prime Minister Sharett had declared that Israel felt entitled to request binding, formal guarantees for the integrity of its frontiers, as well as direct assistance to maintain the balance of arms. It seemed obvious to all but the major Western governments that if no response was given to these requests, Israel would be forced into drastic options. After all, the Arab states were now divided between those receiving arms from the United States and those receiving them from the Soviet Union. They were united only in their implacable hostility to Israel.

'When sorrows come, they come not single spies, but in battalions.' The Shakespearian definition seemed to have special application to Israel in those clouded days. The border conflicts were threatening Israel's short-term tranquillity, while the pursuit of Arab favour by the Powers was undermining its long-term security. As if this were not enough of a burden on Israel's jangled nerves, there now came the third element in the nation's discomfiture: a resolute attempt by two of the Western Powers to press Israel for territorial concessions.

The United States' move came in August 1955, when Secretary Dulles made a major policy speech in New York. It later became evident that he was trying to forestall the Soviet arms transaction by sending out signals to Egypt of American support for territorial concessions by Israel.

Dulles' speech did not ignore Israel's security problem. He even held out the possibility of the United States entering into formal treaty engagements guaranteeing the boundaries of Middle Eastern states. But he added: 'If there is to be a guarantee of borders there should be prior agreement upon what the borders are. The existing lines . . . were fixed by the Armistice Agreements of 1949. They were not designed to be permanent frontiers in every respect.' He went on to advocate the fixing of permanent boundaries; and, in a clear allusion to the Negev desert, he added: 'The difficulty is increased by the fact that even territory which is barren has acquired a sentimental significance.'

The atmosphere of the speech, and of the concurrent diplomatic talks, pointed to territorial concessions by a very small Israel to a vastly bigger Egypt and Jordan. On the problem of refugees, Dulles came nearer to Israel's position in advocating that 'these uprooted people should through resettlement and, where feasible, repatriation, be enabled to resume a life of dignity and self-respect'. The accent had rarely been removed from repatriation to this extent. Dulles went on to offer an American loan to Israel to enable it to pay compensation to refugees remaining in Arab states. But, in Israel's eyes, the implication that the armistice lines were not to be finally recognized and that the Negev was up for bargaining overshadowed the more positive elements in the speech.

If Israel had been disturbed by American 'hints' on the status of its frontiers, it was shocked by the speech of the British Prime Minister, Anthony Eden, at the Guildhall on 9 November 1955. In even more forthright language than that used by Dulles, Eden called for a compromise between the boundaries of the 1947 UN resolution and the 1949 armistice lines. In simple terms, it became evident that London and Washington favoured Israeli concessions in the Negev to Egypt and Jordan, so as to enable them to establish a land-bridge to each other without passing through non-Arab territory. For Israel this was tantamount to the loss of its exclusive control of the Negev, which had been the main benefit secured in the political struggles of 1947–9. In the Knesset on 15 November, Ben Gurion firmly rejected Eden's offer to mediate on this basis, since it was designed 'to truncate the territory of Israel for the benefit of her neighbours' and therefore had 'no legal, moral or logical foundation'.

Israel's general response to the situation created by American and British initiatives was a careful balance between moderation and tenacity. It was presented in a letter by Foreign Minister Sharett to Secretary Dulles on 19 December 1955, after sustained discussions between the Israeli Embassy in Washington and the State Department.

The main points were that Israel would agree to mutual adjustments of the 1949 armistice line for purposes of security and improved communications, but would not consider negotiating on the basis of the 1947 partition line. Israel would consider granting the Arab states transit rights for the free flow of commerce from north to south between Lebanon and Egypt and across the Negev between Egypt and Jordan; and Jordan would be offered free-port facilities in Haifa and the necessary transit rights to reach the port by land. Sharett also confirmed that Israel would be willing to raise funds to compensate the Arab refugees and accepted the United States offer of a loan to help in the work of resettlement and rehabilitation of the refugees in the Arab states. Israel also accepted the Jordan River development plan drawn up by Mr Eric Johnston, the United States envoy, whereby Israel and the Arab states would share the waters of the Jordan and Yarmuk rivers. She considered this a concession because more than half the water supplies would go to the Arab states.

On the other hand, it was made clear that Israel would not retreat from her previous position on the following points:

A group of Israeli soldiers after their return from a reprisal raid against Khirbet Tawfiq in 1955

1 She would not agree to any unilateral concessions and would expect minor adjustments in the armistice line would leave Israel's total territory virtually the same.

2 She would not relinquish the port of Eilat on the Gulf of Aqaba.

3 In granting transit rights to Jordan and Egypt across the Negev, she would not permit the creation of any extra-territorial corridor.

4 She would continue to oppose the internationalization of Jerusalem.

The year 1955 passed away unregretted; but during the first half of 1956 the clouds never seemed to go away. The border violence was unremitting, and Israel's heavy retaliations were not having any lasting effect. Above all, the arms imbalance remained uncorrected; and the actions of the Powers were all destined to appease the Arabs, not to reassure Israel. There was a volcanic atmosphere in Israel, and the only question was how and when the explosion would come. The answer was provided by startling events which unfolded in July 1956. Thereafter, the Egyptian-Israeli conflict became a subsidiary act in a greater drama involving the Major Powers in a sudden rearrangement of their policies and alignments.

The United States' attempts to draw closer to Egypt had failed because Washington could not compete with Moscow in rearming Egypt without

any thought of Israel's future. There was more hope in economic competition. It was thought in Washington after the Soviet arms transaction that Egypt's economic future could be linked in such degree to the United States and other Western Powers as to save Cairo from becoming totally subservient to Soviet policy. For many weeks negotiations had gone forward for the financing by the World Bank, with heavy American participation, of the High Dam at Aswan, on which Egyptian planners relied for the increase of agricultural productivity in the next decades. In the spring and summer of 1956, the United States had discussed this project at length with Egyptian representatives, who had every reason to assume that their consent was now the only condition for the approval of the plan.

But in the meantime second thoughts had arisen in Washington. Egypt was exercising strong and hostile pressure on Israel; it was also making overt attempts to undermine King Hussein in Jordan. The weakening of Israel's security and the establishment of Egypt's leadership over other Arab states were no part of American policy. Washington and Cairo thus had divergent views and interests on the regional plan. In addition, Nasser, especially since the Bandung Conference of non-aligned states, had been following a Soviet direction in most international questions. He had established relations with Communist China, which was then anathema in American eyes. He was showing hostility to nearly all the aims that the United States pursued across the world. This had generated antagonism to Nasser in the United States Congress, whose support would be needed for the vast appropriations that the World Bank project would demand of the American taxpayer. The Egyptian Ambassador to the United States, Dr Ahmed Hussein, had not followed this change of atmosphere; and on 7 July, after returning from Cairo, he publicly announced that Egypt had decided to accept the help of the United States and British governments in carrying out the Aswan Dam scheme through the World Bank. He added that he intended to see Mr Dulles in order to speed up negotiations for a financial agreement.

In the Ambassador's meeting with the Secretary of State on 19 July, a sharp reversal was announced: Mr Dulles stated bluntly that the United States did not regard American and British participation in financing the High Dam as 'feasible in present circumstances'. The withdrawal automatically prevented the World Bank from addressing itself to the project.

The cancellation of the Aswan Project was Nasser's first serious setback. He was no less affronted by the manner of the annulment than by the act itself. On 24 July he reacted in a speech of unrestrained virulence: 'If rumour in Washington tries to make out that the Egyptian economy is not strong enough to warrant American aid, I reply, choke with rage, but you will never succeed in ordering us about or in exercizing your tyranny over us.' He added: 'We Egyptians will not allow any colonizer or despot to dominate us politically, economically or militarily. We shall yield neither to force nor to the dollar.' In later years he was to invite political, economic and military domination by the Soviet Union; and what he had not yielded to the dollar he would surrender to the rouble.

Nasser's first reaction to Dulles' refusal was to look around for ways of dealing a blow at the Western world. In a speech in Alexandria on 26 July, the bombshell burst. Nasser announced that the Egyptian Government had nationalized the Suez Canal Company and would use the income from the Canal – about $100 million a year – to build the Aswan Dam. Describing the Suez Canal Company as 'an exploiting company' and a 'state within a state', Nasser declared that it had been nationalized 'in the name of the nation' and that all its assets and commitments would pass to the Egyptian state.

Although the explosion had arisen from a decision by the United States, it was on Britain and France that the splinters fell. Both countries now found themselves dependent for their major supplies, especially of oil, not on an international waterway in which they had a controlling interest, but on Egyptian goodwill, which was clearly dubious.

In London financial measures were taken against Egypt, and all exports of war material were stopped. The reaction of France was parallel and no less violent. On 27 July the Foreign Minister, Christian Pineau, declared that France would not accept the unilateral action of Colonel Nasser. On 30 July Guy Mollet, the Prime Minister, described Nasser as an 'apprentice dictator whose methods were similar to those used by Hitler, the policy of blackmail alternating with flagrant violations of international agreements'. Early in August an announcement from Paris said that the French Mediterranean Fleet was assembling at Toulon and had received orders to prepare to sail. The British Admiralty and War Office announced naval movements and other precautionary military measures. Both the French and British governments seemed resolved to pry the Suez Canal loose from Nasser's hands by military force.

The American reaction was not nearly as clear-cut. On 29 July Secretary Dulles, returning hastily from South America, condemned the Egyptian Government's action as 'a grievous blow at international confidence'. But it was not part of United States policy to make or encourage recourse to armed force. Dulles now began to weave a web of intricate and constant diplomatic activity around the crisis, beginning with Three Power discussions on 29 July in which the British and French Foreign Ministers were joined by Robert Murphy, the United States Deputy Under-Secretary of State. At these talks it was decided to convene an international conference of twenty-four countries in London on 16 August 'to consider the establishment of an international body or agency for the Suez Canal to ensure that freedom and security of transit were preserved to the shipping of all countries with due regard to the interests of Egypt'. This statement was read with scepticism in Israel, to which navigation in the Suez Canal had been illegally denied ever since its existence, notwithstanding an injunction by the Security Council in September 1951.

If anyone doubted that the Middle East had become the focus of a major Great Power struggle, all doubts were set at rest by the Soviet reaction. In Moscow on 31 July, Mr Khrushchev said that he saw 'no cause of alarm in the Egyptian Government's action' and that 'the nationalization of the Suez Canal does not affect the interests of the peoples of Britain, France, the United States and other countries'. The Soviet press warmly praised the Egyptian Government's action and gave voice to warnings against any tendency by Western Powers to use force for restoring the previous situation.

In August and September, Britain and France went forward with military warnings and preparations. The London Conference of Suez Canal Users came to an end with a proposal to send a mission under the Australian Prime Minister, Robert Menzies to negotiate in Cairo. Meanwhile, Egypt was keeping its eyes closely on the United States. There is no doubt that Dulles, at certain stages, saw the tactical wisdom of not releasing Egypt from apprehension of an Anglo-French armed attack. He had told the British and French governments that 'Nasser would be forced to disgorge'. But while Menzies was in Cairo, a statement by President Eisenhower on 3 September made it quite clear to Nasser that the United States would not favour armed action. Nasser naturally put up an obdurate front to Menzies, whose negotiating position had been undermined. Egypt rejected even the minimal compromises that might have preserved a semblance of international supervision of navigation while leaving the assets of the Suez Canal Company, including the Canal, in Egypt's hands. And so the rift between the United States and its two European allies grew wider, until it had cut a gulf of mutual suspicion and distrust into the very heart of the Western alliance.

October was the crucial month in which French and Israeli hostility to Nasser converged towards united plans of resistance, while the intense heat of Sir Anthony Eden's indignation burned away the reserve which Britain had hitherto maintained towards Israel.

The influence of France on Israel's policy was not solely the result of having a common adversary. In the early months of 1956, France had rescued Israel from the decline of its relative military strength by an unprecedentedly lavish supply of armaments. In a speech to the Knesset (October 1956), Ben Gurion felt able to refer cryptically to the fact that Israel would soon have an 'ally'. When the first arms shipments from France reached Israel, the event was rhapsodically celebrated in verse by the Hebrew poet Natan Alterman. Intimate cooperation in arms supply and political planning had already developed between the General Staffs and the Ministries of Defence of the two countries. Both governments played their cards very close to their chests. By the time Nasser made his dramatic speech on the nationalization of the Suez Canal on 26 July, the idea that France might help Israel to resist Egyptian pressure was already familiar in some echelons of both governments. Israel was so confident of French arms supplies that in the late summer, when Secretary Dulles eventually encouraged the release to Israel of twenty-four F-84 jet fighters manufactured in Canada under American licence, the Israeli Government felt able not to take advantage of the offer.

Meanwhile, Nasser was simultaneously harassing the French in Algeria and the Israelis along all their borders. He seemed to have no intuition that the two victims of his assault might make common cause against him. His speech in Alexandria turned the Franco-Israeli alliance from an idea into a solid intention. Moreover, the British Government had been so affronted by Nasser's actions that when Pineau gave word to British ministers of France's intention to help Israel withstand Egyptian aggression, there was a surprising atmosphere of acquiescence.

In early October, France and Britain still went through the motions of seeking an international remedy that they did not really want. They presented their case to the Security Council in a fruitless debate which ended in the formulation of six points accepted by Egypt. These points reasserted the freedom of navigation for all shipping through the Suez Canal and the insulation of the Suez Canal from all external political influences. But a paragraph which would have enabled France and Britain to open negotiations on a special status for the Canal users was vetoed by the Soviet Union. France and Britain were learning what Israel had long understood – that the Security Council offered no remedy to nations whose policies were opposed by the Soviet Union. The stage was now set for the decisive act in the drama.

Israel was to face its decisions and opportunities after three years of social and political turbulence. Political stresses were to some degree offset by recovery in economic life, marked by greater freedom from restraints. There was an increase in foreign-currency assets and a great stimulus to communications and industry through the early implementation of the German Reparations Agreement. By 1954 there was an abundance of jobs and a steady decline in austerity. These tendencies became so marked that Ben Gurion found it necessary to issue an urgent appeal to Israeli youth from his retreat in Sdeh Boker to avoid the blandishments of careerism and to maintain the tradition of idealism and public service. The hope and consolation of Israeli Jews continued to lie in the development of solidarity with Jewish communities abroad. The American Assistant Secretary of State, Henry Byroade, struck exactly the wrong note in 1954 when he counselled Israel to loosen its ties with world Jewry and to regard itself as an exclusively Middle Eastern state. Israel's ties with world Jewry are amongst its primary spiritual and material resources; and it is the Arab states, not Israel, who deny Israel its Middle Eastern character.

Frontier violence, Egyptian rearmament, Soviet alienation and American frigidity had all come together to drive Israeli opinion towards embattled militance. This found particular expression in the policies followed by the Ministry of Defence under Pinchas Lavon. A quality of impetuous desperation permeated some decisions, such as that which led to a notorious 'security mishap' in Cairo. This was an ill-conceived operation, marked by explosions in public places in the Egyptian capital in conditions calculated to embroil Egypt with the Western Powers. It led to the execution of some Jews in Egypt and the prolonged imprisonment of others. The ambiguity about the source of the instruction for these acts was to haunt Israel for many years. It was one of the factors which led to the resignation of Lavon, whose relations with Prime Minister Sharett and other colleagues had in any case passed the breaking point. In February 1955, at the urgent insistence of Mapai leaders, Ben Gurion returned to the government as Minister of Defence in Sharett's administration.

Despite these shocks and alarms, the Israeli instinct for construction and social expansion was always looking for outlets during Sharett's administration. The Yarkon Pipeline Project was completed and the way lay open for the more ambitious scheme designed to bring water from the Sea of Galilee to the Negev. Immigration, which had been pitifully low in 1952 and 1953, still reached the figure of only 18,000 in 1954. Thereafter, with the rise of confidence in Israel's economy and security, the pattern improved. There were 37,000 immigrants in 1955 and 56,000 in 1956. Elections were held in November 1955, with Ben Gurion in his traditional place at the head of Mapai's list. Mapai declined in strength and lost five seats, and an even more catastrophic fall took place in the representation of the General Zionists, who from the giddy heights of twenty seats sank to a representation of thirteen.

Nevertheless, Ben Gurion was able to form a government on 29 November 1955. By now the tormenting pressure of raids by Egyptian and Jordanian forces and *fedayeen* groups had taken its toll of Israeli nervous energy. It also provoked deep divisions within the Israeli leadership about the scope, range and intensity of armed retaliation. Ben Gurion and Sharett were often at variance on this point. Even more serious was the development of independent initiatives in international policy by the Prime Minister and Ministry of Defence officials, without the coordination with the Foreign Ministry that would have been natural if temperamental tensions between the Ministers concerned had not become extreme. By June 1956 Ben Gurion and Sharett, who had worked for many decades together, reached a point of separation. Sharett resigned at Ben Gurion's specific request and was succeeded in the Foreign Ministry by Golda Meir.

This proved to be the end of Moshe Sharett's participation in governmental leadership and of his stewardship of Israel's relations with the outside world. He had been one of the formative influences in the establishment of Israel and in the fashioning of its policies in the first eight years of its existence. He was a man of large gifts. He stood out amongst his colleagues in the beauty and precision of his language, his intimate links with Arab culture and the tenacity with which he upheld the vision of ultimate Arab-Jewish cooperation. He was far from being an unconditional pacifist. During his premiership he had given his consent to many military operations of great daring and scope. Indeed, he was one of the architects of Israel's military tradition, for he had the main responsibility for securing the establishment of a Jewish Brigade in the Second World War. He was also the driving force in the Israeli delegation which triumphantly fought the battle for partition in the 1947 General Assembly of the United Nations. He had laid the foundations of Israel's Foreign Service with paternal care and indefatigable zeal. His burning love for the national culture in all its ages gave a special nobility to his demeanour and expression. He had a fundamentally ethical approach to the central problems of the state. He was a vigilant guardian of Israel's relations with Jewish communities abroad, to whom he came as a respected and welcome emissary. His intellectual experience was broader than that of most of his contemporaries. He was both a man of the world, at home in universal concepts and ideas, and a patriotic Hebrew citizen in full communion with his people's heritage. He gave more weight than did Ben Gurion to the need for conciliating world opinion; and he never allowed the current hostility of the Arab world to divert him from the ambition of ultimate Arab-Jewish harmony. He saw most problems in their full complexity, while Ben Gurion's genius was to simplify them to their essential core, so as to ignore the obstacles in his path.

It was clear that this honest intellectual torment, the insistence on following decisions through their entire chain of likely consequences, the tendency to sacrifice present advantage for ultimate good must have had an inhibiting effect on Ben Gurion's more dynamic temperament. Sharett's meticulous disposition and fanatical pursuit of exactitude were not always endearing to his colleagues, who lived in a world of broad, generalized concepts. The truth is that the two men, because of the very sharpness of their divergences, would together have formed a balanced team. What one of them lacked the other made up in abundant measure. The conflict between their views was sharpened by an even more acute conflict of personalities. A point had been reached at which they had an almost chemically negative reaction to each other. In later years, Sharett, from the vantage point of an elder statesman, was to act as the conscience of his party and his nation. But people do not always like to be prodded by their own conscience. Sharett afflicted Israelis with moral predicaments from which many sought to escape into Ben Gurion's world of simpler certainties. In view of Ben Gurion's rising eminence and domination of the national life, Sharett's departure may be seen as objectively inevitable. But there is no doubt that its general effect was to impoverish the Israeli leadership and to deprive it of one of its most ennobling dimensions.

Freed from Sharett's restraining hand, Israeli policy in 1956 went straight out for physical security and short-term relief. Once French and Israeli policies had converged, Britain was drawn inexorably into their magnetic field. France had long since reached a point of complete exasperation with Egypt. Apart from concern for its own interest, the French Government was sincerely disturbed by Israel's peril, and especially by the imbalance of arms between Israel and Egypt, through Russian supplies of bombers and other weapons to Egypt. There was a strong disposition to support Israel in any military response it wished to make to Egyptian pressure. There was also the indignant ambition to recapture the French position undermined by Nasser's nationalization of the Suez Canal.

On the other hand, it appeared from the September meeting that France did not wish to act alone. It had despaired of any American understanding for the use of force; but it had observed the sharp upheavals in British policy created by Nasser's actions. It would not be easy to bring Britain into harmony with French and Israeli interests. For one thing, most of the pressure on Israel's borders came from Jordan, to which Britain was almost endemically attached. But Paris was confident that London was moving in its direction.

Nasser was so busy goading Israel and France into a paroxysm of hostility

Outgoing Prime Minister Moshe Sharett and his predecessor and
successor to the position, David Ben Gurion, at the opening session
of the Knesset in August 1955

that he may not have observed a development in London. On 3 October, British disenchantment with United States policy became complete. Secretary Dulles had made a statement in Washington to the effect that the plan to put the Suez Canal under the control of the Canal Users' Association could not be said to have had its teeth drawn 'because it never had any teeth!' Eden's conclusion was that Dulles' previous assurances to him of a determination to make Nasser 'disgorge' his gains had been opportunistic and insincere. He developed a burning distrust of his American colleague, together with an urge to prove that Britain could still act independently in defence of its interests. He began to hint to his colleagues that while Britain would resist Israeli encroachments on Jordan, it would not look with displeasure on tough Israeli response to Egypt's pressure.

The day after a Conservative Party Congress, Eden, together with his Foreign Secretary, Selwyn Lloyd, was taking secret counsel in Paris with Mollet and Pineau on the possibility of an Anglo-French operation designed to recapture the Suez Canal. The operation would be explained as intervention for the purpose of preventing the outbreak of an Israeli–Egyptian conflict.

Thus events moved towards a climax at which French leaders found themselves in consultation not only with Israeli leaders, but with British representatives at increasingly high levels. Nasser had succeeded in getting three countries of sharply divergent interests into a parallel position on a single point: Nasser must be stopped.

The decisions and options now lying before Israel had become almost simplified by the sudden rush of events. Raids by Arab armies and *fedayeen* were taking a heavy toll; it was becoming unsafe to live in an Israeli border settlement and insecure to go about one's business in the interior of the country; the blockade of Eilat by sea had been compounded by the promulgation in Cairo of regulations against flying over the Straits of Tiran to or from Israel; Nasser was holding the French and British economies at ransom and was choking Israel out of any link with the southern and eastern worlds. And now, on 25 October, a military alliance against Israel was announced between Egypt, Jordan and Syria. The noose was tightening around Israel's neck. If resistance were not made now, a future decision to make it might be too late. The nation's security, interest, honour and morale could not indefinitely withstand the forward surge of Nasser's arrogance. Moreover, for the first time, there was a prospect that if Israel struck out in her own defence, she might not be alone. Others would understand her and perhaps give her aid.

When one reflects on Israel's complex of solitude in the preceding years it is easy to understand the exhilarating effect of the prospect that other powers would regard Israeli action as legitimate and salutary. This chance had become real by the early days of October. General Dayan has recorded in his book the *Diary of the Sinai Campaign* that on 2 October 1956, he told his staff that 'as a consequence of British and French reactions to the nationalization of the Suez Canal a situation might emerge in which Israel could take military action against the Egyptian blockade of the Gulf of Akaba. My news electrified the meeting.' Only a year before, the Israeli Cabinet had considered a proposal for taking independent action to open the Straits of Tiran. The proposal had been rejected, largely because Israel had no hope of support and would have been exposed to the full fury of Egyptian air attack. Now it seemed that through a strange convergence of opposing interests, the dangers of solitude might have been removed. Israel, long choked by a sense of impotence and encirclement, had a unique chance of tearing the hostile fingers from its throat. Later, in a debate of high drama in the General Assembly, Israel's representative tried to explain his country's predicament:

It is perhaps natural that a country should interpret its own obligations for the preservation of security more stringently than those who enjoy greater security far away. If we have sometimes found it difficult to persuade even our friends in the international community to understand the motives for our action, this is because nobody in the world community is in Israel's position. How many other nations have had hundreds of their citizens killed over these years by the action of armies across their frontiers? How many nations have had their ships seized and their cargoes confiscated in international waterways? How many nations find the pursuit of their daily tasks to be a matter of daily and perpetual hazard? In how many countries does every single citizen going about his duties feel the icy wind of his own vulnerability? It might perhaps require an unusual measure of humility and imagination for others to answer the question of how they would have acted in our place: nobody else is in our place and is, therefore, fully competent to equate the advantage and the disadvantage of our choice. Surrounded by hostile armies on all its land frontiers, subjected to savage and relentless hostility, exposed to penetration, raids and assaults by day and by night, suffering constant toll of life amongst its citizenry, bombarded by threats of neighbouring governments to accomplish its extinction by armed force, overshadowed by a menace of irresponsible rearmament, embattled, blockaded, besieged – Israel alone amongst the nations faces a battle for its security anew with every approaching nightfall and every rising dawn.

On Monday, 29 October, when Israeli forces swept into Gaza and Sinai, the siege was broken.

8

The Sinai Campaign and Its Aftermath

History would have a very mystical
character if there were no room in it for
chance.   Karl Marx

Could it all have been avoided? The question must arise after any war, especially one which seemed obscure in its aims and its results. Israel's action in October 1956 had not been unanimously endorsed at home. It was opposed in the vote by the Mapam ministers who, nevertheless, did not resign; and it was criticized afterwards by the former Prime Minister, Moshe Sharett. It does not have quite the same unanimous, unquestioned place in Israel's memory as do the wars of 1948 and 1967. Yet as one looks back, it seems that there was not a wide area of choice. In the absence of some sharp change of fortune, Israel's eruption from siege could at most have been postponed. By October 1956 the policies of Israel's foes and Israel's friends converged to destroy all other possibilities. On 25 October the establishment of a joint High Command to control the Egyptian, Syrian and Jordanian armies dispelled any remaining doubt about the gravity of the nation's plight and the need for urgent response.

Of the three adversaries that rose up against Nasser, Israel alone had a clear notion of what it was trying to achieve. At a Cabinet meeting on 28 October a Mapam minister asked Ben Gurion: 'What is the ultimate objective of this invasion? Let us assume it goes off as planned. Do we wish to annex the Sinai Peninsula or any part of it, and what will happen to the Gaza Strip?' Ben Gurion replied:

I do not know the outcome of Sinai. We are interested, first of all, in the Straits of Eilat [Tiran] and the Red Sea. Only through them can we secure direct contact with the nations of Asia and East Africa . . . The main thing, to my mind, is freedom of navigation in the Straits of Eilat. As far as the Gaza Strip is concerned, I fear that it will be embarrassing for us. If I believed in miracles I would pray for it to be swallowed up in the sea. All the same, we must eradicate the *fedayeen* bases and secure peaceful lives for the inhabitants of the border areas.

Egyptian President Gamal Abdul Nasser, whose personality and
policies dominated Middle Eastern affairs for almost two decades
and twice plunged the area into war

Thus when Israel's forces under General Dayan burst into Sinai and Gaza on 29 October they were at least acting in the service of coherent and limited aims. If at the end of the operation Israel had secured freedom for its shipping through the Straits of Tiran and had eliminated Gaza as a source of frontier harassment, it could be said to have achieved its legitimate purpose.

No such clarity marked British and French aims. The central idea was to recapture the Suez Canal and establish an international régime for its management. A corollary objective was to bring about Nasser's collapse. But could an Egyptian régime installed by their military power have had an effective lease of life? This was only one of the awkward questions which Paris and London chose not to face. They were stirred as much by emotion as by any lucid vision of their objectives. In each case, the government had reason for believing that its people stood behind it. This was especially so in France where all parties supported resistance to Nasser.

In Britain, things were more complex. In the first hot flush of indignation after Nasser's nationalization of the Suez Canal, Labour Party spokesmen, such as Hugh Gaitskell and Herbert Morrison, supported a militant response. Indeed, Gaitskell was one of the first to draw the parallel between Nasser and the dictators of the Second World War. Later, he and most of his party were to object vehemently to the British military action and to part company with their Israeli friends. There was an inconsistency here. If Nasser was a dictator on the Hitler-Mussolini pattern, it could hardly be wicked to resist him before his appetites and achievements became invincible.

Eden had played the October preparations very close to his chest. He had cut off most of his ministers, nearly the entire Foreign Office and the United States' Attaché from their normal contact with events. He was soon to crumble in failure, not only because of American pressure, but also because nearly half of the British Parliament turned in fierce hostility against his surreptitious action. All this, however, belonged to an unknown and rancorous future on 29 October when the tensions exploded.

In February 1956 an Egyptian Divisional Commander had issued a blunt directive:

Every officer must prepare himself and his subordinates for the inevitable struggle with Israel, with the object of realizing our noble aim, namely, the annihilation of Israel and her destruction in the shortest possible time and in the most brutal and cruel of battles.

Not for the first time or the last, there was a grotesque chasm here between

An Arabic translation of *Mein Kampf*, which was issued to Egyptian officers and found in their positions during the Sinai Campaign

Egyptian rhetoric and Egyptian performance. The Israeli operation – known by the code name 'Kadesh' – achieved its objective within a hundred hours. The object was not so much to capture territory as to break the Egyptian Army, which numbered 45,000 men, mainly in the Gaza Strip and the Rafah–Abu Ageila–El Arish triangle. The Israeli thrust had an element of surprise. The main pressure on Israel until that time had been the Jordanian frontier across which bitter battles had been waged, culminating in the Kalkilya operation. Tension had grown in the Jordanian sector with the Iraqi entry into Jordan. There had been an Israeli protest and the British Government warned Israel against taking action against Jordan, which was protected by a British defence treaty. The Jordanian front was so central in Israel's concern that Ben Gurion had caused domestic and international surprise when he said in the Knesset in October 1956 that Israel's 'main danger' lay in Egyptian blockade, encirclement and aggressiveness. When a massive call-up of Israeli reservists took place on 27 October, President Eisenhower and Secretary Dulles addressed general statements of alarm to the Israeli Embassy in Washington. Their fear lay in the possibility of a large Israeli operation against Jordan. Israel had to make provision for the possibility that Egypt would be assisted by Jordan and Syria, with whom there was a joint command. Only a section of the Israeli armed units were available for the Egyptian front It had been agreed that the Israeli air force would not initiate operations, but would only respond if the Egyptian air force went into battle.

All was ready for the forward leap. It began with a brilliant movement in which a paratroop battalion was dropped near the Mitla Pass about 20 miles east of the Suez Canal and 100 miles beyond the Israeli border. Egypt's troop concentrations and fortifications were now outflanked from the rear. The next task was for the main body of Israel's air-borne brigade to make contact with the paratroop battalion. The Israeli Government and command kept many options open. They were acting on the assumption that international pressure would give very little time for military action; whatever could not be secured in a few days would have to be renounced.

The appearance of the Israelis at Mitla stirred the Egyptians to panic. Here was the enemy a short distance from the Suez Canal, threatening the major Egyptian supply lines in Sinai. There was a furious Egyptian counter-attack which the Mitla battalion was able to resist. Twenty-four hours later the Israeli offensive branched out in two directions. Southwards, a brigade equipped with civilian transports made its way along the western shore of the Gulf of Aqaba until it overran the Egyptian positions at Sharm el-Sheikh and opened the Red Sea to Israel. Little resistance had been encountered in this operation. The position was different in the north, where the heaviest fighting took place with many casualties on both sides. The capture of Rafah was difficult because of its advantageous strategic position and the fact that it was surrounded by skilfully located minefields. Once Rafah had been taken, the Gaza Strip was cut off from contact with Arab forces or territory anywhere; not surprisingly, it soon fell with little further resistance. There were some notable air battles from which Israel's French-built aircraft came out victorious against the Soviet Migs. There were even successes on the sea, for the Israeli navy captured an Egyptian destroyer which had sailed northwards to attack Haifa. By 5 November the operation was over. The Israelis had lost 180 killed and four prisoners-of-war. They had routed the whole Egyptian force of the Suez Canal, leaving a thousand Egyptian dead and taking six thousand prisoners-of-war, as well as capturing large masses of armament and equipment. The Egyptian forces avoided even heavier casualties only by the rapidity of their flight.

Here was Israel in command of all of Sinai up to 10 miles from the Suez Canal, of the whole Gaza Strip and of Sharm el-Sheikh, controlling the entry to the Straits of Tiran. It was a sharp turn of fortune. To understand what now occurred one must glance back to the political background of the 29 October thrust. France and Britain had mounted an expeditionary force which was to seize possession of the Suez Canal along its entire length, utilizing the Israeli attack both for its diversionary effects and because it offered an international pretext for British and French intervention. While the Security Council was in session debating an irascible American resolution calling for Israeli withdrawal, the British delegate, Sir Pierson Dixon, asked for a short recess. When he came back he had sensational news: the British and French governments had decided to issue an 'ultimatum' to Egypt and Israel, through their representatives in London, ordering them to withdraw 10 miles from the Suez Canal; unless they agreed, the Anglo-French forces would occupy the Suez Canal along its entire length. The ultimatum was not very plausible, since Israel was being asked to 'withdraw' 10 miles from the Canal when its forces were still 40 miles away. In effect, the ultimatum was directed at Egypt alone. The British and French Governments described their action as an effort to prevent the danger of Egyptian aggression against Israel. They also said that without their intervention the war would be enlarged and thereby threaten international traffic. More convincingly, they stated that the United Nations had proved ineffective in stopping the mounting tide of violence in the Middle East.

Few people could have predicted the international pandemonium that broke out on the first day of the Sinai–Suez Expedition. In the Security Council, Britain and France were able by the use of their veto to block resolutions calling for withdrawal of troops. The United States, however, supported a majority of the member states in convening a special session of the General Assembly which, under the Uniting for Peace Resolution of 1951, had ascribed to itself powers to take enforcement action. The debate was markedly hostile to Britain and France and somewhat less so towards Israel. The central political development, however, was the convergence of the United States and the Soviet Union in combined pressure against Britain, France and Israel.

The harmony of the two Major Powers was all the more remarkable since they were at daggers drawn in the same General Assembly hall on the issue of the Soviet invasion of Hungary. In the next few weeks, the United Nations was to show its impotence to act against the Soviet Union. This only seemed to inspire it to vehement action against the three democratic states. On 2 November the General Assembly called for an immediate cease-fire and prompt withdrawal of all the forces that had gone beyond their boundaries on 29 October.

Israel had by now secured its major interests and agreed to the cease-fire on condition of reciprocity. The British and French operations were bogged down miserably in poor organization and extravagantly cautious tactics. It should have been obvious that the time available for the establishment of any military positions was short. Nevertheless, the decision had been taken to 'soften up' Egypt by prolonged bombing operations before any infantry landing designed to secure possession of the Suez Canal. Nasser was greatly flattered by this strategy. The assumption was that his army had all the skill and ferocity of Hitler, against whom Britain and France seemed to be fighting a belated action. Eventually, British and French forces took key positions, such as Ismailia and Port Said. Egypt immediately closed the Canal to all traffic by sinking ships and other obstacles into its waters. It thus stimulated all the states that depended on the Suez Canal supply line to press for the end of hostilities.

Not all the voices heard in the General Assembly were in favour of restoring the previous explosive position. The Canadian Foreign Minister, Lester Pearson, and, to some extent, Secretary Dulles wanted the withdrawal of forces to be accompanied by the creation of more stable conditions than those which had existed before. The result was a Canadian proposal to establish a United Nations Emergency Force that would move into areas to be evacuated by British, French and Israeli troops. Britain and France were by now in no condition to get much advantage from this remedy. Britain, in particular, lived some of the most tortured days in its national history. The United States was exercising pressures to the point of hostility. American representatives refused even to speak to those of the United Kingdom at UN meetings. President Eisenhower declined to receive Prime Minister Eden. Most decisive of all, the United States took financial measures to weaken the British foreign currency position and to withhold oil supplies alternative to those cut off by the Arab states. At the same time, opposition in Britain itself had grown to fever pitch. There were demonstrations in Trafalgar Square. The Labour Party was in full hue and cry against what it regarded as an illicit war.

Many of these obstacles might have been surmounted had the military action been effective. But nothing fails like failure. A Britain divided within itself, humiliated by military defeat and squeezed by the United States in its most vital economic nerves abandoned the purposes for which it had sent its troops into action. The nervous and physical collapse of the Prime Minister compounded and illustrated its agony. The Imperial Power was never to be imperial again.

France's leaders were in a more vigorous mood; yet they reacted with exaggerated seriousness to Soviet threats to drop rockets on Paris and London.

It should have been obvious that American deterrence would prevent the implementation of any such menace. In any case, French robustness would have counted for little with the British resolve crumbling hour by hour. In the end, Britain and France accepted a farcical procedure; the United Nations Emergency Force took over their positions only to hand them back to Egypt a few days later. The United Nations Emergency Force refused not only to internationalize the Canal, but even to salvage some remnant of French and British honour.

Thus Israel's position on 7 November seemed too bad to be true. Its government was receiving letters of violent intimidation from Soviet Prime Minister Bulganin, with implied threats of physical action. In Washington it was alternatively cajoled and bullied: cajoled by promises of greater concern for Israel's security after withdrawal; and bullied by American threats to acquiesce in Israel's expulsion from the United Nations and in the imposition of economic sanctions. Public opinion was coming to Israel's support in all free countries, and especially in the United States; but this development had not taken effect by 7 November. Two days earlier, Ben Gurion had defiantly stated that Israel would not allow any foreign forces to set foot in any of the conquered territories. But he had to retreat from this attitude on 7 November. The issue before the Israeli Cabinet was not whether to withdraw, but whether it was possible to salvage something in the withdrawal. It empowered the Ambassador in Washington, in the light of his appraisal of the situation, to decide between a text offering unconditional withdrawal and one which would have made the withdrawal conditional on 'the conclusion of satisfactory arrangements for the deployment of the United Nations Emergency Force.' The latter formula would allow Israel a chance to establish a system of free navigation in the Straits of Tiran and to ensure that Gaza would remain free of Egyptian troops. There were some in Jerusalem who feared that the conditional answer might provoke dissatisfaction in Washington and thus invite vengeful action from Moscow. In the end, the United States Government and the Secretary-General of the United Nations received and accepted the formula for conditional withdrawal, subject to satisfactory arrangements for the deployment of the United Nations Emergency Force.

Israel now undertook a political struggle aimed at realizing the aims for which the campaign had been fought. It was obviously not possible, or even desirable, to remain in most of Sinai. The decision was to delay and stagger the withdrawal while mustering support for international control both in Sharm el-Sheikh and in the Gaza Strip. It was felt that if this could be achieved, the sacrifices of the war would not have been wasted and Israel would have emerged from the years of torment with some tangible gains for peace and security. Early in January, intensive negotiations began between Secretary Dulles and the Israeli Ambassador on safeguards which would justify Israel in completing its withdrawal. These hinged on the Gaza Strip and Sharm el-Sheikh. The withdrawal was slowed down so that public understanding could be mustered. It soon became clear that Israel's cause on these two issues was stronger in public opinion than had previously been assumed. The detachment of the Israeli cause from British and French interests was now a helpful factor. Israel's case was that international statesmanship should correct, and not just restore, the conditions out of which the explosion had come. It urged that it would be a far-fetched interpretation of legalism to insist that the *status quo*, including the illegal parts of it, should be unconditionally restored. On 11 February the breakthrough came. Dulles addressed a memorandum to the Israeli Ambassador undertaking that if Israel withdrew to the previous lines, the United States would support the stationing of the United Nations Force at Sharm el-Sheikh to ensure non-belligerency and in the Gaza Strip to prevent *fedayeen* raids. While offering these important inducements the United States was also utilizing its possibilities of pressure. On 24 February, while the Israeli Ambassador was holding consultations in Jerusalem, President Eisenhower made a speech strongly hinting that he might support UN sanctions against Israel. This evoked a roar of protest from American opinion and especially from the Senate leaders William B. Knowland and Lyndon B. Johnson, who insisted on an American effort to bring about an agreed solution with Israel. This trend was reinforced when French Prime Minister Guy Mollet and Foreign Minister Christian Pineau arrived in Washington on a previously planned official visit in the last days of February 1957. It was at this stage that the United States and France undertook commitments to Israel that would be untested for ten years and would become the focus of the international crisis in 1967. The United States, in clear terms, and France, in even more vigorous language, stated that they would give support to Israel if she exercised her right of self-defence against any renewal of the blockade in the Straits of Tiran or any resumption of *fedayeen* raids from Gaza. The 'hopes and expectations' that Mrs Meir expressed in her speech to the General Assembly on 1 March were drafted in consultation with the United States and were endorsed in accordance with preconceived arrangements by the United States, France, Britain and all the major maritime nations.

The United States and France had assumed solemn commitments by endorsing Israel's conditions. The Israeli position as outlined on 1 March 1957 stipulated that on Israel's withdrawal, the United Nations Emergency Force would be deployed in Gaza and that the takeover of Gaza from the military and civilian control of Israel would be exclusively by the United Nations Emergency Force; that the United Nations would be the agency responsible for administration; and that UN responsibilities in Gaza would be maintained until there was a peace settlement or a definitive agreement on the future of the Gaza Strip. Israel warned that if conditions were created in the Gaza Strip which indicated a return to the previously existing situation, Israel would reserve its freedom to act in defence of its rights. On the Gulf of Aqaba, Mrs Meir declared that Israel was ready to withdraw immediately from Sharm el-Sheikh 'in the confidence that there will be continued freedom of navigation for international and Israeli shipping in the gulf and through the Straits of Tiran'. She went on to say:

Interference by armed force with Israel ships exercising free and innocent passage in the Gulf of Aqaba and through the Straits of Tiran will be regarded by Israel as an attack entitling her to exercise her inherent right of self-defence under Article 51 of the Charter and to take all such measures as are necessary to ensure the free and innocent passage of her ships in the gulf and in the straits.

While the American statement of 1 March had been satisfactory on Aqaba, it had not fulfilled Mr Dulles' promise to support a UN administration for the Gaza Strip. Accordingly, Israel delayed its withdrawal until this matter was clarified between Secretary Dulles and the Israeli Ambassador. As a result of these talks, President Eisenhower addressed a message to Ben Gurion reaffirming the American commitments in solemn terms and stating that Israel would have no cause to regret its withdrawal.

The bitter pill of withdrawal could be swallowed only because of these assurances and, more particularly, in the light of the prospect that a new dimension would be added to Israel's international position through the opening of the blocked artery leading into the Red Sea and beyond. Careful agreements were negotiated with the United States to ensure that President Eisenhower's commitment to Ben Gurion would find concrete expression. It was agreed that a tanker flying the American flag would be one of the first to exercise free passage and to pass under the eyes of the UN Emergency Force into the Israeli port of Eilat. The symbolism of this journey by *S. S. Kernhills* in April 1957 did much to raise Israel's drooping spirits. These had plunged even lower towards despair when, a few days after Israel's withdrawal, Egypt sent its administration back into Gaza despite the 'assumption' that the Gaza Strip would be left under international control. There were even some voices in Israel in favour of going back and reconquering Gaza. Ben Gurion, however, noted that the Egyptian Army had still not entered the Gaza Strip; the United Nations Emergency Force was the only army on the scene. Without protection by Egyptian forces it was unlikely that the *fedayeen* would find Gaza a congenial base. Ben Gurion now embarked on one of his most difficult exercises in domestic persuasion. He sought to convince the Israeli public that the fight had not been in vain; that concrete results had ensued from it; and that the alternative course of standing in embattled defiance of world pressures offered no constructive issue. For in the four months during which Israel was developing its diplomatic battle at the United Nations, in Washington and across the world, the country itself was in sad condition. It was cut off from its commercial contacts. The Soviet Union and other Communist countries had withdrawn their Ambassadors. Tourism was virtually at a standstill. The rhythm of construction had died down, and the country took on a dark, empty and inert aspect alien to its dynamic nature. It became physically evident that Israel was the kind of organism that could only flourish in close connection with the outside world.

In the end, he carried the day – as he so often had before – and subsequent events vindicated his judgment. For the next ten years there was not a single violent collision between Israelis and Egyptians from the Gaza Strip; and during that period Israel translated its navigation rights in the Straits of Tiran from an abstract principle into a living reality expressed in hundreds of sailings under dozens of flags and in the swift development of Eilat as Israel's outlet to the southern and eastern worlds. To these gains in Tiran and Gaza was added the psychological boost which Israel derived from its successful military operations. So, in the end, the balance sheet in March 1957 was in decisive credit. The result had been secured by what was to become a familiar Israeli

technique: tenacity was maintained on the ground despite heavy pressures, and, at the same time, serious attempts to conciliate world opinion were being made. Eventually, the Sinai Campaign secured the two ends which Ben Gurion had prescribed for it in his reply to the Mapam ministers on 28 October. While Britain and France had come out empty-handed and humiliated, Israel emerged with its banner flying high and with its main objectives secured.

There was to be a paradoxical development in the following year. The main divergence between Israel and the United States had been on the question of whether Nasser's expansionist policy justified forceful reaction. In 1956 the United States had given a negative answer. But in the summer of 1958, when Nasser attempted to impose his domination on Arab countries outside Egypt and to overthrow all Arab régimes uncongenial to his philosophy and his leadership, the United States became as irritated as Israel, France and Britain had been in 1956. The Iraqi Government was overthrown and Iraq's leaders brutally murdered; and pressure was exercised both on Lebanon and Iraq to fall in with Nasser's pattern of domination. This time the United States took the kind of action which it would have seriously criticized a year before. On 15 July 1958 American marines landed in Lebanon, while Britain took up corresponding military positions in Jordan. Here two Western Powers were acting in a frank effort to obstruct Nasser's expansion. For Nasserism had become something far more than a doctrine of Egyptian revolution. Its central theme was hegemonistic. Cairo saw itself not only as the capital of Egypt, but also as the centre in which all Arab policies should be determined. Nasser's policy was one empire, one nation, one leader; and there was no difficulty in diagnosing who he thought the leader should be. Wherever there was a government in the Arab world dedicated to traditional Moslem values, or to cordial relations with the West, or one which declined to accept Nasser's pretensions to leadership, he and his agents would move for its overthrow. After the landings in Lebanon and Jordan, the United States and Britain faced an Emergency Session of the United Nations in loud affirmation of their right to intervene at the request of sovereign governments for the maintenance of their integrity and independence. Israel kept in close touch with these developments. Indeed, without the use of its air space it would have been impossible to supply Jordan. Quite apart from its intellectual satisfaction, Israel drew practical relief from this robust American insight into Middle Eastern realities. Economic aid was renewed and the United States developed a sharper sensitivity than before towards the problems of Israeli defence. The road was open for a full decade of consolidation and growth.

The embryo port of Eilat in the early 1950's. Since then Eilat has become a major outlet for Israel's trade with Africa and the Far East

9

Between The Wars, 1957–1967

*He who does not remember the past is
doomed to repeat it.*   Santayana

Few people expected the Sinai Campaign to mark an upward swing in Israel's
fortunes. The commentators and columnists looked wisely at the clouds
and predicted unceasing rain. They argued that Israel, after all, had withdrawn to its previous positions without any substantive gain; that it would
henceforth be identified in the Arab mind with the colonial powers; that
the partnership with France and Britain had given credibility to the image
of an 'imperialist tool'; and that Israel would now be sternly shunned by
the developing world.

   None of this came to pass. The decade which opened in 1957 was charged
with vitality and optimism. There were still many ordeals ahead; but it seemed
that the nightmare of weakness was over. In the period before 1956, many
in the world still doubted Israel's durability. The country always seemed poised
on the brink of bankruptcy. Its international stature had been limited. Nobody
in the world had made much effort to sooth its irritations; it had aroused none of
the salutary apprehension which protects a nation against contempt or outrage.
But after 1957 the prospect brightened; Israel's sharp reaction to prolonged
belligerency had certainly evoked disapproval in many places, but it had also
inspired an uneasy respect. It was likely that Israel would, at least, be taken into
serious account and that its reactions to danger or provocation would be more
carefully measured.

   With every year that passed, the country seemed to lose something of its
fragility. The population grew from 1,900,000 to 2,800,000. The rate of
economic expansion had few parallels. More eloquent than statistics of growth
was the visible evidence of a landscape across which a green carpet of cultivation
moved like an advancing tide. In the growing cities and suburbs there were signs
of relative affluence, with the rise of a mercantile and professional middle class.
Israel's agriculture celebrated many triumphs; its talent for profusion stirred
the mind and hope of many nations in a famine-stricken world. From a million
cultivated acres, Israel was producing eighty-five per cent of the food consumed
by two and a half million people at a high level of nutrition, while also ex-

Upper Afula with Mount Tabor in the background. During the
long period of economic consolidation and development, dozens of
new towns like this sprang up throughout the country

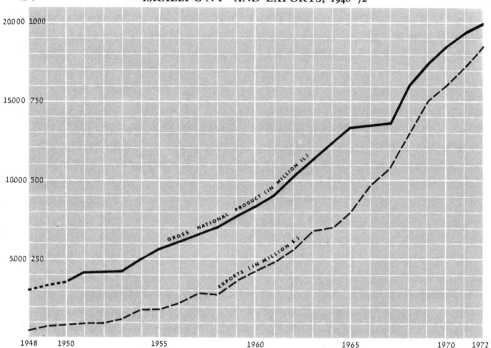

MILLION
IL $

20,000 1,000

15,000 750

10,000 500

5,000 250

GROSS NATIONAL PRODUCT (IN MILLION IL)

EXPORTS (IN MILLION $)

1948 1950   1955   1960   1965   1970 1972

porting $130 million worth of agricultural products to the world markets. The industrial apparatus, too, became more elaborate and diverse. The defence establishment made heavy demands on technical precision and inventiveness, and the challenge was, for the most part, successfully met. The average *per capita* income moved towards European levels. Israeli research was honoured in the scientific world. Much in Israel was still imperfect, lacking outward form and inner harmony; but the country's aspect was becoming less rigorous, its culture less parochial, its energies more robust.

There is an instructive symbolism in the fact that archaeology and science were the main intellectual enthusiasms of Israeli youth. Here was a people straining to transcend its smallness by an appeal to historic lineage and intellectual vitality. Israel was commonly regarded as a progressive community with a modern scientific outlook; but it was also gripped by a constant search for its roots in a distant past. Much of Israeli life is taken up with reconciliation between past and future; between the old inheritance and the new potentiality; between religious tradition and modern progress; between Western pragmatism and Eastern spirituality; between free enterprise and collective ideals; Contradictions are sharp, and the tang of Israeli life is heightened by them. Above all, there was usually something in the national enterprise which expressed the instinct for innovation. Across the Gulf of Aqaba from Eilat, a bridge of commerce and friendship was patiently constructed towards the eastern half of the globe. In June 1964 the National Water Carrier was impressively completed and Galilee waters flowed southward to irrigate Negev fields. For many years the fear of Arab displeasure had prevented the full development of Israel's diplomatic links. But from 1960 onwards, the country was bountifully visited, inspected, explored, praised and often flattered by heads of states and governments and by leading spokesmen of the world's intellectual community

The sources of this fascination were complex. The building of new communities has always appealed to man's creative dreams. But in the 1960's Israel had a particular message in the context of its times. In the advanced countries there was no longer a mystique of struggle. Life had lost its rhapsodical sense. On the other hand, the developing states had let their early exaltation give way to bitterness and despair, for institutional freedom had not been accompanied by any parallel growth in economic resources or social dynamism. The flags were obviously not enough. The emblems of sovereignty were moving, but they could not bridge the humiliating gulf in capacities and resources between the privileged and the disinherited states. Thus the advanced countries admired Israel for her pioneering vitality, while new nations probed the reasons for her accelerated development. Some envied Israel for what she had already accomplished; others for what she still had to do. To Jewish communities, Israel imparted a sentiment of kinship, pride and mutual responsibility.

Israel's struggle against the Arab siege in 1956 had not changed its physical map. The borders were exactly as before. Free navigation in the Red Sea and tranquillity in the settlements near the Gaza Strip were tangible assets, symbolized, though not created, by UN troops. But these gains themselves could not explain the new buoyancy in the national temper. The real transformation was in Israel's vision of itself. This had evolved from self-doubt to something like national confidence.

In its international relations, Israel had come out of the Sinai Campaign with an improved prospect. The kinship with France was very close. In 1961 de Gaulle had assured Ben Gurion of French 'solidarity and friendship' and had then raised his glass to 'Israel, our friend and ally'. Israelis had not heard such words since the establishment of their state. Israel's cooperation with the Fourth Republic until 1958 might have been explained as a marriage of convenience, for the two countries had common foes in Cairo and other Arab capitals. But the Algerian war, with the resultant tension between Paris and Cairo, had been over for some years when, in June 1964, President de Gaulle reaffirmed to the Israeli Prime Minister, Levi Eshkol, that Israel was still a 'friend and ally' to whose progress France was deeply committed. French arms supplies prevented the collapse of the military balance under the weight of Soviet arms deliveries to the Arab states. France also promised support for Israel's efforts to integrate itself into the new European community. A cultural agreement was signed in 1959, and French and Israeli warships exchanged courtesy visits in 1961. At the 1964 meeting in Paris, de Gaulle urged Eshkol neither to provoke the Arab governments by excessive severity nor to tempt them by military weakness. At that time he saw no contradiction between traditional French interests in the Arab world and the cultivation of strong relations with Israel. On the contrary, the very intimacy of France's relations with Israel spurred the Arab states to a competitive quest for her favour and assured her, for the first time since the Second World War, of a central place in the Middle Eastern power balance.

Britain did not maintain the same intimacy as during the few days of common struggle; but it never reverted to the old frigidity. There was no embargo on the purchase of Centurion tanks and other equipment, and economic ties were close and mutually fruitful. Public opinion admired Israel's military performance, perhaps with a twinge of envy, and reacted sharply against Nasser's continued militance.

The United States and Israel had fallen apart in their policies at the end of 1956; but within a few months their harmony had been renewed and, in some ways, deepened. American policy would clearly be more alert to the danger of neglecting Israel's security needs. Washington now understood that embattled solitude was not the condition most likely to breed patient counsel in Israel. In the summer of 1958, Secretary Dulles was telling Israel of United States opposition to Nasser's 'radical' pretensions to establish his hegemony over other nations and régimes in the Middle East. The United States actively supported Israel's right to use her due share of the Jordan-Yarmuk waters; and the Eisenhower Doctrine, confirmed by the United States Congress in 1957, promised support for any Middle Eastern state threatened by aggression from a state dominated by international Communism. By the early 1960's, the United States was expressing its support of Israel's independence and integrity more openly. In 1962 President John F. Kennedy told Foreign Minister Golda Meir that the United States was, in effect, Israel's 'ally', joined to her in a relationship of special intimacy. With the sale of Hawk missiles and Patton tanks, American components were to become a salient part of Israel's deterrent strength.

Sherman tanks on parade after the Sinai Campaign

At the same time, the Kennedy administration was trying hard, through massive economic aid, to curb Nasser's militance and to turn his mind towards the solution of Egypt's social problems. These attempts were vain: Nasser's pan-Arab appetite was irrepressible. Instead of developing his economy, he threw himself into a sterile war in the Yemen to ensure the rise of a pro-Nasserite régime in place of the traditional rule of the Imams. He thereby threatened Saudi Arabia and the Gulf principalities and, consequently, became a source of danger to American interests. The Johnson administration reacted by a more open application of the 'balance of power' doctrine. In 1965 and 1966, it decided to supply Israel with more advanced weapons, such as heavy tanks and Skyhawk fighter bombers. At the same time, American-Egyptian relations declined. The United States cut down its wheat supplies to Egypt. Nasser retaliated with strong verbal attacks on the United States and its President, in terms reminiscent of his assault on Britain and France in 1956. 'Let the Americans drink the sea water' was one of his memorable epigrams; he had a liking for schoolboyish expressions of defiance. The sea water remained unconsumed, but Israel's stability became more appreciated in the West.

In her second decade Israel built an impressive structure of relations with the developing states. It had begun in the 1950's with isolated ventures in cooperation with Burma and Ghana; but it now evolved into a vocation of international scale. A state with a population of a little over two million, scarce in resources, was promoting the development of dozens of other countries in three continents of the world. Hundreds of Israeli technologists, scientists, doctors, engineers, teachers, agronomists, irrigation experts and specialists in youth

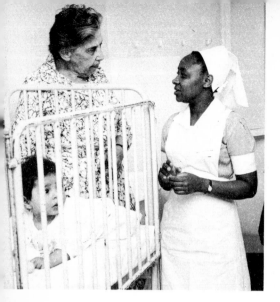

left A nursing trainee from Gabon at the Hadassah Medical Centre, Jerusalem. Thousands of Asian and African students have undergone practical training in Israeli educational establishments *right* Prime Minister Levi Eshkol with President Jomo Kenyatta of Kenya on a state visit in 1966. More than 60 countries in Asia, Africa and Latin America have received technical aid from Israel

organization were sharing the lessons and experiences of Israeli pioneering with other developing nations. Israel's development role had three expressions. First, there were the Israeli experts working singly or in teams in the developing countries themselves. Then, there were almost 9,000 men and women from some eighty countries who in the years 1957 to 1966 received training in Israel's institutions of higher learning or in special courses related to development. Finally, there were international conferences which brought exponents of the natural and social sciences together with leaders of new nations in a dialogue on Israel's soil. The Rehovot Conferences on Science and Development gave a theoretical background to Israel's more empirical contributions to the progress of developing nations.

The Israeli examples in Burma and Ghana were contagious. The arrival of Israeli diplomatic missions and technicians became almost an integral part of the ceremonies marking the independence of new African states. A few years after Sinai, Israel was giving assistance of one sort or another to some sixty-five countries in Africa, Asia and Central and South America. This was an imaginative use both of capacities and limitations. Israel had the advantage of being a small country not suspected of domination. But it was also a developing country, so that the relevance of its experience was greater than that of more developed societies. Moreover, Israel had no 'master race' attitude. Its people had known suffering and persecution, and it had preceded the other new states in its struggle for recognition and acceptance by the international community. Its work in developing countries helped Israel to transcend the regional 'isolation' imposed by the Arab states and to extend its vision beyond its frontiers. There were some political repercussions as well. At the UN General Assembly in 1961 sixteen nations, mostly African, submitted a

resolution calling for direct negotiations between the Arab states and Israel.

It was clear as the years went by that the Arab view of Israel as a dark conspiracy, a rapacious colonial adventure or a regrettable but temporary Crusader occupation had been rejected by the opinion and emotion of mankind. There were forces at work in the life of the region and the world which outweighed the factors on which Arab nationalism had relied in its dream of Israel's eclipse. Arab leaders could not count, as they had once hoped, on Israel's spontaneous disintegration, or on the help of the world community to bring about Israel's ruin. If they were to succeed in 'destroying Israel', they would have to do the job by their own strength and counsel.

Israel's security was seen as a function of her own independent military strength and of her international friendships. Of these, the first loomed largest in her mind. Israel had no automatic commitment from any power to come to her aid if she were attacked or if her vital interests were violated by Arab states. Everything depended on her own capacity to deter and contain the regional hostility by maintaining adequate strength. The task was hard but feasible. The commitment of two million Israelis to their own defence was more absolute and far more passionate than the commitment of one hundred million Arabs to Israel's destruction. Indeed, the numerical equation was misleading. Most of the hundred million Arabs, especially those far away, were not aware of any personal obligation to sacrifice themselves for Israel's liquidation. For the Arab nation, with its own survival assured in so many states, Israel's submergence was optional. Thus, Israel's defence was pursued with intense fervour, while the Arab threat to her existence was mainly expressed in rhetoric which offended Israel's pride, but left her body and spirit intact. To the advantage of morale we could add the reinforcement of technology. In modern strategy, the value of more numbers tends to decline as scientific skills grow. When technical methods become more sophisticated, the quantitative element loses its decisive importance; the possibility of a small community holding its own against heavy demographic odds becomes more tangible. This is not to say that it is preferable to be small. But it is, at least, a tolerable destiny. In Israel's national memory David's victory over Goliath was a result not of his smallness, but of his compensating agility and talent for improvisation.

In the 1960's Israel's security doctrine was rooted in the idea of an independent deterrent power. This policy seemed to respond to broader international interests. Events in Vietnam, Congo, Cyprus, Yemen and Kashmir illustrated the dangers which threatened world peace whenever there was a lack of internal stability in small states or a deficient equilibrium between them. A small nation announcing its resolve to ensure its own defence without falling on the responsibility or conscience of others could expect to hear a sigh of relief go up from harassed and over-committed powers. For none of Israel's friends wanted to expand its direct strategic engagements. Israel's policy of self-reliance could, therefore, count on some support. The embargo atmosphere of the 1950's began to clear away. The Israeli defence establishment under Levi Eshkol's leadership embarked on a programme of modernization and intensive procurement. Another aim was to variegate Israel's sources of supply. There was no reason in the early 1960's to be sceptical about French support; but many Israelis thought it wise to avoid the concentration of all one's eggs in a single basket. New prospects of armoured and air strength were thus pursued in the United States. The result was that by 1966 the power of Israel in relation to any Arab force likely to be arrayed against her in the coming years was no less effective than ten years before.

The Arab states had not won military superiority; and to make matters worse for them, their pretence of union was collapsing. Rival régimes, contrasting ideologies, competitive bids for hegemony and diverse international orientations tore the Arab world apart. The Yemen war, which had raged since 1961, found the Arab 'family' divided into three fronts: the supporters of the Royalist forces, headed by Saudi Arabia: the allies of the 1962 Republican Revolution, led by Egypt; and the uneasy neutrals in between. Jordan was at daggers drawn with Syria and Egypt. Morocco and Tunis were in conflict over Mauretania. Only three Arab states (Libya, Kuwait and Sudan) maintained normal relations with all other members of the Arab League. In 1958 it was believed that the leftist Kassem régime in Iraq, having overthrown the pro-Western monarchy, would be subservient to Nasser. When it showed an unexpectedly independent spirit, Nasser turned on it with furious invective, thus offending the Soviet Union. Similarly, when Syria, which had formed a union with Egypt in the guise of the United Arab Republic in 1958, broke away from Cairo in 1961, it was met with the full blast of Nasser's disapproval. Nasser was tolerant only of those Arab régimes which accepted his leadership. Whenever regional and particularist tendencies asserted themselves against Cairo's control, he became vituperative. Nothing divided the Arab world more than the attempt to unite it. The atmosphere of disruption was made more intense by personal rivalries among Arab political leaders. When they embraced each other at airports on official visits, the eyes across each other's backs and shoulders had a cold glint of suspicion.

The failure of the Egyptian-Syrian union was therefore predictable. So also was the refusal of many Arab states to become provinces subject to Cairo. At first glance, it might seem that Israel should have been no more than the interested spectator of these events. In fact, it was profoundly involved in all their consequences. Unable to rally the dispersed and quarrelsome Arab states under his banner, Nasser looked around for a unifying theme. He found it in the vocabulary and idiom of anti-Israel rhetoric.

In the sequel to the 1967 war, Nasser and his sympathizers made many efforts to obscure his record of verbal extremism. They cultivated an impression that only firebrands like Ahmed Shukeiry and the radio commentators indulged this vice. But it is Nasser's quiet, silky voice that Israelis remember in association with the most violent assaults on their peace and dignity. It was Nasser who said: 'The establishment of Israel is the greatest crime in history.' And again – implausibly – 'Ben Gurion is the greatest war criminal in this century. (The fact is that few statesmen, including Nasser, had evoked more respect than Ben Gurion outside their countries). In Nasser's speeches the quarrel was not with Israel's policies, but with Israel's right to live. The very existence of Israel is 'a stain', 'a shame', 'a disgrace', 'a bleeding wound'. On 20 May 1965 we hear him proclaim that 'Israeli aspirations regarding Egypt reach as far as the Al Sharqiyya area because the children of Israel lived in the district before their departure from Egypt'.

Far from 'aspiring to the Al Sharqiyya district of Egypt', most Israelis would have been hard put to say where that district was. All of them at that time would have been prepared to support a peace treaty with Egypt without territorial changes. Similarly, they would have looked in vain for the 'map extending from the Nile to the Euphrates', which Nasser solemnly told foreign visitors was carved on a wall in the Knesset building. There is no map in the Knesset building. The climax of Nasser's verbal assault came on 4 October 1958 in his endorsement of the anti-Semitic *Protocols of the Elders of Zion*, which has probably caused the murder of more people than any document in history: it is the spiritual basis of European and, especially, of Nazi anti-Semitism. More copies of it have been sold in Egypt in the last two decades than in all the countries of the world put together since it was forged in the early years of the twentieth century. It is only a short step from this to the communiqué signed jointly by Nasser and Iraqi President Aref in 1963 proclaiming, that 'The aim of the Arabs is the destruction of Israel'.

Nasser's most delicate problem arose when he discovered that the total effect of this ugly stuff was to arouse revulsion but not fear in Israel – and a measure of scepticism in the rest of the world. His response was to call a 'Summit Meeting' in Cairo in January 1964. It was attended by the heads of thirteen Arab states commanding an area of 4 million square miles and a population of eighty million. The motive of their disquiet was their failure to intimidate a small country one-fortieth their size in population and one-five hundredth their size in area.

   The alarm bell which shook the Arab leaders to a realization of their own impotence was Israel's completion of the National Water Carrier in 1964. This project was of high value to our economy. In scale and technical imagination it would have done credit to a larger state; in human terms it carried the special appeal which belongs to the sudden eruption of verdure in a wilderness. But its implications went deeper. What was ostensibly an engineering enterprise had now become a decisive political issue. For the Arab governments had publicly sworn that the Galilee water would never flow southwards. Israel, for her part, had defined the free use of her share of the Jordan water as a vital national interest which, like the integrity of her territory and the freedom of passage in the Gulf of Aqaba, would be defended at any cost. Thus the Arab states and Israel faced each other across the ancient river in a test of resolve and deterrent power. If this Arab threat proved hollow, why should any other Arab menace be believed? And if Arab declarations lost their intimidatory force, would not Israel's consolidation go forward in swift and decisive thrust?

   The Arab governments could not have chosen less favourable ground than the water project to call world opinion to their cause. The enterprise was radiantly innocent. It caused no harm to anyone, and the threat to oppose it by force was regarded by most of mankind as senseless malice. In January 1964, while waiting for Pope Paul VI at Megiddo, where he was to begin his pilgrimage to the Holy Places, the Soviet Ambassador in Israel, of all people, informed

One of the most significant projects in the development of the economy was the completion in 1964 of the National Water Carrier, which transfers water from the Jordan and the Sea of Galilee to the Negev

Prime Minister Eshkol that 'Israel had a right to its share of the Jordan waters'.

The Upper Jordan, Sea of Galilee and the Yarmuk were the primary sources of fresh water for irrigation projects in Israel and Jordan. There was, at most, a possibility of some marginal use of this water in southern Syria and Lebanon; it would have been legitimate for the riparian Arab states to press their claims for larger allocations. But it was quite irrational to affirm that Israel, through whose territory the Jordan flowed for 65 miles, had no right at all to divert a single cubic metre to its arid territory in the south. Moreover, an objective external adjudication had been made with the support of international opinion. In 1958 Eric Johnston, as President Eisenhower's emissary, had presented a plan formulated by irrigation engineers and legal experts. This allotted each country enough water for its needs according to normal international criteria. Even Arab engineers had admitted that this suggestion was objectively fair. But their governments had refused to ratify the agreement on avowedly political grounds. Yet the objective judgment stood on public record and had its effect. Israel, although not formally bound by a plan which her neighbours had refused to sign, decided voluntarily to accept the limitations which it imposed. It was disappointing that the plan gave Israel no more than thirty-five per cent of the total resource. But in a bid for world support, Israelis preferred the political advantages of third-party arbitration to the unilateral assertion of their own claims.

For several years Israeli engineers had been building a pumping station to raise the water 1,100 feet above the Sea of Galilee and have it flow in a series of pipes and aqueducts towards the northern and central Negev. The United States was associated in every stage of the enterprise, to which Presidents Kennedy and Johnson committed their written support. Arab governments had failed to win approval anywhere for their desire to obstruct the project. It must have been plain to Nasser by early 1964 that Israel would not endure thirst and aridity merely to gratify his malice and that when the switch was thrown and the water gushed southwards, most of the world would applaud. Thus he could neither thwart the enterprise by military force nor impede it by international pressures. On 11 June 1964 the water began to flow in the National Carrier. The Arab threat had been quietly but firmly frustrated.

The Arab Summit Conference in 1964 was followed by another in 1965. It reacted to the Arab dilemma by a doctrine of delayed response. On 11 July 1965 Nasser said: 'The final account with Israel will be made within five years if we are patient. The Moslems waited seventy years until they expelled the Crusaders from Palestine.' Two years later Nasser was to take a more impatient view of his options; but for the time being he played a waiting game.

In reply to Syrian pressure for immediate war, he said with complete veracity: 'We cannot use force today because conditions are not ripe.'

Evidently the will to make war was strong but the capacity was deficient. Therefore a Palestine Liberation Organization was formed at the Summit Conference to fight Israel in the undefined future and destroy King Hussein's régime in the more immediate present. A Joint Arab Command was established under the command of the Egyptian General Abdul Hakim Amer to plan the eventual military assault. And instead of preventing the flow of water to the Negev by making war immediately, it was decided to choke off Israel's irrigation channels by a perverse and expensive diversion of the Upper Jordan streams into areas of Lebanon and Syria which had no need of them. The singularity of Arab policy was revealed here in typical form: the aim was not to advance Arab interests, but to harm those of Israel.

Thus the Arab Summit Conferences of 1964 and 1965 sought to postpone the armed conflict in practice, to keep its prospect alive in policy and rhetoric and to stir enough irritation to prevent any long-term tranquillity. The plan sounded impressive, but its weaknesses were great. It reflected a tendency in Arab politics to prefer the form of things to their substance; for none of the instruments created at the Summit was as formidable as it tried to appear. The Palestine Liberation Organization was ferocious enough in pamphlets and broadcasts, but its martial qualities were dubious. Indeed, the organization derived a comic-opera aspect from the spectacle of its leader. Mr Ahmed Shukeiry's corpulent gait, pompous demeanour and blatant concern for his own vanity and comfort were reassuring to his prospective victims. Israelis reflected that if Shukeiry was their chief danger, they must be tolerably safe.

Similarly, the Joint High Command soon ran adrift. Its budget was in constant deficit; and other Arab states politely declined to have Egyptian troops on their soil. There remained the plan for diverting the Jordan at its source. But this depended on the unlikely condition of Israel's acquiescence. Geographical conditions were such that the work of throttling Israel would have to be conducted within range of Israel's tank fire; and, ultimately, the diversion could only be carried out by building a canal within a few hundred yards of Israel's border. In November 1964 Israeli aircraft and tanks, responding to Syrian fire in a border clash, scored hits on Syrian machinery at work in the survey stage of the diversion. The Syrian project was again interrupted by Israeli fire in March 1965. What grounds were there for believing that more substantive efforts to steal the water would pass unscathed?

As a design for keeping the fires of hostility aglow, the Summit decisions and all their apparatus were comprehensible; as a programme for Israel's liquidation they were a failure. At any rate, Israel's flesh simply refused to creep. Within a few years, the Summit technique had played itself out; and with Arab states polarized between the 'conservatives' and the 'revolutionaries', it became impossible for their leaders to meet at all.

A general election was held in Israel in November 1965, and Levi Eshkol's new administration was formed two months later. It began with an effort to judge the prospects of continuing stability in the coming years. Most political and military intelligence reports pointed to the likelihood that there would be continuing tension, falling short of explosion. Nasser's caution at the Summit Conferences resulted from his sober estimate of the military balance, which seemed unlikely to change. In February 1966 French Ministers assured Israel of uninterrupted support for its defence. Their only criticism was directed at what they called an 'excessive Israeli nervousness' about the durability of the French alliance. An exchange of views with Maurice Couve de Murville in February 1966 revealed no major divergence in the two countries' policies. Israel was responsive to French views about the need for Israel to explore the possibility of Soviet support for Middle Eastern stability. In Washington a few days later, President Johnson and Secretary of Defence Robert McNamara gave their formal assent to the purchase of Skyhawk aircraft. At Warsaw in May 1966, the Polish Government, through Foreign Minister Rapacki, assured Israel of steadfast links based on the memories of 'a common struggle and a common agony'. A few weeks later, Israel's envoy to Bucharest was instructed to formulate an integral programme of cooperation with Rumania, going beyond the normal diplomatic ties. Israel also sought a wider application in Latin America of the development projects which it had been carrying out in many countries of Africa. Agreements were soon to be signed with the Organization of American States and its financial organs. Even in Southeast Asia there was a disposition to strengthen ties with Israel. In March 1967 official visits were paid to Thailand, Philippines, Japan, Burma and Cambodia, as well as Australia and New Zealand. In Singapore, the Defence and Foreign Ministers were eager to draw on Israel's experience in economic development and the organization of a citizens' army; and plans were laid for the gradual development of commercial and diplomatic relations. In October 1966 Israel applied for associate membership in the European Economic Community; it had been sounding out this matter for several years. A few months later the Commission of the EEC recommended a favourable response; and in 1970 Israel was able to sign a preferential agreement with the Community.

Opportunities seemed to beckon wherever Israel looked. Every seed of new effort seemed to bear some fruit. In March 1965 President Habib Bourguiba of Tunis shattered the conventional Arab ideology by appealing for 'moderation and logic instead of passion', and urging a negotiated settlement with Israel. Even the Israeli dialogue with the Soviet Union was correct, if not warm. During that year, two thousand Jews reached Israel from the USSR. The trickle was small; but it came after decades of absolute drought. If it could be gradually pumped to a greater profusion, a new vision of national growth would come into Israel's view. But clouds were gathering on this horizon. In May 1966 Mr Kosygin set out on his voyage to Cairo. Thereafter, the Soviet Union proclaimed Arab slogans and thought Arab thoughts; it was later to incite the Arabs to violent deeds as well.

Despite occasional setbacks the popular mood at home was favourable to a broad consolidation of Israel's international links. Criticism came only from a few areas of dissent. There were some in the opposition Herut Party who traditionally advocated military retaliation against most acts of Arab provocation. The government's responses were more selective. Its object was to keep the Arab attacks within bounds while saving military strength and political sympathy for larger ordeals. Some of the leaders of Rafi (which had split from Mapai) still thought it possible to rely exclusively on France for Israel's air strength and were hesitant about expanding security ties with the United States. They also showed little sympathy for attempts to achieve a thaw in relations with Eastern Europe. The government, for its part, did not delude itself about the prospect, but believed that it was morally imperative to explore it. Setting its face against all restrictive 'orientations', the government's foreign policy was set on a universal quest for friendship, commerce and understanding wherever they could be found. The strategy was plain: instead of allowing Arab hostility to isolate Israel, the government would try to isolate Arab hostility until it choked for lack of sympathetic air.

Nothing in the early months of 1967 seemed to refute this prospect. The argument among Israeli experts and commentators was about whether Israel could count on a continuing respite for five years – or ten. At the beginning of the year, almost every Israeli political and military leader publicly predicted that 1967 would not be a year of war.

To explain why all this rationality came to nought, one must turn to Damascus and Moscow. Across three of Israel's borders there were Arab governments which, for divergent reasons, seemed reconciled to temporary stability. In the south, Nasser, embroiled in Yemen, managed to combine verbal extremism against Israel with tactical prudence. Israel, in his view, must 'eventually' be destroyed; but the battle would be joined only when Arab armies were ready and when Arab unity was complete. The second condition seemed so remote that it seemed to convert the threat of Israel's annihilation into a theological idea. Nasser did not give up the dream of war. But while awaiting it, he would bide his time in safety. His fanaticism was sometimes tempered by empirical prudence: he had survived because he sometimes understood the valour of which discretion is the better part.

Meanwhile, the King of Jordan was being described by Nasser, his future ally, as 'the Hashemite harlot', 'the imperialistic lackey' and 'the treacherous dwarf'. King Hussein understood that the terrorists of El Fatah and of Shukeiry's Palestine Liberation Organization were a sharper threat to his kingdom than was Israel, which was ready to negotiate a peace treaty with him on honourable terms. He generally managed to hold his ground against Cairo, Damascus and the more militant terrorist groups; but sometimes the Jordan authorities lost control of areas in which terrorists operated against Israel. In November 1966 the village of Samoa, near Hebron, suffered loss and havoc when Israeli forces moved in to clean out terrorist bases. For some hours the Jordanian régime seemed to be in danger, and in Israel itself many uncomfortable questions were asked about the scale and intensity of the raid. But there was no Israeli intention to go beyond isolated reactions into a sustained invasion; and the armistice lines, as well as the integrity of the Hashemite Kingdom, remained intact. Indeed, Jordan's integrity was paradoxically guaranteed by Israel's physical presence; for without the intervening slice of Israeli territory in the Negev, the military and demographic power of Egypt would sooner or later have swamped Jordan. All this time Lebanon was occupied with its internal balance and growing mercantile success and gave no indulgence to military or subversive assaults against Israel. Alone among Israel's neighbours, she maintained a policy commensurate with her means. Thus from three directions, the Arab war against Israel was being waged with purely verbal heroism. If Syria had been content with a similar passivity, 1967 – and the succeeding years – would have rolled on tense and rancorous, but without war.

In September 1961, after three years of uneasy union with Egypt, Syria had broken away from the United Arab Republic. In March 1963 the Ba'ath ('Socialist Renascence') movement seized power in Damascus and Baghdad. Its revolutionary dogma and socialist phraseology gave it a somewhat eccentric aspect in the Arab world. It had started out as the advocate of pan-Arab solidarity and the opponent of separate nationhood, which it condemned as 'regionalism', but in its rivalry with Nasser for supremacy in the Arab world, it soon developed a separatist policy. Nasser at that time was in favour of tactical

School children participating in the 'Adloyada' parade on Purim. The challenge to Israel's educational system is to strengthen links with the past while preparing for a creative future

restraint in relations with Israel; so the Ba'ath sponsored revolutionary activism. At the Arab Summit Conferences of 1964 and 1965, and thereafter, Syria alone called for immediate confrontation. All the other Arab governments preferred Nasser's more comfortable philosophy of a distant and ultimate expulsion of Israel from the Middle East. In February 1966 there was yet another revolution in Damascus, and the Syrian pendulum took an even more drastic swing to the left. The new leaders, Nureddin el Atassi, Yusuf Zuayin, General Salah Jedid and Ahmed Suweidani, urged that war against Israel must not be a distant dream; something must be done every day to give it reality and substance. If the balance of arms made the clash of regular forces unrewarding, it could be evaded and transcended by guerilla techniques.

It was, of course, absurd to imagine that terrorist infiltrations and attacks could by themselves 'destroy' anything as solid as the State of Israel. On the other hand, Israeli acquiescence to them was inconceivable. They reminded Israel deeply and permanently of its unique vulnerability. A country of broad expanse and ample configuration might have been relatively tolerant if a narrow and remote border area were less than completely secure. Israel, however, consisted entirely of border areas. Nowhere in the country could a man live and work far from the shadow of hostile guns. If the borders themselves could be breached at any point convenient to the guerilla command, the whole nation would be obsessed by insecurity. In the last months of 1966, terrorist units of a few dozen men had achieved the following results: the railway between Israel's capital, Jerusalem, and its largest town, Tel Aviv, had been made unsafe for regular travel; residences had been blown up within a few hundred yards of the Knesset; several roads in the north could only be traversed after initial probing by mine-detecting vehicles; a youth was blown to pieces while playing football near the Lebanese frontier; four soldiers were blasted to death in Upper Galilee and six others killed or wounded in the area facing the Hebron hills. If such results could be achieved by a few dozen infiltrators, what would remain of tranquillity if the terrorist movement were allowed to expand and to deploy its activities over a broader field? The unpleasant fact was that the Syrian leaders and the terrorist groups had uncovered Israel's most vulnerable nerve. No country in the world was more exposed to a form of aggression so cheap in risk and requiring such small investment of military valour and skill.

Israelis could remember a time when international opinion had been more indignant about terrorist actions than it later became. General Burns of Canada, the Chief of Staff of the United Nations armistice machinery in the Middle East had this to say:

The Technion, Israel's largest scientific institution of higher
learning, was established in 1912 and has developed a world-wide
reputation for its high standards

'I felt that what Egyptians were doing in sending these men, whom they dignified with the name of 'fedayeen' or 'commandos', into another country with the mission to attack men, women and children indiscriminately, was a war crime. It was essentially of the same character, though less in degree, as the offences for which the Nazi leaders had been tried in Nuremberg, to cite the most recent example (*Between Arab and Israeli*, 1963, p. 88).

Nobody in those days equated murder with progressive national sentiment.

Apart from the sabotage technique, there was another area of confrontation in which Syria had a special advantage. The collective farming villages (kibbutzim) in Upper Galilee and the Jordan Valley are the jewel in Israel's crown. Set in a frame of serene physical beauty, they represent the pioneering values which have given Israeli society much of its originality. They lie among the verdure of well-watered lowlands. On the hills, looking down upon them with rancorous vigilance, were the Syrian gun emplacements and fortified positions on the Golan Heights. Part of the area to the west of the Syrian frontier had been defined in the 1949 Armistice Agreement as a 'demilitarized zone'. In Israel's interpretation, demilitarization meant nothing except the absence of armed forces: it did not imply that development activity was prohibited. Syria, on the other hand, asserted that the area, being demilitarized, was of undefined sovereignty and might again come under Syrian rule in the 'eventual peace settlement', which Damascus paradoxically asserted would never come. Meanwhile, the Arab governments insisted that the area must remain a desert. The United Nations resolved this obscurity with typical ambivalence. The problem of sovereignty was left in suspense so as to satisfy Syria's claim or, at least, not to refute it. On the other hand, the Security Council ruled to Israel's advantage in 1951, and again in 1953, that the demilitarized status of the zones could not be invoked to impede 'normal economic development'. There were two sides to the question, and this time the United Nations was on both of them.

Late in 1966 and throughout the first part of 1967, the prospect of a tranquil Arab-Israel frontier was shattered by terrorist raids and by Syrian gun bombardment of Israel's northern settlements. On 14 July 1966 a Syrian Mig 21 was shot down by an Israeli Mirage. On 15 August Syrian aircraft attacked a disabled Israeli motor launch on the Sea of Galilee; one Syrian Mig 17 was brought down by anti-aircraft fire from the vessel, while a Mig 21 was destroyed by Mirage fighters. The Syrians were unvarying both in the constancy of their assaults and in their operational inefficiency. Yet their political logic was sound: the aim was to prevent any stabilization of the frontier, and this was without any doubt achieved.

The security of the settlements in the northern Galilee was constantly threatened by bombardment from Syrian positions on the Golan Heights

It was clear that sooner or later Syrian pressure would either have to subside or be resisted. Because the contingencies were grave, Israel decided to exhaust other remedies. On 14 October the Security Council, on Israel's initiative, discussed the murderous Syrian attacks. After many laborious weeks, a resolution was drafted expressing criticism of Syria in terms so mild as to be almost deferential. It was sponsored by nations from five continents – Argentina, Japan, the Netherlands, New Zealand and Nigeria. It expressed 'a regret at infiltration from Syria and loss of human life caused by the incidents in October and November 1966'. The adoption of this text would have consoled no widows or orphans in Israel. It would have saved no lives. At most, it would have given a harassed nation the minimal comfort which comes from an enlightened human solidarity, however vaguely expressed. But even this was to be denied. The Soviet Union vetoed the resolution on the grounds that it dared to imply an absence of total virtue among the implacable colonels in Damascus. A similar fate had befallen a December 1964 resolution expressing regret at the shelling of Dan, Dafna and She'ar Yashuv by Syrian guns. As far as the Security Council was officially concerned, there was an open season for killing Israelis on their own territory, whether the killing was done by regular armies or by 'guerrilla' groups.

Syrian aggression and Soviet bias thus intersected at a signpost pointing to danger. Since 1953 the Soviet Union had blindly supported every Arab cause in the controversy with Israel. But from 1963 onwards Moscow added a new refinement. While all Arab nations would be aided in their conflict with Israel, special favour and protection would be offered to the 'progressive' régimes in Damascus, Cairo, Republican Yemen, Algiers and Baghdad, which were aligned against the West in the Cold War. These would receive a more fervent Russian embrace than that offered to 'reactionary' Arab states, such as Saudia Arabia, Jordan, Lebanon, Tunisia and Morocco. In the Soviet vocabulary, a 'progressive' Arab state was one which devoted all its resources to arms, neglected social progress and made war against Israel the central aim of its policy. An 'independent' state was one whose policy was dependent on that of the Soviet Union. By these standards, Syria was the most 'progressive' and 'independent' of any state that had ever existed in the Middle East. It would be nurtured by the Soviet Union in all its ordeals and protected by Moscow from the results of its excesses.

The Moscow-Damascus equation was the heart of Israel's dilemma. The most violent and aggressive of Israel's adversaries operated against her from the vast shadow of Soviet protection. Syria could thus combine a heroic posture with an unheroic absence of risk.

But when the Syrian Prime Minister declared in October 1966, 'We shall set the whole region on fire,' events were to prove him right. The threat to Israel's security came not from single exploits, but from their accumulation. Machine-guns and artillery on the Golan Heights gave Syria a local advantage, while the El Fatah groups, operating through Lebanon and Jordan, enabled Damascus to harass Israel over a broader front. Israel could never predict at what part of her body the rash of violence would erupt. It could certainly expect no permanent relief from insecurity until Damascus underwent a change either of heart or ideology. Neither contingency seemed probable. On 13 March 1966 the Syrian newspaper '*Al Ba'ath*' had written:

The revolutionary forces of the Arab homeland, the Ba'ath at their head, preach a genuine Arab Palestine liberation on the soil of Palestine; and they have had enough of traditional methods. The Arab people demand armed struggle and day-to-day incessant confrontation through a total war of liberation in which all the Arabs will take part.

This became the central theme of Syrian policy in 1967, and no Arab government was prepared to speak or work against it.

If 'all the Arabs' were going to take part in an assault on Israel it is relevant to ask whether 'all the Israelis' would be united in effective resistance. We must now retrace some of the developments within Israeli society during the decade between the wars. Most of the population lived those years in peace, with no constant sense of being physically threatened. There was therefore greater preoccupation with the country's internal problems. But quite apart from this, Israel was ripe for changes in the colour and shape of its society. New problems had collected, and many of the attitudes on which the national unity had been based were no longer as secure as before.

Austerity was no longer an ideal. The nation's resources were growing; but so also was its determination to live beyond them. Standards of consumption were rising faster than the rates of productivity; and towards the end of the decade economic difficulties were to become intense. With the recession came a growth of unemployment. As many as 50–100,000 workers, a significant percentage of the total labour force – were out of work. The impact of the crisis was softened by two major achievements in Israel's foreign relations. The first was the maintenance of the American aid programme which brought hundreds of millions of dollars of aid in grants and loans. The other was economic co-operation with the Federal Republic of Germany, based primarily on the investment of $700 million in twelve years, in addition to large sums devoted to personal restitution. Thus between 1955 and 1968 $1 billion reached Israel from Germany. The overall result was a growth of industrial energy and an improved balance of payments; there was also a sharp expansion of exports. But while the statistics looked good on the books, they did not reflect an egalitarian distribution of benefits. Social divisions were beginning to cause concern. The fact that immigrants from oriental countries were in the lower reaches of the economy gave a disquieting ethnic aspect to economic inequalities.

Israel society was now more complex, diverse and sophisticated than before. The intimate family atmosphere had been transformed by urbanism and economic diversity. Israel was open to winds of opinion from outside, and the impact of years was breaking up the old patterns of thought and custom. The younger citizens of Israel had been raised in an atmosphere of sovereignty, and the heart-rending nostalgia of Zionism did not speak to their hearts or their experience. They were sometimes impatient with the old ideological sanctities. Their way of thinking was concrete and pragmatic: they did not share their elders' passion for abstract ideas or social doctrines. Zionism, in their eyes, had fulfilled its aim and should now be left to the appraisal of history. The word even became the target for benevolent jokes. Socialism, too, was all very well, but would have to be diluted in order to allow the growth of an industrialized economy, which demanded more freedom for competition and private enterprise. The test of a policy was not whether it conformed to doctrine, but whether it worked in practice. The Utopian vision of sending out a 'light to the nations' seemed pretentious and burdensome to young people who thought that they had carried too many burdens already. Many of them would be satisfied with the more modest ambition of making Israel a decent, ordered, agreeable land in which to live. Even in the kibbutzim, pioneering simplicity was no longer universal. As wealth increased, the buildings and gardens became more lavish. Some of the air-conditioned dining-halls, cultural centres and coffee-bars would have done credit to the fine hotels and summer resorts, which, incidentally, were also expanding in number and comfort in the hope of attracting and maintaining the tourist trade. The phrase 'Espresso Generation' was coined to describe a youth that was prepared for sacrifice if necessary, but was insistent on living in ease and relative affluence if they were possible.

At the same time the new immigrants, especially from oriental lands, were claiming their inheritance. They had graduated from municipal responsibilities to a demand for due representation in the country's central government and political life. In the early years most parties had included representatives of these communities in their lists in order to attract votes and to avoid the dangers of

The focal point of the 'Espresso Generation': Dizengoff Street, Tel Aviv. Members of this 'generation' bore the brunt of the fighting in the Six Day War

separate political organization. Yet most of these representatives were not newcomers but veterans who had long merged into the establishment.

As in all immigrant societies, there were genuine causes for social tension, but the main complication was psychological. Not all the immigrants recognized that the gap between themselves and the established population had been created not by Israel, but by the pre-State history of the Jewish people. That history had sent some Jewish masses into countries where the economic and technological rhythm was dynamic and where liberalism provided at least occasional possibilities for Jews to share the general progress of ideas and material wealth. Others had been living for centuries in countries in which the results of the industrial and scientific revolutions had not been felt either by Jews or by anyone else. Thus Jews came to Israel with a gap of standards and capacities already built in. Israel always moved to eliminate the gaps, not to create them. But since the differences in educational standards lay at the heart of the problem, it was plain that the solution would have to be organic, and therefore not immediate. In the meantime the gap endured. The nation's political and educational leaders drew satisfaction from the thought that it was becoming narrower; the immigrants saw only that it still remained. Some of them ascribed this not to objective conditions arising out of long-rooted diversities, but to favouritism or prejudice or snobbery. As a judgment of Israeli policy, this was preposterous. The establishment of development towns, the immense housing programme which brought immigrants from ship to home without the intervening *ma'abarot* phase and, above all, the special educational programmes and institutions designed to elevate children above the conditions

of their homes all showed a sensitive urgency for the problem of social integration. Nor was there a failure on the level of consciousness. In the early 1960's, Ben Gurion and his Ministers of Finance, Education and Housing were thinking, planning and doing more about this problem than about any other. For some time it occupied the headlines as the chief item of national concern. But this did not mean that there was no emotional malaise. Social barriers existed. Ashkenazi and Sephardi Jews had derogatory epithets for each other which, at best, were used indulgently, at worst contemptuously. The European origins of the pre-State community had created the established patterns, and it was the non-Europeans who had to do most of the adaptation. The educational curriculum, for instance, had placed more stress on the work of the East European Hebrew authors than on that of Jews in Moslem lands. It was sometimes forgotten that Abraham was an Iraqi Jew and Moses an Egyptian Jew. The hierarchy of Jewish values and memories had shifted westwards over the generations. The kibbutz, which still determined the legitimacy of Israeli values, was essentially the creation of European Jews and never played a major role in absorption of mass-immigration from non-European lands.

Fortunately, there were many influences at work in favour of social integration. The army provided the newcomers with an environment of free association with other Israelis. It also conferred a feeling of dignity and vocation, as well as a sense of place and language and unimpeded opportunities of advancement. The school system concentrated, by lavish stipends, on bringing a larger proportion of oriental Jews into the secondary and higher educational institutions. There is no deep-rooted plutocracy in Israel and, of course, no tradition of inherited nobility, so that educational performance is the main key to upward social mobility.

Another unifying factor was the common heritage to which all Jews could reach back across the intervening diversities of exile. The educational system concentrated on the diffusion of a Jewish consciousness; and from the Tenth Anniversary celebration in 1958 onwards the Youth Bible Contest entered the national folklore. Bible groups and societies flourished in every town and village, and the long tradition of piety among oriental Jews carried them to the highest levels.

Israelis are unanimous in recognizing that their nation could not have been reborn without the persistence of religious memory and practice. Even the most secular nationalists pay tribute to the constancy with which the flame was kept alive against all attempts to extinguish it. To this extent the religious heritage is a unifying force. But the application of religious doctrine, the forms

Immigrant school children on an outing in the early days of Kiryat Gat. Social integration has often proved to be a greater problem than economic development

and institutions which expressed it, and the degree of compulsion which the
State may properly enlist for its observance are all held in dispute.

   The religious controversy was active throughout the decade between the
wars. Orthodox Jews were in the minority, but their cohesion and zeal gave
them a strong tactical position. Few governments or municipalities could form
a leadership without them. They naturally did their utmost to impose rabbinical law on the public sector. At the same time a spirit of pragmatism and
scientific empiricism was seizing hold of the younger population. Religious
disputes were waged in heated arguments and street demonstrations. Public
Sabbath observance, transportation on Sabbath (especially in Jerusalem),
the right to sell non-kosher meat, the status of the religious schools and the
permissibility of mixed bathing (especially in Jerusalem) were all debated
with a vehemence that surprised many foreign observers. In Jerusalem the
discussion between the orthodox and the non-observant was polarized
by a fanatical ultra-orthodox group, Neturei Karta, which believed that
the State of Israel was conceived in original sin. It had pre-empted divine
revelation by coming into existence through human decision, instead of
awaiting the coming of the Messiah. The Neturei Karta treated the state as a
hated occupying power and went on praying for the restoration of Zion, which
'unfortunately' had already been restored. They ignored the immense weight
given by biblical and rabbinical authority to the ingathering of the exiles and
the restoration of Jewish freedom. Sometimes the religious debate invaded the
the political arena. The parliamentary crisis of 1958–9 revolved around the
question 'Who is a Jew?' The controversy arose out of the prosaic problems of
registration. The question was whether a Jew, as the Minister of Interior said,
should be defined as somebody who asserted his Jewish consciousness, or
whether the condition was more rigid – the circumstance of having been born
of a Jewish mother. It is interesting to recall that in this period Prime Minister
Ben Gurion consulted Jewish scholars all over the world and most of them
argued in favour of the traditional definition. A formula was found, tradition
triumphed and the crisis was resolved. No other people in the world so
constantly kept asking itself who it was and in what manner its identity should
be defined.

The fact is that by the mid–1960's Israel was less cohesive than it had been in its
first decade. Israelis stood together for life and death, but in their less extreme
ordeals they were conscious of the things that divided them. The word
'gap' began to figure endlessly in Israel's constant exploration of itself. There
was the gap between the new urban middle class and the old rural élite based on

the kibbutz movement. There was the gap between both of these and the struggling disinherited proletariat in the slum areas and shanty towns. There was
the gap between the European-educated population and their sabra offspring
and the oriental immigrants with their special pieties, loyalties and family
traditions. There was also a generation gap: the young Israeli generation born
in the sun and under the open skies was given to a simpler, less tormented, but
more superficial intellectual outlook than that which had been common to
the pioneering generation. There was also a gap of alienation between young
matter-of-fact Israelis and the more sentimental, complicated, introspective
but creative Diaspora Jews.

And yet there were common memories which often reminded Israelis that
history had dealt with the whole of the Jewish people in a special way, so that
in the last resort they were indivisible in their fate. One of the moments of
unifying truth came with the capture and trial of Adolf Eichmann who had
been in charge of the department appointed by Hitler in 1944 to carry out
the extermination of the Jews in Nazi-occupied Europe. Eichmann had done
his work with horrible competence. After the defeat of Germany in 1945,
he had gone into hiding for five years and in 1950 had escaped to Argentina
where he lived under the name Ricardo Klement. Israeli and other Jewish
volunteers and organizations had kept up the search. The idea that the murderer
of millions of men, women and children was walking the earth in peace and
impunity was infuriating to the Jewish conscience. Ben Gurion put the full
weight of his authority behind the world-wide effort to track Eichmann down,
and Israeli intelligence services were decisive in his discovery and capture. One
day in May 1960 when 'Ricardo Klement' was walking home from a factory
in which he worked in Buenos Aires, he was captured by Israelis who put him
on an aircraft for Israel. There were complications in Israel's relations with
Argentina, which asked that the Israeli Ambassador be recalled and brought a
complaint to the UN Security Council. But the formal irregularity of the capture struck most of the world as subsidiary to the greater drama. Here was an
arch-criminal, an assassin of Jewish masses, brought to trial in a Jewish homeland. A free Israel could now offer redress and honour to the afflicted Jewish
people.

The trial was exemplary in its dignity and judicial precision. The court of
three judges, under the presidency of Justice Moshe Landau, heard hundreds of
witnesses who unfolded stories so macabre and agonizing that the whole nation
was stunned by a new flow of grief. The Israeli Attorney General, Gideon
Hausner, rose to lofty and sombre heights in bringing the indictment in the
name of six million accusers 'whose blood cries out but whose voice is stilled'.

Sentence of death was passed and upheld in the Court of Appeal, and for the only time in Israel's history, presidential clemency was withheld. But of far greater significance than the justice meted out to a single odious monster was the electrifying effect of the trial on world opinion and on Israel's young generation. The mystery of man's infinite degradation was unfolded in gory detail day by day, together with the nobility and despair of Jewish resistance. A sharp light was thrown on the role of the Jewish people as history's most poignant victim. One of the underlying sources of Israel's struggle for freedom and security was brought into view. At one session, Attorney General Hausner recounted the story of sleepy Jewish children being rounded up at dawn and put on buses on the pretence of being sent on picnics, and then being herded into gas chambers for asphyxiation. One could feel the world shudder in a paroxysm of shame. The Eichmann trial had risen above the level of retribution, vengeance and even formal justice.

It was clearly inevitable that the new pluralism of Israel's society should come to expression in the nation's political life. There were also normal biological influences at work. Ben Gurion's temporary retirement in 1954 had reminded Israel that the pattern of their leadership was not set for all eternity. As the 1959 elections approached, the problem of eventual succession arose

above The cataclysmic effect of the trial of Adolph Eichmann in 1961 served to remind the world and teach the younger generation of Israelis about the Nazi horror

within the Mapai Party. Ben Gurion wished to replenish the party leadership by drawing on some of its members and adherents who had become prominent outside the party in military, diplomatic and government service. The ladder to the summit had previously been composed of well-defined rungs, leading from local party branches to professional service in party or Histadrut bodies. There was apprehension that Ben Gurion's move would disturb the routine order of ascent. It was also feared that he was veering from loyalty to comrades of his own generation towards men three decades younger than himself. In the event these tensions were reconciled, and Mapai appealed to the electorate in 1959 with a team carefully balanced between fidelity and innovation. It was rewarded by a crushing victory which gave it forty-nine seats. This was more than Mapai had ever attained, although it was not sufficient to ensure adoption of the party's programme for a change in the electoral system. The electoral verdict took Ben Gurion's domestic prestige and international fame to its highest peak, and he was able to wield the Premiership with imposing authority. There seemed good reason to anticipate a stable period in Israel's domestic life. But this hope was shattered by the Lavon Affair or, more accurately, by the intensity of Ben Gurion's reaction to it.

As Israelis look back beyond the screen of the Six Day War it seems incredible that we should have been stirred to such passion by the matters that pre-occupied us before 1967. Only the absence of any urgent challenge from outside can explain the intensity with which Israelis debated the Lavon Affair. It erupted in the autumn of 1960, but its roots go back to 1954 when Pinchas Lavon was Minister of Defence in Sharett's Cabinet.

The central event was a so-called 'security mishap'. In 1951 an intelligence unit was established in Egypt consisting of young Egyptian Jews. By 1954 Nasser had confirmed his authority and was in the final stages of his treaty negotiations with Great Britain. This treaty provided for the withdrawal of all British troops from the Canal zone. There was anxiety in Israel over the strategic implications of the British withdrawal and concern for the possibility that vast stores of equipment would fall into Nasser's hands. The British military presence in the Canal zone had served as a buffer between Egyptian and and Israeli military forces; there would now be proximity instead of separation. The Anglo-Egyptian Treaty was regarded by Israel as a change in the regional balance of power. The Israeli Government did not crystallize any decision, but in July 1954, after explosions in Cairo and Alexandria, eleven Jews were arrested. It was assumed that the intelligence unit had carried out operations and had failed. The question in Israel was who had given the instruction? Neither the Prime Minister nor the Cabinet had been informed or consulted. In an effort to determine who had given the instruction for the 'security mishap', Prime Minister Sharett nominated a 'Committee of Two' in October 1954.

Meanwhile, on 26 October 1954 the Moslem Brotherhood had made an attempt on the life of Nasser. There were mass arrests and trials, followed by executions of Moslem Brotherhood leaders. To counter-balance this treatment of the Moslem Brothers, Nasser ordered the trial of the eleven Jews involved in the events of 15 July. It began on 4 December 1954. The 'Committee of Two' in Israel concluded its investigations by the statement that they 'had not been convinced beyond a reasonable doubt that Lavon had not authorized the operation'. A shadow thus lay on Lavon's role as Minister of Defence, especially as he had declared categorically that he had not authorized the operation.

On 27 January 1955, the Cairo trials were over. Two of the defendants were sentenced to death and executed on 31 January 1955. The other accused received very long terms of imprisonment. On 2 February Lavon submitted his resignation to Prime Minister Sharett. Quite apart from the 'Affair' and the 'security mishap', there had been tension between the army and the Minister, and morale was disturbed. Sharett, with the support of Mapai leaders, decided to recall Ben Gurion to the Ministry of Defence. Lavon's career seemed to have ended. But his dynamism and talent elevated him within a year to the position of Secretary-General of the Histadrut. In the Israeli system this post is equivalent in stature to that of a senior Cabinet Minister. The 'Affair' seemed to have been left behind.

It was not to be. In 1959 an Israeli officer who had commanded the operation known as the 'security mishap' and managed to escape from Egypt was brought to trial in Israel on charges unrelated to the 'security mishap' and sentenced to a long imprisonment. Some revelations concerning the 'security mishap' of 1954 were made during his trial. Lavon considered that he had new evidence which would remove the question-mark left behind by the 'Committee of Two'. On 26 September, 1960 he asked the Prime Minister for a statement clearing him of responsibility. But Ben Gurion refused to make a judgment, pointing out that he had no judicial capacity and had not even studied the 'Affair'. Lavon proceeded to place the issue before the Knesset Security and Foreign Affairs Committee. Most of the press supported Lavon, claiming that he had been wrongly accused and implying that there had even been a 'conspiracy' against him. Ben Gurion's response was consistent: the only way to establish the facts was by a formal judicial enquiry. The majority of his Cabinet thought that the matter should be investigated by a Cabinet com-

mittee, including the Minister of Justice. This committee, composed of seven ministers, reported its findings to the Cabinet on 25 December 1960. Its report formally exonerated Lavon from any responsibility for the 'security mishap', and its verdict was endorsed by the Cabinet, with three abstentions and without Ben Gurion's participation in the vote. Ben Gurion was resentful of this result.

At the end of January 1961, he resigned but continued as head of a caretaker government. Feeling himself defeated in his own Cabinet, he turned to the party. On 4 February 1961, by a party vote of 159 to 96, Lavon was dismissed as Secretary-General of the Histadrut. Soon afterwards Ben Gurion withdrew his resignation. It was generally believed that there had been no original intention to dismiss Lavon from the leadership of the Histadrut and that this vote was taken primarily in order to prevent Ben Gurion's departure from the party leadership.

On the surface this was a debate about a security error six years before on

above Foreign Minister Golda Meir with ex-Minister of Defence
Pinchas Lavon. The so-called 'Lavon Affair', which forced Lavon's
resignation, had political repercussions of long standing

which full certainty was unlikely to be established. Even the documentary evidence, which by the nature of intelligence operations was meagre, came under accusation of forgery. In parts of Israel's legal community there was some scepticism about whether a Committee of Inquiry headed by a judge was so different from a Cabinet committee headed, in effect, by the Minister of Justice as to justify so much tension. But beneath the outer layer of discussion lay issues which were to be endlessly agitated in the public arena. Ben Gurion's principle was that a political body such as a Cabinet committee could not exonerate anybody, since this was a judicial function. The balance of Israel's democratic structure had thus been violated. Moreover, Ben Gurion argued, if Lavon was exonerated it followed that the officer subordinate to him was virtually accused and condemned for having given a fatal order without authority. To condemn by political decision, without judicial authority, was even worse than to exonerate by such means. Ben Gurion thus presented the action of the Cabinet committee as a major corruption of the democratic process and of juridical integrity. He pursued this theme in writings of unbelievable vehemence and profusion. He also began to express disparaging sentiments about the Committee of Seven, especially his Finance Minister, Levi Eshkol, and the Minister of Justice, Pinchas Rosen. Ben Gurion's critics had a more varied indictment to make: he was exaggerating the importance of a formalistic and debatable issue, upsetting the national priorities and preventing the nation from getting on with its vital work. By creating a choice between dismissing Lavon or renouncing his own leadership he was facing his party with the need to vote against its objective judgment; for in its heart it probably wanted both Ben Gurion and Lavon to continue their respective tasks. Leading academic figures entered the fray to allege the existence of charismatic and authoritarian elements in Ben Gurion's leadership. They raised the question whether any leader should refuse acceptance of a collective Cabinet, parliamentary and party decision (for the Knesset endorsed the exoneration of Lavon by the 'Committee of Seven'). Ben Gurion found himself beleaguered by public opinion after many years of general adulation.

So the argument flowed on. For the historian of this period, the major consequence of the 'Lavon Affair' was that it expedited Ben Gurion's departure from the national leadership. There were other points of tension between him and his party, but it was the controversy over his treatment of the 'Affair' that tore his mind away from central national issues to brood darkly on something in which most Israelis wanted to lose interest. After the 1961 election in which Mapai retained power but lost seven seats, there was an ardent resolve to have done with the whole issue. The public had a feeling that Israel would

After the Six Day War, the children of Kibbutz Gadot were able to walk down to the Jordan River, which adjoins their home, for the first time in their lives

lose its sanity unless it abandoned the 'Affair', which was eating away at its heart and mind like a curse in mediaeval demonology.

Ben Gurion weathered this and other storms, but he was now estranged from many of his contemporaries, apathetic about many of Israel's parliamentary conflicts, wounded by the rejection of his position on the 'Affair' and full of dark fears about the future. In April 1963, when Egypt, Syria and Iraq announced one of their periodic paper 'federations' with the usual dire threats of Israel's destruction, Ben Gurion reacted in an apocalyptic spirit that contrasted with his usual confidence. He sent letters to over a hundred heads of government, sometimes expressing doubt about Israel's ability to exist in the future. One morning in June 1963, he opened a Cabinet meeting with the casual remark that he would resign as soon as the meeting was over. An era of large and vivid leadership had come to an end.

J. L. Talmon, a leading Israeli historian has written:

> The wonderful gallery of great and colourful personalities thrown up by Zionism will stand comparison with any of the finest and ablest leaders amongst the nations: Herzl with Mazzini, Weizmann with Cavour or Masaryk, Ben Gurion with Bismarck or Pilsudski, Jabotinsky with Nehru . . . (*Israel Among the Nations*, 1970, p. 133).

Some of these comparisons are more apt than others, but the passage has an accurate sense of dimension. Ben Gurion had a more profound impact on his nation's formative years than did either of the European statesmen with whom he is compared. He occupied a larger area of the national consciousness than the Premiership strictly required. His squat, short figure, beetling eyebrows, white tufts of hair, staccato form of speech and, above all, his quick, jerky manner of moving about gave an infectious impression of clarity and purpose. He had a talent for animating the national will. He created a permanent sense of excitement about those objectives which he deemed central and decisive at any given time. He had a broad, simple vision of Israel's destiny. He saw modern Israel as the descendant of the ancient prophetic Israel, harbinger to the world of the messianic dream. By developing its intellectual and moral resources, Israel could again become a nation of special vitality, able, despite its smallness, to impress itself on history and to ensure its security against heavy material odds. Ben Gurion was ubiquitous and all pervasive in Israeli life. He had something to say about biblical research, science, history, education, religion and, of course, military strategy and organization. His intellect was vigilant and lively though not formally disciplined. He was perennially open to new interests and enthusiasms. He tended to sharpen his judgments so as to exclude subtleties or

Controversy over the role of religion in the state has flared up periodically and threatened Israel with a *kulturkampf*. These *yeshiva* students, however, study both secular and religious subjects

ambivalence. He felt that not much could be done about peace with the Arabs until Israel was unbreakably strong; he therefore excluded this problem from his active concern and gave an impression of being unconciliatory. The impression was inaccurate.

In point of fact his international policy, although sometimes expressed in barks of defiance, was essentially moderate. His immense domestic prestige gave him a wide discretion which he sometimes used in order to withdraw from untenable positions. He was sometimes more categoric in his definitions than the facts seemed to warrant. He asserted, for example, that the United Nations had played no positive role in Israel's emergence. A more accurate analysis would admit that there is no single line of truth on this issue; the United Nations was extremely important for Israel in some ordeals (as in 1947–9) and ineffective in others. Similarly, Ben Gurion's declaration of autarchy ('What matters is not what the nations of the world [*goyyim*] say, but what the Jews do') was probably more extreme than he seriously intended. He knew in his heart that Israel had been more dependent on outside support – and more successful in obtaining it – than any other state faced with similar hazards. But his aim was didactic. He was trying to get Israelis to understand the need for self-reliance and autonomous decision. His method was to concentrate a powerful searchlight on one aspect of a problem, even if it meant creating darkness in surrounding areas.

The issues selected for bright illumination were usually the right ones: military strength; mass-immigration; social integration; educational progress. Ben Gurion had less fortune in domestic conflict. He fully understood the mechanics of power but was limited in his talent for personal relations. He was lonely, introspective, uninterested in outward forms and impatient of small talk. He did not suffer fools gladly. There was no particular reason why he should; after all, the only people who suffer fools gladly are other fools. But in the end, Ben Gurion placed himself on roads where none but the most uncritical of his devotees were willing to follow him. The public refused to understand his excessive emphasis on the 'Affair'. Israeli society was emerging from innocence to sophistication and was finding Ben Gurion's paternalism too stringent and authoritative. It admired his leadership but secretly longed for the experience of breathing for itself. His attacks on Eshkol were ascribed by most Israelis to the human failings which afflict many strong men in their relations with successors. Ben Gurion had subconsciously come to identify himself with Israel's rebirth to the point where he could not easily admit that the national history would one day have to flow without him. His final months in office and the first two years outside it were unhappy and contentious, but long after they were over his brilliant leadership lived on in Israel's memory and gratitude. He was a leader cast in large dimensions, and he endowed Israel's early years with originality and vital power.

Levi Eshkol, who had been Finance Minister for a decade, stepped into the vacant place with an air of assurance. He had been the choice of everyone, including Ben Gurion, who would indeed have preferred him to Moshe Sharett as the custodian Premier in 1953. He was Ben Gurion's loyal disciple and had carried many burdens for his chief, including the distasteful task of settling the Lavon Affair. His methods and mannerisms were so different from those of his predecessor that there was no danger of imitation. Eshkol was in his late sixties when he took office, and his place in Israel's history had been won not in the heady atmosphere of strategy and international politics, but in the dust and heat of pioneering and economic construction. He was the first authentic kibbutznik to take the supreme office, and the agricultural community and labour movement sustained him with fraternal pride. He had no charismatic pretensions. He sought not to dominate, but to persuade. He could rightly feel that every mile of waterpipe, every growing village, every bungalow in Lachish, every factory owed something to his accumulative and constructive zeal. He could look out on the whole landscape of Israel like a man surveying his own handiwork but without any loss of simplicity or balance. He knew exactly what he was and what he was not, and he wielded his responsibilities in strict proportion to his gifts. He had been happiest when his gnarled fingers could dig deep into the soil of concrete affairs; he would now have to test his capacities of supervision and command. He had few gifts of expression. Sometimes, to get at his precise meaning was like trying to grasp a cake of soap in a bath. This handicap was grave and nearly proved fatal at moments when the nation expected a trumpet call to summon it to action in the service of clearly defined aims. But he believed that solid, concrete facts had an intrinsic eloquence which would make itself heard where it mattered most. His warm humanism was derived from the traditions first of Yiddish-speaking Russian Jewry and later of the Hebrew labour and settlement movement.

The Eshkol administration had taken over Ben Gurion's team with minimal adjustments. It felt bound to call itself a 'government of continuity' as if to assure the public that everything would still be weighed and decided by consulting Ben Gurion's presumptive wish. This is not really what the public wanted and, in any case, differences of temperament at the summit of power made a change of style inevitable. Eshkol began with domestic conciliation.

He saw no reason to inherit Ben Gurion's quarrels. He authorized the official internment of the remains of Jabotinsky, the Revisionist Zionist leader who had been venerated by the Herut Party and respected by countless others. Jabotinsky had died and been buried in New York, leaving an injunction that he was only to be reinterred in Israel at the behest of a sovereign Jewish government. Ben Gurion had refused to give this authorization. Eshkol had appeased the grievance of his Herut opponents; he also showed more sensitivity than Ben Gurion for the sentiments and complexes of Zionists in the Diaspora. In the same ecumenical spirit he brought about a union between Mapai and Achdut Ha'avodah in a new Labour Party, an objective for which Ben Gurion had laboured in vain. Eshkol was setting his own style and not merely following in his predecessor's steps.

There were fears that Ben Gurion's departure would weaken the state in its international relations by removing the prestige and historic awe which accompanied him across the world. This danger was surmounted. Eshkol became, surprisingly, the first Israeli Prime Minister to be officially invited by a President of the United States to visit Washington. His intimacy with Lyndon B. Johnson was put to work to ensure the expansion of American arms supplies to Israel. President de Gaulle repeated affirmations of friendship and alliance, and Prime Minister Harold Wilson received him with Socialist solidarity at Chequers and Downing Street. He was the first Prime Minister of Israel to make a tour of African capitals; and in 1964–5, when Germany ceased arms supplies to Israel as a result of Arab protests, Eshkol and his colleagues secured an impressive compensation by establishing diplomatic relations with the Federal Republic.

But for some sections of the labour movement, the idea of living without Ben Gurion at the helm was hard to bear. The new Prime Minister was soon beset by violent criticism and challenge from his predecessor. The immediate cause was Eshkol's refusal to revive the investigation of the treatment of the 'Affair' at Ben Gurion's request in 1964. Ben Gurion hinted that Eshkol was seeking to cover up discreditable footprints, including his own. For good measure, Ben Gurion stated darkly that Eshkol had jeopardized unspecified 'security matters'. By 1965 Ben Gurion's assaults on Eshkol were unbearably severe. In loyalty to him, some of his strongest supporters, including Moshe Dayan, Shimon Peres and Yosef Almogi, had left Eshkol's administration. In 1965 they formed a separate party (Rafi) under Ben Gurion. Labour unity had been wrecked, and the nation entered a phase of unprecedented acrimony.

Eshkol met these adversities with outward calm: but they were eating away at his physical and nervous strength. In 1965 in a massive counter-stroke, he took his depleted Labour Alignment into electoral battle, defeating Herut and overwhelming Rafi, which emerged with a meagre eight per cent of the popular vote, despite the allure of its two leading names. Eshkol had reached his highest peak, and with a powerful majority at his command he could speak not as Ben Gurion's appointed successor, but as the people's choice.

Yet he was still pursued by virulent abuse. There was a wide chasm between his government's real achievements and the negative image which its opponents managed to create. In addition to his successes in Washington, Paris and Bonn, he had carried the National Water Carrier to fulfilment. He had shown courage and resolution in authorizing Israel's controlled military reactions; and the economic measures devised by his Finance Minister, Pinchas Sapir, though irksome in the short run, were really his government's most creditable achievement. They were an honest attempt to correct Israel's disturbed balance of payments by a period of thrift and accumulation, in place of easy-going improvidence. He was calling for immediate sacrifice in the name of ultimate economic strength. The electorate had shown a penetrating understanding of his achievements, even when his opponents were portraying him as a weak and ineffective successor to a giant-size statesman.

It is possible that this disparaging picture of the Israeli Government was at work in the minds of Egyptian and Soviet leaders when they began to put pressure on Israel in May 1967. Nasser may have believed articles in the Israeli press about Eshkol's alleged weakness; he would be proved wrong when it was too late.

Yet at the beginning of May 1967 there was no premonition of crisis. The national mood was as close to normalcy as could be expected by a people born in war and nurtured in siege. Israelis realized, of course, that there would be the usual quota of murderous infiltrations. Now and then a flame of violence would erupt and soon subside, leaving some death and wreckage in its wake. This was the familiar rhythm. The special dignity of Israeli life comes from the large place that it gives to sacrifice. Israel lives intimately with danger, so that the very permanence of it dulls its edge and breeds a special adaptability to assault. But by the third week of May, Israel was going to face something radically different from the usual ebb and flow of intermittent violence. All possibilities, including the most unthinkable, would suddenly come into view.

10

1967: Nasser – To the Brink and Beyond

*The aggressor is he who makes war
inevitable.* Taine

Independence Day in 1967, as in previous years, opened with a military review in Jerusalem and ended with a public competition in biblical knowledge among pupils of secondary schools. This is the duality of Israel's experience; it swerves between physical danger and the symbolism of normality and peace. The biblical competition is followed on the radio with the kind of partisan tension that most other nations reserve for major sport events. When it ends, the holiday is over. The road becomes dense with the traffic of citizens scattering to their homes, and Jerusalem goes back to its placid sobriety. It was thus that on 15 May the last year of Israel's second decade began its course.

Israelis would thereafter divide much of their experience between what preceded that day and what came after it. For the ordeal that came upon Israel in May 1967 grew and erupted with extraordinary suddenness; there was nothing in that month's beginning that gave augury of its end.

The early months of 1967 had been turbulent, but no more so than at many other times. There seemed no reason to expect that the usual raids and reprisals would set off a total clash of arms. The border tension was serious in the north, but so had it always been. This time, however, there was a chain of mutual commitment between Syria, the Soviet Union and Egypt to keep Israel under murderous harassment while protecting Syria from reprisals. Out of this tangled relationship a major war would grow.

The first link in the chain was Syria, which had been brooding in diminished pride over the debacle of its air force on 7 April 1967. After several terrorist raids, the Syrians had attacked Israeli farmers in the Sea of Galilee area. The exchange of fire escalated from machine-guns to artillery and from artillery to aircraft. Six Syrian Mig aircraft were brought down, two of them in the territory of Jordan, whose government made little attempt to hide its satisfaction. The extent of the Syrian defeat was unexpected even in Israel. Elsewhere in the Arab world, the response to Syria's discomfiture ranged all the way from open derision in Amman to embarrassed silence in Cairo. Egypt hastened to explain

An Israeli armoured unit regrouping by the main square of Gaza
after the fall of the town in the Six Day War

that its commitment to aid Syria, if attacked, referred only to sustained warfare and not to 'spasmodic incidents'. The 7 April air encounter had not been expensive in lives to either side. No civilian suffering was involved, and Israeli representatives reported a satisfied reaction in most capitals. There were overt congratulations in Paris, where the victory of Mirages over Migs had kindled technological pride.

But there was no good humour in Moscow. If the Kremlin's favourite régime could be routed with impunity, why should any Arab state place its trust in Soviet protection? The Soviet leadership at this time was disturbed by the tendency of its 'progressive' friends to get into trouble. In Algeria, Ghana and Indonesia, the radical leaders Ben Bella, Nkruma and Sukarno had been driven from power. In other developing states, political leaders were asking themselves whether Russian sponsorship brought them real advantage or security. There is little doubt that the Soviet Union had decided to make the preservation of the Syrian régime a principle of its wider strategy. If Syria could not look after itself, somebody else would have to come to its rescue. But since direct Soviet participation in fighting might invite a confrontation with the United States, it was better in the Soviet view for pressure on Israel to be exercised by someone else. The USSR would, therefore, call on Cairo to rescue Damascus from its self-inflicted humiliation. In mid-April 1967, prodded by Soviet leaders, Egyptian political and military missions went to Damascus, where they deepened their commitment to protect Syria from Israeli reaction. A war alignment was taking shape.

While the Soviet Union stirred Egypt to greater militance, Cairo was at first reluctant to respond. In early May 1967, Israel's main concern was still shifting to and fro between Damascus and Moscow, with little concern for the southern border. Terrorist raids from Syrian territory multiplied. At no time did they affect thousands of lives or bring about a collapse of public order. But Israel is a close-knit society. Personal griefs afflicting a kibbutz or a suburb invade the whole public mood. And there was every cause to regard the Syrian terrorism as an early stage of malignancy. It could not be left alone. If it were not controlled it would expand into a fatal derangement of the national life. The logical military course would have been to react against the Syrian camps or army posts from which the terrorists set out. But the Soviet context could not be overlooked; Israel knew that it was not dealing with a problem of local dimensions alone. It therefore decided on a strategy of limited response. We would try, however hopelessly, to restrain the Soviet Union from encouraging the inflammatory policies of Damascus. It would reinforce defensive remedies on its own soil by minefields and barbed wire, and it would interpose a stage of verbal warning to Syria before any military reaction was approved. Only if all this failed and violence had to be met by force would its response come into effect. Even then, it would be swift and of local scope, falling short of a general confrontation and leaving the existing borders intact.

The effort to enlist Soviet influence against terrorist assaults was unrewarding. At first the Soviet Ambassador hinted that the Israeli victims of terrorism might have blown themselves up in a cunning attempt to create an atmosphere of Syrian–Israeli hostility. This was soon abandoned in favour of a more official theory, which the USSR outlined to Israel during April and May. Israel was asked 'to give serious consideration' to the possibility that agents of American oil interests and intelligence agencies, disguised as El Fatah infiltrators, were laying mines on Israeli roads in order to provoke Israel into retaliation which would, in turn, weaken the régime in Damascus! Israel, for her part, asked the Soviet Union 'to give serious consideration' to a less sophisticated idea: that when the Syrians and the terrorists said that they were laying mines, they really were. It added that 'if it were made clear to the Syrians that the USSR opposes terrorist acts, it is probable that these would be stopped'.

Nothing of the kind was 'made clear'. Instead, the Soviet Union began to incite Egypt against Israel so as to involve Egypt in the burden of protecting Syria. In Moscow on 12 and 13 May, an Egyptian parliamentary delegation, headed by the President of the National Council, Anwar Sadat, had been told to 'expect an Israeli invasion' of Syria immediately after Independence Day,

above Anwar Sadat became President of Egypt in September 1970 following the death of Gamal Abdul Nasser
right Nureddin El Atassi, President of Syria, the Soviets' 'pet' state in the Middle East before the Six Day War

with the aim of overthrowing the Damascus régime. The Soviet Union was appealing to Cairo for a show of solidarity with the 'threatened' Syrian Republic. After the war, Nasser never concealed that Soviet informants had spurred him to the course on which he had embarked. At midnight on 22 May, when imposing the blockade at the Straits of Tiran, he said:

On 13 May we received *accurate information* that Israel was concentrating on the Syrian border huge armed forces of about eleven to thirteen brigades. These forces were divided into two fronts, one south of the Sea of Galilee and one north of the lake. The decision made by Israel at the time was to carry out an attack on Syria, starting on 17 May. On 14 May we took action, discussed the matter, and contacted our Syrian brothers. The Syrians also had this information.

This speech is a central document for understanding the Soviet role in the 1967 war. The mobilization of 'eleven to thirteen Israeli brigades', to say nothing of their concentration on a narrow front, would have had a conspicuous effect on Israel's life. No newspaperman or foreign mission in Israel could have been unaware of it. The disruption of normality in so many families would have been registered in all the chanceries and newspapers of the world. On 11 May Eshkol had invited the Soviet Ambassador and his attachés to get into a car, without prior notice, and to search for the 'massive Israeli concentrations' which they said were lurking in the north. The Ambassador had primly replied that his function was to communicate Soviet truths, not to test their veracity. But the UN observers had investigated Soviet and Syrian reports on the ground in the second week of May; and the Secretary-General of the United Nations was to report publicly on 18 May that no exceptional troop concentrations existed at all. It is thus impossible to believe that Soviet warnings to Egypt and Syria about Israeli troop concentrations could ever have been inspired by genuine belief. If the USSR was spreading false rumours of Israeli troop concentration . . . there could be only one conclusion: an explosive charge of falsehood was being laid at the foundations of Middle Eastern peace. The wick was to be three weeks long.

Once suspicion about Israel's troop concentrations was sown in Arab hearts, everything said and done on the Israeli side was automatically invoked to support it. Israel's political and military leaders were trying to dissuade the Syrians from terrorist acts by warnings that her capacity to endure the murder of its citizens had its limits. These warnings were not always co-ordinated; and some of them, such as that by Mr Eshkol on 12 May, were not intended for public ears at all. Zealous press officers had released an intimate background talk by the Prime Minister in a party forum. On 14 May three

The May 1967 Independence
Day Parade in Jerusalem

newspapers simultaneously carried interviews with General Rabin warning
Damascus that the régime bore responsibility for continued terrorism. This
was interpreted as an Israeli intention to enter Damascus and set up a more
congenial régime. At Independence Day meetings, many Israeli public
figures, in addition to those responsible for security and foreign policy, had
made the conventional speeches of embattled defiance. And a briefing of
foreign military attachés was made in Tel Aviv on 11 May, in terms which
some of them understood to augur a major counter-attack if Syrian raids
continued.

All these speeches, statements and briefings were clearly intended to deter
Syrian attacks and thus prevent the need to react against them. And all the
statements were models of temperance in comparison with the threats of total
annihilation by which Israel herself was being assailed. Yet in the atmosphere
created by Soviet information about Israel's imminent attack on Damascus,
routine Israeli warnings of localized response seem to have been received in some
Arab capitals with something close to panic. Nothing was done by any Arab
leader to cool the heated air.

Even acts of studied Israeli moderation were misconstrued. For example,
it had been decided to hold the Independence Day parade in Jerusalem without
planes, tanks or heavy armour in order to avoid litigation with Jordan in the
United Nations. The Israel-Jordan Armistice Agreement limited the number
and categories of weapons that could permissibly be maintained in the Jerusalem area. It was evident that these provisions referred to weapons capable of
shooting, not to demonstrative, unarmed and vulnerable equipment on
ceremonial parade. But the Israeli Cabinet decided to keep within the letter
of the contract, despite domestic criticism.

Israel's abstention from putting her major weapons and military units on show had a sequel. By all normal standards this was a conciliatory decision. It showed concern both for juridical correctness and for the sensitivities of Arab states. In the event it was given a sinister interpretation. Nasser and other Arab leaders professed to believe that if Israeli armoured and air units were not on parade in Jerusalem, they must be nefariously concentrated for action against the Arabs somewhere else! The modest dimensions of the Jerusalem parade were even invoked to support the Soviet story that Israeli troops were all in the north, poised to conquer Damascus. In the unique atmosphere of the Arab-Israeli conflict, it is often impossible to do anything right.

As Israel went about its celebration in minor key, passions in Arab states mounted towards frenzy. On the day before the parade, Mohammed Fawzi, the Egyptian Army Chief of Staff, flew to Damascus to co-ordinate plans with the Syrian Government. The Soviet Union was clearly interested in this co-ordination. Henceforth, any dangers, real or imaginary, facing the Damascus régime – including those provoked by Syrian terrorism – were no longer to engage the responsibility of Moscow alone. Cairo, too, was involved. One of the most effective false alarms in history was doing its work; Egypt was poised to forestall an Israeli 'assault' on Damascus that had never been intended, or even conceived.

The 1967 Independence Day parade was a rather depressing occasion. Without the glitter of planes and tanks, there was a lean aspect to the infantry columns. As the Ministers watched them go by, they began to receive messages which became more and more ominous as the day went on. Infantry and armoured units of the Egyptian Army had moved to the Suez Canal and were crossing into Sinai with ostentatious publicity. Large convoys were deliberately being routed through Cairo's busiest streets on their way to Ismailia. The Egyptian parliamentary delegation led by Anwar Sadat had returned to Cairo from Moscow, fed with Soviet information about Israel's imminent plan 'to conquer Syria'. All Egyptian armed forces were alerted to a state of emergency because of what was described in Cairo as 'the tense situation on the Israel-Syrian armistice lines'.

The scale of these movements created no immediate military threat; but their political implications were grave, and the emotional accompaniment even graver. A torrent of invective against Israel poured from all the radio stations in the Arab world. Lebanon, Iraq and Jordan declared states of alert. Israel responded with quiet measures to reinforce its dispositions in the south.

In Washington and London, Israeli diplomats were told that the Egyptian troop movements were only 'demonstrative' and without military intent. This calm diagnosis did not seem unreasonable at the time. Many remembered how in February 1960, after some clashes across the Syrian-Israeli boundary, similar movements had been made by Egyptian armies in Sinai; yet a few weeks later they had returned to their bases west of the Suez Canal. On 15 and 16 May the consensus in Western capitals was that Israel faced a political manoeuvre rather than a military threat. Nevertheless, it was decided to prepare for worse possibilities; with so many hot words in the air, even a 'demonstrative' intention could pass into active folly.

And so it did. On the morning of 16 May graver possibilities came into view. The commander of the UNEF, Major General Rikhye of the Indian Army, received a message from General Fawzi, the Egyptian Chief of Staff, asking for the withdrawal of all UN forces along Egypt's borders. The reason given was 'that the Egyptian armed forces had been ordered to prepare to go into action against Israel in case, and whenever, it launches an act of aggression against any Arab country'.

General Rikhye pointed out, correctly, that the procedure adopted by Egypt was irregular. The political direction of the UNEF was not his responsibility but that of the Secretary-General, who was the only man from whom he could take orders. The procedural point was correct, but it counted for little. On the same day U Thant received a cable from Egyptian Foreign Minister Riad telling him that the Egyptian Government had decided to 'terminate the presence of the UN Emergency Force in Egypt and the Gaza Strip'. Mr Riad recalled that UNEF had been stationed there at the invitation of the UAR and that its continued presence would not be possible without Egyptian approval. He was now asking that it should be withdrawn 'as soon possible'.

On the evening of 16 May the Secretary-General had already given Cairo a clear impression that he would not feel able to oppose its demand. He had told the Egyptian Representative that 'a request by the UAR authorities for a temporary withdrawal of UNEF from the armistice demarcation line and the international frontier, or from any parts of them, would be considered by the Secretary-General as tantamount to a request for the complete withdrawal of UNEF from Gaza and Sinai, since this would reduce UNEF to ineffectiveness'. Having thus excluded any possibility of a partial withdrawal of UNEF, U Thant had gone on to say: 'If it was the intention of the government of the United Arab Republic to withdraw the consent it gave in 1956 for the stationing of UNEF on the territory of the United Arab Republic and Gaza, it was of course entitled to do so. On receipt of such a request the Secretary-General would order the withdrawal of all UNEF troops from Gaza and Sinai, simultaneously informing the General Assembly of what he was doing and why.' Thus the time between the unofficial and official Egyptian request for the removal of UNEF had been used by U Thant to assure Cairo that he would promptly do what Egypt wanted, so long as the request was absolute and couched in proper form. On the dimensions of UNEF's withdrawal, he had adopted an 'all or nothing' attitude that excluded any compromise. By the time that he conferred with his Advisory Committee, with the Israeli representative and with delegates of the Major Powers on 18 May, U Thant had, in effect, committed UN action in advance. Two representatives, those of Canada and Brazil, urged the Secretary-General to temporize without denying the juridical validity of Egypt's request. It was, however, too late for any manoeuvre. On the evening of 18 May, the Secretary-General sent a reply to the Egyptian Foreign Minister, informing him that the Egyptian Government's request would be complied with and that instructions would be issued without delay for the orderly withdrawal of the force.

No action by the United Nations has ever been more contentiously discussed by governments, the world press and public opinion. The United States, the United Kingdom and Canada, as well as Israel, were among the countries whose leaders expressed their disquiet. In a heated response to his critics on 27 June 1967, U Thant ascribed the criticism to 'distortions of the record which in some places apparently have emanated from panic, emotion and political bias'. In the more tranquil parts of his memorandum, the Secretary-General gives a moving account of the pressures which compelled his action. He had no alternative in law but to accede to a request rooted in Egypt's sovereign rights; the countries which supplied contingents would accede to the Egyptian request whatever the Secretary-General said or did; this applied especially to Yugoslavia and India, whose soldiers accounted for more than half of the force and whose governments had decided to accept Egypt's expulsion order, irrespective of what the Secretary-General chose to do. Egyptian troops were in any case physically expelling UN units from their main observation posts in Sinai; the assumption that there would be time for international consultation if a request for withdrawal were made had always been vague and elusive. (Some months later the Secretary-General contested an astonishing claim by Nasser to the effect that he had not intended his request for withdrawal from Sharm el-Sheikh to be acted on at all.)

But perhaps the most convincing sentence in U Thant's report was that which referred to the essentially fragile basis for UNEF's operation throughout its existence. The plain fact is that a withdrawal could have been requested and obtained by Egypt at any moment during the decade of UNEF's operation. But it is precisely the lesson of 'fragility' which was thereafter to inspire Israel's refusal ever again to place its vital interests in the United Nation's hands. What had for ten years appeared to be a stable international reality turned out within two hours to be as insubstantial as a spider's web. Thereafter, all proposals for ensuring peace through UN 'forces' were viewed by Israelis as evidence of a strange tendency to reject experience.

With the UNEF withdrawal, Israel found itself in a new and graver phase.

above Secretary-General U Thant flew to Cairo in May 1967 in an attempt to prevent the outbreak of hostilities. On the same day, Nasser declared a blockade of the Straits of Tiran

It was still not easy to calculate what Nasser's precise intentions were. Indeed, at that stage, he himself probably had no clear idea of what he was about. He was moving step by step, testing the ground with each advance. He may have been surprised at the lack of restraining obstacles. The ease with which he had sent the United Nations packing must have kindled in his mind the idea that it was less dangerous to exert pressure on Israel's vital interests than he had ever believed. Actions which he might previously have avoided as rash and fraught with penalty were now reaping enormous success.

Above all, they went forward in complete impunity. Might not Western support of Israel's security be more a fiction than a reliable fact? Prospects which but a short time ago had seemed unattainable had now come exhilaratingly within his view.

The urgent question, of course, was whether Nasser would actually impose a blockade on Israeli shipping in the Straits of Tiran. There was a slender chance that he might be content to keep Israeli shipping under constant threat without actively obstructing it. After all, even a lack of certainty about whether the maritime channel was open would hinder Israel's development of her Red Sea outlet. By this time, however, Nasser was playing for higher stakes than he had thought possible a little while before. If fortune had been kind to him, why should he not bask in its smile? By now he was concerned not with a blockade, but with Israel's total humiliation and defeat.

Everything came together to make the question of Sharm el-Sheikh fateful for Israel and the world. If the blockade were actually imposed, Israel would have to decide whether to defend or abandon a vital national interest. The juridical implication of a blockade would be that Nasser did not recoil from an active state of war. And a blockade in the straits and the gulf, unlike the troop concentrations in Sinai, would take Israel to a point of no return. Troop movements, after all, could be ordered and later dispersed, without loss of face or implication of retreat. But once a blocade was imposed, its cancellation would be inconceivable, except under pressure or threat of physical force. Moreover, any submission by Israel to a blockade of the Straits of Tiran would do more than threaten a concrete economic interest. It would mean the collapse of Israel's deterrent power, for there was no issue in which Israel had pledged its honour in more irrevocable terms. A nation which could not protect its basic and vital maritime interests would presumably find reasons for not repelling other assaults on its rights. Unless a stand were made here, nobody in the Arab world, and few people beyond it, would ever again believe in Israel's power to resist, and therefore to survive. The Munich parallel is often overworked, but in this case it was perfectly valid. Economic, maritime, regional, juridical, international and psychological considerations had made Nasser's intention and Israel's response on the Tiran blockade an issue of destiny for Egypt and Israel alike.

Most human tragedies are self-inflicted. Nasser was now to be driven by elements in his own nature towards the brink of a precipice – and beyond. During the night of Monday, 22 May, despite Israeli and other warnings, he announced his fatal decision to impose a blockade. The next day at dawn his ominous words were to shake every Israeli into the recognition that the issue of physical survival was now posed for the whole nation.

The fact is that Nasser was utterly resolved to have his war and to be satisfied with nothing less. He had written years before of 'a hero's role searching for an actor to play it'. Now the dream would unfold with himself in the central part and with the whole world as the stage. He presented the blockade not as a single stroke of malice, but as a challenge to total combat. The choice for Israel was drastic – slow strangulation or rapid solitary death:

We are in confrontation with Israel. In contrast to what happened in 1956, when France and Britain were at her side, Israel is not supported today by any European Power. The world will not accept a repetition of 1956. We are face to face with Israel. Henceforward, the situation is in your hands. Our armed forces have occupied Sharm el-Sheikh. We shall on no account allow the Israeli flag to pass through the Gulf of Aqaba. The Jews threatened to make war; I reply *Ahlan Wasahalan*; Welcome, we are ready for war, The water is ours.

The speech had been made to officers of the Egyptian air base at Bir Gafgafa in Sinai, 100 miles from Israel's south-western border. A few days later the commanders of this airfield, and of others, were to receive operation orders listing the targets in Israel they were to bomb. To their valour and efficiency, still unproved, Nasser had committed the outcome of his most daring enterprise. He owed them whatever a leader's authority could do to enlarge and galvanize their powers. But far beyond his fervent audience in the baking desert heat, he was appealing to the whole domain of Arabism, calling its sons to such display of union, sacrifice, hatred, resilience and selfless passion as they had not shown since the ferocious days of their early history. An opportunity little imagined a few weeks before had somehow taken form and substance. If lost, it might never be reborn. Turning his back on a whole decade of prudence, he now uttered a courtly and exultant welcome to the approaching war. '*Ahlan wasahalan*': it was as if he were greeting the unexpected appearance of a cherished and long absent guest.

Nasser's blockade decision had been taken and announced while the Secretary-General of the United Nations was in the air on his way to Cairo. Neither U Thant nor either of his predecessors had ever been treated quite like this. The United Nations was the victim of a confidence trick on an international scale. The action which U Thant could have hoped to prevent was taken in advance of his arrival, and his visit was thus reduced to futility in advance.

International apathy now created a vacuum in which the hope of peace could no longer breathe. The governments which in 1957 had solemnly pledged themselves to oppose a blockade in the Gulf of Aqaba shrouded their policies in prudent and discreet silence. But if the flight of the Powers from their commitments was implicit and private, the abdication of the United Nations was explicit and overt.

The Security Council was convened by Canada and Denmark on 24 May. It is difficult even some years after the event to read its proceedings without a gasp of disbelief. One must remember that it met two days after the imposition of the blockade in the Gulf of Aqaba. Powerful Egyptian concentrations, including armoured columns, were pouring into Sinai. Military airports were being made ready for the assault. Speeches had been delivered by President Nasser which, by any classical definition, would have been regarded as declarations of war. The aim of securing Israel's 'destruction' had been frankly stated. Israeli mobilization in reaction to the Egyptian troop movements had gained momentum. After ten years of sentinel duty, UNEF had been humiliatingly banished. Secretary-General Thant had gone on a desperate journey to Cairo in an effort to salvage the declining peace. Arab masses in the streets were hanging Israel in effigy. The whole Israeli nation was laying down the tools of peace to take up instruments of defence. And the crisis had gone far beyond the scope of governments: it had seized the imagination and concern of multitudes of people. At no time since the Second World War, except during the Cuban Missile Crisis of 1962, had the headlines of newspapers expressed a sharper accent of tension. It is not an exaggeration to say that hundreds of millions of eyes and ears were focused expectantly on the horseshoe table at the United Nations Headquarters in New York.

In these conditions of emergency, the Security Council convened at 10.30 a.m. on 24 May. The first words spoken by the representative of the Soviet Union set what was to be the prevailing tone of farce: 'The Soviet delegation deems it necessary to stress that it does not see sufficient grounds for such a hasty convening of the Security Council and for the artificially dramatic climate fostered by the representatives of some Western Powers

which are probably counting on an exaggerated effort in the staging of this meeting.' The Bulgarian representative, without any movement of his impassive features, went on to declare: 'The delegation of Bulgaria believes that at the present moment there is really no need for an urgent meeting of the Security Council.' The Indian representative then stated with bland solemnity: 'The situation on the ground, while potentially dangerous, is still not clear; therefore, an urgent and immediate discussion is unwarranted'.

The world community was in full flight. One representative after another asserted that the mere imminence of war was no reason for convening the tribunal charged with the preservation of peace! Eventually, after further talking to and fro, the Chairman caused the agenda to be adopted. The Danish Ambassador took the floor to ask: 'What should be our attitude in the face of this grave danger? Should the Council just stand by, see what happens, and hope for the best? That is hardly, I believe, what world opinion would expect of us.'

The harsh fact is that by this time world opinion expected the Security Council to perform any folly of which human beings are inherently capable. Three hours after it had assembled, the Security Council rose, having done and said nothing except to adopt its agenda. It was to hold meetings intermittently until 3 June; not for one hour did its proceedings rise above the ineptitude of its first session. After doing nothing on 24 May, the Security Council

Above President Zalman Shazar with members of the victorious
General Staff following the Six Day War

adjourned until the afternoon of 29 May. The crisis was to mount from stage to stage without any UN action at all.

Meanwhile, in Cairo, U Thant was being rebuffed. He was told that Egypt 'would not take any armed action'. This, of course, was beside the point. The matter at issue was whether Egypt would cancel the aggressive action that it had already taken in the form of a maritime blockade and troop concentrations, the continuation of which was deliberately designed to provoke Israel's resistance. If there had been any hope in the Secretary-General's visit, it would have been in his arrival in Cairo before the blockade was imposed. Egypt had callously frustrated this prospect, and U Thant returned dejected to New York.

The mood was heavy on 23 May when Israeli Ministers met to consider Nasser's blockade. There was hot crisis in the air, and Prime Minister Eshkol took counsel with the parliamentary leaders of all the major parties. It was decided to regard the blockade as a declaration and act of war requiring the fulfilment of Israel's announcement on 1 March 1957 that it would fight against such a measure. Other decisions were to intensify military readiness and to dispatch the Foreign Minister to Washington and other capitals to seek support for Israel's resolve not to submit to blockade and encirclement. Both the military and political ground would be prepared before active resistance was to be initiated.

The waiting period put an excruciating burden on Israel's nerves. It was dictated for the first few days by a need for military measures; thereafter, by the traumatic memories of 1956–7, when, after a spectacular military victory, Israel had been forced to withdraw from all its gains by a combined pressure of the United States and the Soviet Union. It had learned that no military victory is stable unless it is ratified by political success. Now Israel had strong cards to play, especially in Washington. Ten years before, President Eisenhower had publicly recognized that the reimposition of the blockade in the Straits of Tiran would oblige Israel to protect its maritime rights. In the meantime, what had then been a juridical principle had become a concrete national interest. Through the Straits of Tiran to Eilat came the tanker traffic bringing all Israel's needs in fuel; and a pipeline from Eilat to the Mediterranean coast had made Israel an exporter of surplus oil to Europe. Moreover, Eilat was the point from which Israeli diplomacy, development aid and commerce reached out across the Red Sea to East Africa and Asia. To abandon this maritime outlet meant that Israel would lose its major geopolitical asset. It would become a diminished force, thrown back to exclusive dependence on its Western connections. The development of the Negev as Israel's window to the southern and eastern worlds would become paralyzed. Not least, Israel would lose the credibility of its deterrent power, on which its whole security depended. Thus the humble port at the Negev's tip had become the point at which the national duty and interest converged with particular intensity. Egyptian statements gave clear evidence that Nasser's aim was to take Eilat and the southern Negev from Israel, in order to establish a continuous land link between Egypt and the Arab states to Israel's east and north.

There were still two questions to elucidate. Must Israel act alone, or with the sympathy of governments which had committed themselves to this cause ten years ago? And, even if they were inhibited by caution or self-interest, or Arab intimidation, from giving Israel the support which they had solemnly promised, would they at least expiate their passivity by not seeking to annul whatever Israel could achieve by itself? These questions, in their turn, would largely depend on whether Israel could arouse a large volume of public opinion on her behalf. And, finally, there was the looming shadow of Soviet hostility. If the Soviet Union had prodded Egypt into the war, could Israel assume that Moscow had decided to let the war be lost? The Soviet presence in the Mediterranean was a new factor which had not existed in 1956. Yet even in 1956 a series of verbal and epistolary threats from Moscow had precipitated Israel's withdrawal from Sinai without an attempt to secure a peace settlement. Could Israel ensure that Soviet pressure would be neutralized this time? This depended on the United States alone.

It was to bring these matters to clarity and decision that the Israeli Government had sent its Foreign Minister to Paris, London and Washington between 23 and 26 May. During those days the attitudes of the Western powers became lucidly clear. The most ominous news for Israel was the change in France's attitude. In 1957 the French commitment to support Israeli resistance if the blockade of the Straits of Tiran were renewed had been more dramatic and unequivocal than any other. But President de Gaulle now pointed out that 'guarantees were not absolute and the situation had evolved'. The implication was that France had drawn nearer to the Arabs since the end of the Algerian war; at the same time Soviet policy now had a larger weight in de Gaulle's calculations, which excluded any idea of 'Western solidarity'. His advice to Israel, in effect, was to swallow the blockade until or unless it could be rescinded by the concertation of the Four Powers. The idea of the Soviet Union joining with the West to defend Israel's vital interests against an exultant Arab world seemed unrealistic. And so it turned out to be. Within a few hours, the Soviet

Union formally rejected any Four Power consultation. The French fear seemed to be that if Israel resisted Egypt, or if the Western Powers themselves tried to break the blockade, Soviet intervention was likely, and Eilat would become the Danzig of the Third World War. Events were soon to refute this apprehension. But for Israel in her solitude and agony to be abandoned by the Power which supplied her most important armaments was a hard and unexpected blow.

More favourable winds blew in London, where Prime Minister Wilson had voiced stringent criticism of Nasser's blockade. There was even talk of mounting an international maritime patrol to ensure that the straits be opened in defiance of Nasser's edicts. But this was made explicitly dependent on American leadership and support and on international action.

Washington held the key to the future and was to keep it for many years. In President Johnson's speech of 26 May, Israelis could discern the augury of a new alignment which, this time, might bring the greatest of the Powers to her side. For Johnson had condemned the blockade as an illicit and provocative act. He asserted his intention to carry out his commitments and those of his predecessors to maintain Israel's security. He stated to Israel that he would use any or all possible measures to keep the straits open. These assurances were only partially offset by his refusal to share Israel's prediction of an imminent Egyptian armed attack. His advisers were convinced that if war broke out, Israel would win, in spite of Egypt's preponderance of weaponry. In any case, the President needed congressional and international support to bring his policies to fruition. He told the Israeli Foreign Minister that 'Israel would not be alone unless it decided to go alone.' The main point was that on this occasion, unlike 1956, the United States had formally recognized Israel's status as the victim of an aggressive assault.

It was not clear whether these favourable American policies would be of tangible use to Israel in the immediate ordeal; but it was now evident that Israel could count on a better international balance than in 1956. If the United States was willing in principle to take any or all measures to open the straits, it could hardly censure Israel for defining its own policy in similar terms – and with more effect.

In the event, Nasser's momentum of aggression was too swift for anything to overtake it. He was now expressing his resolve 'to restore the situation to what it was before 1956', which meant, at least, that Israel must lose its maritime outlet to the Red Sea. From this he went on to declare the ambition of 'restoring the situation to what it was before 1948', which simply meant that the Middle Eastern map would not contain a 'State of Israel'. In one of his daily speeches to hysterically screaming crowds he said that if war broke out the issue would be not the Gulf of Aqaba, but 'the destruction of Israel'.

There had been times, of course, when Arab rhetoric promised more than Arab courage seemed likely to attempt. But in May and early June 1967, the rhetoric sounded very serious indeed. Delegations from all the Arab countries were flocking to Cairo to pledge their participation in the kill. Iraqi troops arrived in Syria on 25 May. Egyptian troops were recalled from Yemen. On 30 May King Hussein flew to Cairo, where he signed a Defence Pact with Nasser. Article 7 of the pact placed Jordanian troops under Egyptian command. Later, on 4 June, an Iraqi delegation signed a similar pact in Cairo. By the first week in June, Egypt had received and deployed contingents from Kuwait, Algeria, Sudan and Iraq. Libya and Tunisia allowed Algerian troops to cross their territory. On 1 June President Aref of Iraq said: 'There is resolve, determination and unity to achieve our clear aim: to remove Israel from the

left Prime Minister Levi Eshkol and President Lyndon B. Johnson confer in January 1968. As the pre-war tension grew, the US had appealed to Israel to exercise restraint and thus became involved in the besieged country's fate
right King Hussein brought Jordan into the Six Day War after deciding to disregard Israel's offer to avoid acts of hostility

map . . . It is the day to wash away the stain. We shall, God willing, meet in Tel Aviv and Haifa.' The Palestinian Arab leader Ahmed Shukeiry said that after victory the Arabs would allow only those Israelis who had been born in Palestine to remain. 'But', he added with macabre relish, 'I estimate that not many of them will survive'.

The notion of a united Arab world rising implacably and cruelly to attempt Israel's destruction had sustained Arab dreams – and Israeli fears – for many years. Now it had erupted from myth into hard fact. Israel's fortunes were declining and her flame was burning low.

When Israeli Ministers took counsel on the night of 27 May they had no doubts about the military possibility of breaking the Egyptian blockade and encirclement. The question was still whether more time should be given to consolidate the political prospect. The Israeli Government was impressed by President Johnson's promise to 'take all and every possible measure to ensure that the Straits of Tiran remain open'. While there were some who thought that any further delay would injure Israel's military position, others believed that the President's assumption of responsibility must be allowed to mature; and that if it failed, after more patience on Israel's part, new political possibilities would open out in the American-Israeli relationship. The next morning there was an almost unanimous vote in favour of a further short period of waiting.

For what had come that morning from Washington was not only President Johnson's exhortation to give more time, but also a message from Secretary Rusk to the effect that the United States and Britain were urgently to prepare an international naval escort plan, and other nations, including Holland and Canada had already promised to join.

This prospect was soon to fade; but an Israeli Government receiving such a message had very few options. On the negative side, to ignore it would open Israel to the charge of having refused an opportunity for international action. On the positive side, international support of a major Israeli interest was more impressively stated here than in any of its previous ordeals.

It turned out that the period of waiting did not injure Israel's military prospects, while it certainly increased her political strength and magnified the sympathy of world opinion. This was a predictable result. By August 1969, a reputable poll showed that sixty-three per cent of Israelis considered that the waiting period was an act of wise statesmanship, while only twenty-four per cent ascribed it to hesitancy and indecision. At the time, however, nervousness about the decision to wait threatened to disrupt Israel's internal cohesion just when the enemy was at the gate. The tension was understandable. Israel was surrounded by greater Arab armies than had ever been arrayed against her. On paper, the numbers of Arab tanks and aircraft poised for attack seemed to augur a possible defeat. Exuberant Arab crowds were dancing in the streets, intoxicated with the prospect of revenge and bloodshed. Senior Israeli officers were pressing strongly for urgent action, and were even predicting that if it were postponed there could be no confidence of complete success. Opposition parties were pressing strongly for changes in the Israeli Government. There were calls to restore Ben Gurion to leadership, even though it was known that he was almost the sole advocate of prolonged abstention from resistance.

Far deeper, and more serious, was the popular demand for relieving Mr Eshkol of his burden as Minister of Defence and consigning it to a specialist in that field. The main candidates were General Yigal Allon, now Minister of Labour, who had led the Israeli striking forces in the War of Independence; and General Moshe Dayan, member of the Rafi Party, who had been Israel's Chief-of-Staff in the Sinai Campaign of 1956. Each of these leaders had his fervent advocates and his militant opponents. Dayan's inclusion would not only enhance military morale; it would also open the way for broadening the coalition beyond the existing parties, so as to embrace the Gahal opposition and Rafi. Thus his addition to the government, apart from its enlivening personal effect, would also bring about an all-party union. The call for this change became stronger when Eshkol, weighed down by fatigue and responsibility, made a speech to the nation on 28 May in a stumbling manner. Later, when Israel achieved spectacular victory, a grateful nation acknowledged Eshkol's role in accumulating Israel's military strength and perfecting the training of the Israel Defence Forces during his stewardship of the Defence Ministry. It also admired the lucidity and calmness of his decisions in the pressure of war. A week before, however, it had felt that the double burden of the Premiership and the Ministry of Defence was too much for him – or anyone – to bear in the absence of a broad parliamentary consensus.

By 31 May, after much political and parliamentary manoeuvring – the issue was resolved by the establishment of a Government of National Unity, including the opposition leader and previous chief of the Irgun Zvai Leumi, Menachem Begin, and Moshe Dayan, who took over the Ministry of Defence under Eshkol's Premiership. The new government was joyously received. The way was now open for the nation to face hard ordeals in unison.

For there was now no doubt that war was close on the horizon. Everything that the Powers did, and omitted to do, in the last days of May and the early days of June seemed calculated to strengthen Israel's sense of solitude. The Arab governments were pushing their advantage to the extreme. Vast crowds gathered in the streets of Cairo shouting: 'Nasser, Nasser, we are behind you. We will slaughter them; we will destroy them. Slaughter, slaughter, slaughter . . .' The official Egyptian radio took care to broadcast these blood-curdling threats to Israel. The Egyptian General Mourtaghi announced: 'In five days we shall liquidate the little State of Israel. Even without a war, Israel will collapse because she will be unable to bear the load of mobilization.'

Five days was evidently too much for the Syrian temper. In Damascus a leading general cried: 'If hostilities break out, Egypt and Syria will be able to destroy Israel in four days at the most.' More ominous than these threats was the fact that on 30 May, King Hussein had flown to Egypt and signed a Joint Defence Pact with Nasser. It was now clear that if war broke out, Israel might well have to fight on three fronts simultaneously.

A sense of vulnerability penetrated every part of the Israeli consciousness like an icy wind. As Israelis looked around, they saw the world divided between those who were seeking their destruction and those who were doing nothing to prevent it. On 2 June France expressed strong reservations about the planned Anglo-American declaration on freedom of navigation in the Straits of Tiran. Despite Washington's confident prediction, Canada had edged away from any intention to support maritime action outside the framework of the United Nations. And the farce in the Security Council was proving every hour that no such thing as a 'United Nations framework' existed. The British attitude had also become more reserved than it had been on the morrow of the blockade. The Foreign Secretary, George Brown, who had reacted so ferociously to the first moves of Nasser's blockade, was now saying cautiously that: 'We regard the United Nations as primarily responsible for peace-keeping.' This was very close to saying that the peace was not going to be kept at all.

Above all, Washington was now less sanguine than a few days before about a possibility of international action against Nasser. President Johnson was encountering reservations in Congress, which felt that American intervention should not even be considered unless Israel's actual survival were in jeopardy. The conviction of the American security authorities was that if fighting broke out, the impression of Arab predominance would prove illusory. A State Department spokesman said that 'the United Nations is the focus of American attempts to solve the crisis', and that his government supported 'the British initiative on a joint declaration for free navigation'. It was not promising to see the credit for this initiative being generously passed by Washington and London to each other. And to say that the United Nations is the 'focus for efforts' was very like saying that there were no efforts and would be no focus.

By 3 June the darkness was even more intense. The military map looked grave. There was a massive Egyptian force in Sinai, with nearly a thousand tanks on Israel's southern border. The Egyptian order of battle, taken together with speeches about Israel's 'illegal' presence in Eilat, pointed to an attempt to sunder the southern Negev from the main body of the state. Egyptian aircraft were coming over the Negev daily to reconnoitre for promising targets. The Jordanian Army was moving into battle positions. Syrian troops glowered down from the Golan Heights upon Israeli settlements in Upper Galilee and the Jordan Valley. In the United Nations, and in many of the world's capitals, Israeli representatives were now being uncomfortably shunned by their colleagues, as if to look them in the eye involved an intolerable ordeal of conscience.

Then came news from Paris that President de Gaulle was suspending all dispatch of arms to Israel. This was bound to have an accelerating effect on Israel's decision to fight, for if, in addition to growing solitude, Israel had reached the zenith of its military strength, the feeling of 'now or never' was bound to be reinforced. If the French motive had been to prevent the war from erupting, its action would have exactly the opposite effect.

So much so that on Sunday, 4 June, the country's mood was strangely tranquil. The day before the beaches had been crowded with soldiers on leave; all tourists had gone. The nation seemed to be basking all alone in the clear light of its duty. And those on whom the burden of decision fell could act as men who had revolved all the hazards and choices so fully that little was left but the formality of action itself. It was as if Israel's adversaries, by their arrogance, and her friends, by their impotence, had narrowed the choices down to a single compulsion.

For was there really any range of choice? Here was Israel with 100,000 Egyptian troops strung out across the Sinai wilderness, organized in seven divisions, with nearly one thousand tanks, while another armoured division was held at a reserve position in the Bir Gafgafa region. If the Egyptians passed to the attack, either as the first move in the fighting or in reaction to Israeli resistance, the chief danger seemed to lie in a swift thrust across the Negev which would join Egyptian and Jordanian armies north of Eilat. Behind the 100,000 Egyptians in Sinai was a reserve of 60,000 men. The adversary's superiority was most marked in the air. The Arabs had the advantage of overwhelming numbers and of alarming proximity to Israel's most sensitive nerve centres. The air-base at Bir Gafgafa was within a few minutes of Tel Aviv, while there was no vital Egyptian target in similar range of an Israeli airfield. The Egyptian air force had some four hundred interceptors and fighter-bombers, and seventy-five to eighty medium and light bombers, which seemed capable of creating enormous havoc in Israeli cities.

As if this were not enough, the peril from Egypt was compounded by the adherence to the Egyptian design of the manpower, armour and air forces of other Arab countries. None of these amounted to a decisive peril in itself; but their combined force and strategic disposition would prevent Israel from putting all its strength to work against the main foe. That Syria would participate in the war was taken for granted. This meant that Israel had to reckon with a Syrian Army of 50,000 men, with at least two hundred tanks of operational capacity and one hundred Soviet aircraft, including thirty-two modern Mig 21s.

Political estimates were still not unanimous in predicting whether Jordan would enter the arena. But military plans had to take this prospect into account. There was a Jordanian Army of 50–60,000 men whose main strength lay in 250 Patton and Centurion tanks. It was only in the air that Jordan was weak. An Iraqi division was taking up its positions on Jordan territory in accordance with the UAR-Jordan Defence Pact, to which Iraq had officially adhered.

Those were the cold facts of the Arabs' numerical superiority. This, in its turn, was enlarged by their topographical advantage and sharpened by a higher morale than the Arab world had known in all its modern experience. Reports were reaching Israel of Egyptian generals, and other leaders, straining hard against the tactical leash which Nasser had imposed upon them. His idea, which Muhammad Hassanein Heykal frankly expressed, was to 'absorb' the first blow, and 'inflict a knock-out' in the second round, after Israel had taken pre-emptive action. 'We have made it inevitable for Israel to fight,' was Heykal's legitimate boast. This strategy required Israel to be goaded into the first attack. But the correspondent of the London *Observer* was telling how tens of thousands of young men across Egypt were forming societies with the aim of forcing Nasser's hand, so that even if he wanted to control them at all it could only be for a short time. After the war, this report was to be supported by Eric Rouleau, a French writer known for his zealous support of Arab causes. In his words, the Cairo atmosphere could be summed up in simple terms: 'We have waited long enough; it serves no useful purpose to wait any longer. Let's finish with Israel and be done with it. No more words. Prompt action is needed. Forward to Tel Aviv.'

It seemed quixotic to await the Arab armies in Tel Aviv. On 4 June, a unanimous consensus developed in the Israeli Cabinet in favour of immediate resistance. There would be a total response to Egyptian blockade and encroachment. By every juridical definition, Egypt was already at war with Israel. Cairo had even circulated a memorandum to that effect to other governments on 1 June. On the other hand, Israel had involved the Americans very deeply. Their political and moral responsibility was much greater in their own conscience than it had been a week before. Israel would not be repeating the experience of 1956, when the United States, shocked by the sheer surprise of Israel's eruption, had joined with the Soviet Union to cancel its results. There was also an unparalleled wave of opinion across the world in solidarity with Israel's plight. The idea that one generation after the Nazi massacre the independent remnant of Jewry could be cruelly threatened sent a wave of horror into many hearts.

Of those who made the decision in Jerusalem on 4 June, some have passed away. Those who still bear the burden are joined in a covenant of memory. They have known the sharing of great things by men set apart from ordinary concerns. Once the Cabinet voted, its members knew that they had expressed a people's united will. For amid the alarms of mid-May, the nation had given birth to new impulses. All the conditions which divide Israelis from each other and give their society a deceptive air of fragmentation, all the deeply rooted Jewish recalcitrance towards authority were now transmuted into a new metal which few had seen or felt before. There had, of course, been some fear, as was natural for a people which had so often endured unendurable things. It seemed that a great doom was sweeping towards them; and in some places in Israel there was talk of Auschwitz and Maidanek. If anything, the anxious sympathy of friends in the outside world had the ironic effect of sharpening the national apprehension. Israelis reasoned, with shrewd perversity, that if even people abroad were showing concern for them, they must be at the very brink of death. So as the last days of May vanished into the haze of memory, the people was gripped by a sudden spirit of union and resolve. Men of military age silently laid down their work in factory, office and farm, took up their reservist papers and disappeared towards the south.

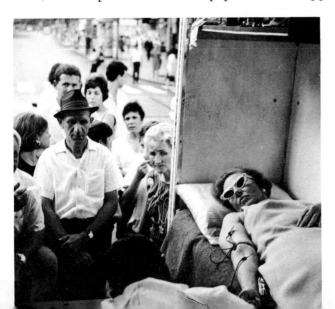

The weeks preceding the outbreak of war were marked by a fervent public desire to take part in the national struggle for survival. Donors queue up at a mobile blood bank in anticipation of the forthcoming war

Hospital beds by the hundreds were made ready with a quiet and almost macabre efficiency. Trenches and shelters had been dug all over the land. Industrialists, noted in better days for their hardheaded thrift, donated legendary sums for the national defence. As the days of suspense went by, the radio brought touching messages exchanged between soldiers at the front and their young wives at home. There were references to children about to be born, or anxious allusions to the oven having been left burning in the haste of departure. The simplicity of these exchanges held a pathos hard to bear. There had been a sudden rearrangement of values, with human affections rising to the top.

The Jewish dispersion, too, was in a ferment of a more dramatic kind. There were the usual ardent rhetorical demonstrations, but there was also more tangible evidence of solidarity. Thousands of young men were crowding the offices of Israeli Consulates and Jewish Agency institutions asking to be sent to Israel for immediate service. And the excitement was not limited to Jews alone. A blind man in Brooklyn offered to send the money that he had saved over twenty years to buy a house, stating that if Israel went under there would be no point in living anyway; and that if Israel succeeded he would surely get his money back. In Scandinavia there were members of Parliament who pondered resignation so as to make themselves available to fight in Israel. An elderly spinster in northern Scotland announced that she could do very little by way of fighting, but that few people could drive an army truck as robustly as she. Amateur technologists sent Israel their obsessive plans for secret weapons which would cause the Egyptian Army to crumble into dust. Scientists and professors by thousands, many of whom had never given a passing thought to Israel, found themselves impelled to sign agonizing appeals for the support of Israel's security. Even sophisticated newspapers, like *The Times*, *The Guardian*, *The Economist*, *The Observer*, *The New York Times* and *Le Monde*, which had long been advocating Israeli concession, were suddenly admitting that one of the ways of dealing with aggression might, after all, be to resist it. There was clearly something in Israel's predicament which touched sensitive chords of humane feeling. From some newly liberated African states came scores of messages from young men who had spent weeks or months in Israel's training courses and for whom it had become an Alma Mater, the nurse and the architect of their skills. In the churches of Holland, prayers were being uttered for Israel's survival. Had the ensuing battle not been so short, the voluntary convergence of men and women from all over the world to Israel's defence might have been without parallel in the history of modern war. In the moment of danger, Israel stood high in the trust and anxiety of peace-loving mankind.

In Israel itself the normal rivalries were softened by acts of mutual tolerance and sympathy which in other days most citizens would have been too shame-faced to offer or to accept. Synagogues all over the land seemed fuller than usual. The air was quiet with courage and simple rectitude. The nation which was supposed to have lost its youthful idealism and pioneering virtues now looked back to the old unifying visions. Israelis and Diaspora Jews found each other anew and rejoiced in the mutual discovery. Responsibility and sacrifice were no longer embarrassing words. It was a moment of special quality which would live on and on, deep in the heart and mind of Israel for generations to come. A new dimension had been added to the national memory and the exploration of it would take many years. The whole nation was convinced of a single stark certainty. The choice was to live or perish – to defend the national existence or to forfeit it for all time.

On Monday, 5 June, the morning heat lay heavy on the land. At 7.50 a.m. the air-raid sirens let out their familiar howl. Men and women going to work and children hurrying to school paid no immediate attention to the sound; only when policemen began to move tensely among them did they sense that something more was afoot than the usual testing of the warning system. The roads began to clear as the crowds moved awkwardly and dubiously towards the few shelters which existed.

Egyptian planes advancing towards Israel had been sighted on the radar screens. This had happened often in recent days. In accordance with the government's decision, Israeli aircraft had gone out to meet the advancing force; but this time our airmen's mission was not tactical or limited as before. They were making a total strike against the intimidating Egyptian air force. Shortly afterwards, the Egyptian ground forces in the Gaza Strip bombarded the Israeli settlements at Nachal Oz and Erez. Israeli armoured units were now responding fully. Israeli and Egyptian forces on land and in the air were locked in mortal combat. The action to which Nasser had been goading Israel for three weeks had now erupted. Israel was hitting back in the air and, from the very first, there was a glow of victory on her wings. Nasser had got the war which he had so insistently sought and passionately welcomed. Heykal's logic was being fulfilled: Israel was doing what he had called 'inevitable'.

Even before the first results of the air strikes were known, Israelis were overcome by a vast sense of relief. Everything that could be done short of war to defend honour and survival had been exhausted. The inevitability of Israel's action would now impress many across the world; the United States could not again question Israel's plight or claim that Israel had not involved it frankly in the dilemma.

In legal terms, Israel was exercising 'the inherent right of self-defence' recognized for all States in Article 51 of the United Nations' Charter. At two o'clock in the morning, in New York, the Israel representative at the United Nations was ordered to convene the Security Council, before which he was to unfold the design of Egyptian aggression and report on Israel's resistance. By 10 a.m. the government was receiving reports of excited head-lines, radio bulletins and television stories all over the world reporting that Israel, which had been assumed to be on the verge of destruction, had risen up in wrathful self-defence. The incomparable Arab radio stations were telling of sensational Arab victories and of Israel's imminent liquidation.

What comes most vividly to recollection is the speed with which Israel passed from peril to deliverance. What was to be the Six Day War was, in effect, decided in the air during the first six hours. There was nothing in objective logic or military experience to prepare anyone for such a result. Most experts believed that the numerical superiority of the Arabs and their ability to press Israel in three directions would at least make them immune from swift defeat and thereafter give them a chance of victory or at least of an honourable stalemate.

But by 11 a.m. on 5 June Israel's destiny had been turned upside down. Re-ports arrived of unbelievable successes in the air. All the Egyptian airfields had been attacked, and most of their planes destroyed on the ground. By noon the number of Egyptian aircraft destroyed ran into the hundreds, and when night fell Israel commanded the skies of the Middle East.

At 10 a.m. on 5 June, the Israeli Government had conveyed a message to the King of Jordan expressing the hope that he would remain outside the conflict and promising him that Israel would attack nowhere unless it was attacked. The hope was rational enough; but the Middle East is so constructed that the rational things are the things least likely to happen. Israel's military authorities fully supported the political move. Faced by eleven Jordanian brigades on the west bank of the Jordan and in the area south and east of the Dead Sea, they could only have made the most modest provision for a holding action. The experience of 1956, the constant hostility between Nasser and Hussein ever since and the fragility of the Jordanian Army had led to the conclusion that despite the 31 May pact, King Hussein might hesitate before entering the fray. But all these calculations were shattered when Jordanian forces opened a heavy bombardment all along the front. King Hussein has himself described the nature of his dilemma:

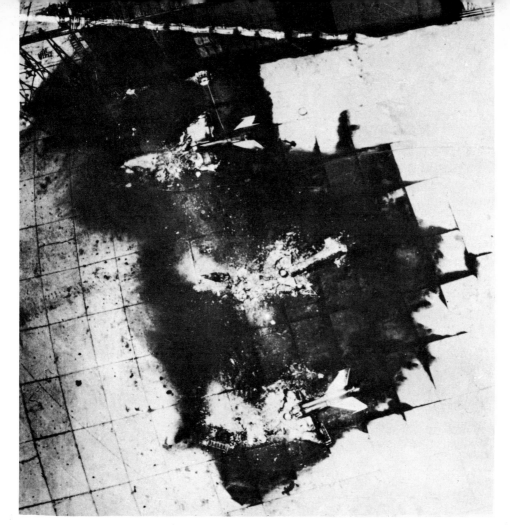

It was at this point that we received a telephone call at air force headquarters from United Nations General Odd Bull. It was a little after 11 a.m. The Norwegian general informed me that the Israel Prime Minister had addressed an appeal to Jordan. Mr Eshkol had summarily announced that the Israeli offensive had started that morning, Monday, 5 June, with operations directed against the United Arab Republic. He then added: 'If you don't intervene you will suffer no consequences.'

By this time we were already fighting in Jerusalem. And our planes had just taken off to bomb Israeli air bases. So I answered Odd Bull: 'They started the battle; well, they are receiving our reply by air.'

The die was cast. Jordanian forces captured Government House in southeast Jerusalem, where the United Nations Truce Organization had its headquarters. Early in the afternoon, the Jordanian Army began moving its tanks opposite north-western Jerusalem. Thus, within a few hours, a danger to Israel's security had arisen at the most unforeseen and vulnerable place. In a swift redisposition of forces, the central sector had to be reinforced.

above The Six Day War was, to all intents and purposes, won during the first six hours, when the Arab air forces were wholly destroyed, mainly on the ground, by massive Israeli air strikes

Amman radio was now making bloodthirsty statements announcing that all Israelis should be 'torn to bits'. The truth is that on Monday, 5 June, more casualties were being inflicted on Israel by Jordan than she was sustaining on the Egyptian front. Israeli forces were now ordered to resist without inhibition; and shortly after 2 p.m. the Israeli air force attacked the airfields at Amman and Mafraq, where nearly all of Jordan's small force of twenty Hunter aircraft was destroyed. In a swift counter-attack, Government House in Jerusalem was recaptured and Jordanian forces expelled.

The entry of Jordan gave the war an unforeseen direction. What had been predicted as a reaction against Egyptian forces in Sinai, with the aim of breaking the ring of strangulation, had now developed into a conflict involving Israeli forces on every front. Now, more than ever, it was evident that without victory there would be no survival. Any success by Arab armies and air forces, however limited in tactical scope, would squeeze Israel from three directions at once. Israel was so placed in relation to its neighbours that the choice under the armistice map was always posed between decisive victory and total defeat. It was clear that a successful campaign against Jordan would bring both victory and many complexities.

Israel would never have reason to regret that even under early Jordanian fire she still presented King Hussein with the opportunity to retreat. It was to become evident after the war that the King was not really free to apply his discretion or to consult his own interest. Egypt's most formidable soldier, General Mahmoud Riad, had been appointed to command the Jordanian sector, and on the evening of 4 June he had installed himself with an Egyptian staff at Operational Headquarters in Amman. King Hussein has described how the Egyptian general calmly took Jordan into his military possession, without taking her into any truthful confidence. He has written:

We were the recipients of false information about what had happened in Egypt since the attacks by Israeli air forces on the air bases in the UAR. A new message from Marshal Amer informed us that the Israeli air offensive was continuing; however, it went on to affirm that the Egyptians had destroyed seventy-five percent of the Israeli air force. The same communication told us that the Egyptian bombers had counter-attacked with a crushing assault on Israeli bases. Amer continued with the information that Egyptian ground forces had penetrated Israel through the Negev. These reports, which were fantastic, to say the least, contributed largely in sowing confusion and distorting our appreciation of the situation. At that point, when our radar signalled to us that machines coming from Egypt were flying towards Israel, no doubt crossed our minds: we were instantly persuaded that it was true. They were Israeli bombers returning after carrying out their mission against Egypt.

So by noon on 5 June Israel had a war with two Arab countries, which would soon be reinforced by contingents from more distant Arab lands. A few hours later, the Egyptian and Jordanian air forces had been destroyed. Israel was advancing deep into Sinai. Heavy casualties had been inflicted on the Syrian and Iraqi air forces. Jordan had opened a murderous assault on Israeli buildings and streets in Jerusalem from guns strategically poised around and between the Holy Places of Christianity and Islam. Israeli forces were moving in from the coast towards Jerusalem to remove what was now the greatest threat to security and survival. There would be five more days of hard fighting, and many would lose life and limb. But no single day in all Jewish history would ever dim the lustre of the one that Israel had just lived. Between a single dawn and nightfall, it had passed from peril to successful resistance. Twenty-four hours before, Nasser had been convinced that he would go down in history like Saladin, the Moslem military hero before whose sword all adversaries and infidels trembled. Nasser's predictions of Israel's destruction had been uttered in full authenticity of belief. Much of the world had been hypnotized by his strength and confidence. Now his dreams lay about his feet in ruins.

The news that the Israeli air force had destroyed over four hundred Arab aircraft in a single day for the loss of twenty Israeli planes sounded wildly improbable. The world lived some hours of confusion and doubt. Those who tuned into Arab radio stations heard Arab governments proclaiming joyfully that 'the battle has come – and be it welcome'. Crowds in the streets of Cairo were celebrating the imminence of Israel's destruction and gloating over the spectacular 'victories' being announced every half hour. In the fantasy world of the Arab communiqués, Arab armies were advancing everywhere towards the realization of the aim that Nasser had defined on 26 May:

The battle will be a general one and our basic objective will be to destroy Israel. I probably could not have said such things five, or even three years ago. If I had said such things and had been unable to carry them out, my words would have been empty and valueless. Today I say such things because I am confident.

This had been a mere twelve days before. When the truth dawned, the speed of the transformation would leave the Arabs stunned for the remaining days of the war, and for many weeks beyond. There would still be hard fighting for some days, but on the Egyptian front the issue had been virtually decided in the first round. Israel turned to other dangers. With a brigade in Jerusalem, an ar-

moured group of reservists from the coastal plain, a parachute brigade detached from the southern front, and a tank force originally intended for the Syrian front, the Israeli Army was able to drive the Jordanians across the Jordan in forty-eight hours. The speed of the Jordanian flight was beyond expectation. The secret lay in the early command of the air which enabled Israeli aircraft to harass Jordanian convoys, penetrate Jordanian defences and reduce the whole Jordanian Army to a tattered shred.

The hardest battle was fought in Jerusalem, where Israeli forces under General Uzi Narkiss and Colonel Mordechai Gur attacked heavily fortified positions and worked their way street by street through urban quarters under constant ambush and sniping. By the morning of Wednesday, 7 June, the Old City was enclosed by the two arms of an Israeli pincer movement. It is certain that with time and patience, East Jerusalem would have fallen

above The united city of Jerusalem with the famous landmarks of the Old City (centre) against the background of modern apartment complexes

by siege. But there was the prospect of a Security Council resolution which
would freeze the military situation with the city still divided. This left Israel
no choice but to expedite its action. It began at 8.30 a.m., and six hours later
all Jerusalem was under Israeli control. The Israeli forces had suffered many
casualties through careful avoidance of the Holy Places. The Jordanians used the
El-Aqsa Mosque as a sniping post and the entire area of the Temple Mount as an
ammunition dump, despite anguished pleas from the Jordanian Governor of
Jerusalem and the Moslem religious authorities. By 10.15 a.m. the Israeli flag
had been raised over the Temple Mount. The Western Wall, the most sacred
place in Jewry, was in Israeli hands. No man of historic imagination could fail
to be awed at this reunion of a people with the relic of its ancient glory. Young
Israeli soldiers, raised in the hard-headed secular mood of their generation,
wept like children as they stood in silence before the massive scarred stones.

Meanwhile, west of the Jordan, General David Elazar's armoured thrust from the north had swept Israeli forces to the river's edge. Israel now commanded the whole length of the Jordan from its sources in Dan to where it goes down into the Dead Sea in the south. Simultaneously, an independent and brilliant campaign was being waged by General Yeshayahu Gavish's forces in the south. His tank commander, General Israel Tal, advanced to El Arish, whence the Israeli assault forked out in two directions: one following the coastal road westwards towards the Suez Canal; the other moving south to attack the most heavily fortified Egyptian positions. Here, a thrust by General Abraham Yoffe across the desert converged with Tal's advance, while General Ariel Sharon's force continued to mop up in the general area of Um Kattef-Abu Ageila and further to the south towards Kusseima.

The third day of the war, 7 June, which saw Jerusalem reunited, was also the day of climax in the Egyptian sector in Sinai. The Egyptian forces were in full retreat across Sinai; and Israeli naval forces steaming up the Gulf of Aqaba were able to take Sharm el-Sheikh, open the Straits of Tiran and thus correct the injury which had been the proximated cause of the war.

By the fourth day of the war, 8 June, there was nothing left to fight on the eastern front. The Jordanian armed forces and tens of thousands of terrified refugees were rushing eastwards across the Jordan bridges, leaving Samaria and Judea under Israel's exclusive control. All preoccupation was now centred on the mopping-up operation in Sinai. Before 8 June was out, General Tal had taken Kantara and Ismailia, while General Yoffe's forces were advancing in a two-pronged attack towards the city of Suez and in the direction of the Bitter Lakes, with another section moving southwards towards Ras Sudar on the Gulf of Suez. The paratroopers who had landed at Sharm el-Sheikh now moved northwards to form a link with the main body of the advancing Israeli Army. The Mitla Pass ravine was the scene of sanguinary battles with a thousand tanks participating. They ended in total victory and the destruction of Egypt's armoured force. Israel's flag flew everywhere along the Suez Canal, the Straits of Tiran were open, the Egyptian air force was destroyed, vast quantities of equipment, including at least eight hundred tanks, were devastated or captured. The totality of the Egyptian debacle almost defied belief.

By the morning of 9 June it seemed possible that the only Arab state to get off scot-free from the war would be the one whose policies had kindled it. But it was not conceivable that Israel, having repelled Arab aggression amidst a mounting tide of world sympathy, would be content to per-petuate the vulnerability of its settlers in the Jordan Valley and Upper Galilee. Syrian forces, with a militance and effectiveness that no other Arab army had shown, were shelling the Israeli villages in the north. The close links between Syria and the Soviet Union provoked anguished debates in Israel about the feasibility of fighting a state which had such ominously direct protection by a Great Power. The majority feeling, however, was that if a quick result could be won, Soviet intervention would be physically impossible; and after the event the Soviet Union would be deterred by American pressures from active interference. Accordingly, the Israeli air force, having no Syrian rival in the air, turned itself into flying artillery to bring the Syrian gun positions under assault. On the morning of Friday, 9 June, the Israel Defence Forces received authority to storm the Golan Heights. The toll of life and blood was high. Every topographical advantage lay with the Syrians. Israel had to attack up-hill against heavily fortified installations situated in the most advantageous positions that nature could offer. Finally, the Israeli armour broke through the Syrian defences when it was itself in a state of depletion. Out of an entire Israeli tank battalion, only two tanks were still in full operation. At a critical stage, General Elazar's assault was reinforced by General Elad Peled coming northwards from the West Bank to attack the area of Tawfiq. By Saturday, 10 June, Kuneitra was in Israeli hands and the road to Damascus lay open.

It had never been Israel's intention to tempt providence (or the Soviet Union) by an assault on the Syrian capital itself. Israeli forces had been sur-prised by the momentum of Syrian retreat, which had almost sucked Israeli for-ces into Kuneitra. Despite angry Soviet threats in the Security Council, the only reaction by Moscow came in the diplomatic field, with the Soviet Ambassador calling on the Foreign Minister on Saturday afternoon to an-nounce the rupture of relations between Israel and the Soviet Union. This example was followed by Poland, Czechoslovakia, Hungary, Bulgaria and Yugoslavia.

So within six days, Israel had exchanged its vulnerability and peril for a position of unprecedented military domination in the Middle East. It had destroyed or captured 430 combat aircraft and eight hundred tanks. It had inflicted fifteen thousand fatal casualties on Arab troops. It had taken 5,500 offi-cers and non-commissioned officers as prisoners. Its own losses were forty aircraft and 676 dead.

A study made by the Institute for Strategic Studies in London, by Mi-chael Howard and Robert Hunter, summarizes the campaign:

The third Arab-Israeli war is likely to be studied in Staff Colleges for many years to come. Like the campaigns of the younger Napoleon, the performance of the Israeli Defence Force provided a textbook illustration for all the classical principles of war: speed, surprise, concentration, security, information, the offensive—above all, training and morale. Airmen will note with professional approval how the Israeli air-force was employed first to gain command of the air by destruction of the enemy air-forces, then to take part in the ground battle by interdiction of enemy communications, direct support of ground attacks and, finally, pursuit. The flexibility of the administrative and staff system will be examined and the attention of young officers drawn to the part played by leadership at all levels. Military radicals will observe how the Israelis attained this peak of excellence without the aid of drill sergeants and the barrack square. Tacticians will stress the importance they attached in this, as in previous campaigns, to being able to move and fight by night as effectively as they did by day. Above all, it will be seen how Israel observed a principle which appears in few military textbooks, but which armed forces neglect at their peril: the Clausewitzian principle of political context which the British ignored so disastrously in 1956. The Israeli High Command knew that it was not operating in a political vacuum. It worked on the assumption that it would have three days to complete its task before outside pressures compelled a cease-fire.

This dispassionate foreign analysis has been quoted because it is hard for an Israeli, or, indeed, for any Jew, to write about the Six Day War without giving way to rhapsodical emotion at the speed and thoroughness of the transition. Nasser and Heykal had written that if war broke out, its original causes – such as the blockade of the Straits of Tiran and the Syrian assaults from Golan – would be over-shadowed by consequences of far greater scope. This was true. If Israel had lost, it would have been the end of a nation's history. Conversely, an Israeli victory was bound to transform the mood and context in which Israel and the Arab peoples would face each other in the years ahead. For one thing, Israel now held 26,476 square miles of territory previously in Arab hands: 444 square miles on the Golan Heights, 2,270 square miles in Judea and Samaria, 140 square miles in the Gaza Strip, and 23,622 square miles in Sinai. More unexpected were the political successes which followed the military triumph – unexpected because in the political arena the Arabs outweighed Israel more crushingly than on the battlefield. With their fourteen sovereign states, vast territory, enormous mineral resources and heavy weight in the scales of world strategy, they must have been confident that their diplomacy would wipe out the losses that they had sustained in war. Why should not 1956–7 repeat itself? Then, too, Israel had won a military victory, but this had been annulled by an Arab political counter-attack supported by the Major Powers.

A tank crew, positioned and on alert, during the long, hot days of waiting which preceded 5 June 1967

Now it was to be different: in the immediate sequel of the war, the adversaries clearly defined their political objectives. The Arab states would try to secure a complete Israeli withdrawal without paying the agonizing price of peace and recognition. Israel, for its part, would recall the traumatic experience of 1956: this time it would cling to its territorial gains not in order to perpetuate them, but in order to translate them into a peaceful order of relations in the Middle East, based on a secure Israel with defensible boundaries to be negotiated within the scope of the peace treaty. But if this aim was to be achieved, the first and most urgent task was to avoid a converging and unanimous international pressure calling for Israel's total and unconditional withdrawal.

The glow of military success was so radiant in those early days of June that the Israeli public hardly noticed its first diplomatic success – the defeat of Soviet proposals in the Security Council on 14 June calling for the maintenance of a cease-fire and withdrawal to previous positions. This time Israel was able to secure American and Western support for a cease-fire based on positions reached in fighting and not linked with a call for withdrawal.

There had been something casual in the progress towards war. Some historians will adduce that the blockade of the Straits of Tiran was its central 'cause'. Others will stress the decision of the Syrian Government to inflame the smouldering conflict by terrorist infiltration. All will assign a large role to the action of the Soviet Union in inciting Egypt to mobilize her forces and apply pressure to Israel in the south. The truth is that these were only the incendiary sparks. Historic events have a broader framework than the immediate one out of which they seem to erupt. The context of the 1967 war, as of its two predecessors, must be sought in the total hostility which marked the Arab policy towards Israel. So long as this intense hostility prevailed, like a bonfire soaked in gasoline, the specific motive of conflagration was a matter of chance and time. The world wars were not 'caused' by Sarajevo and Danzig, but by the international alignments and emotions from which they evolved. Similarly, an Arab-Israel war was bound to arise, sooner or later, from a savage concentration of belligerency, hostility and non-recognition. The hatred was too violent to be contained. It was nourished by a fallacious version of the region which excluded Israel from the Middle East's past, present and future. It was fanned and eventually ignited by a charismatic arrogance and a boastful rhetoric which the Arab masses probably took more seriously than did Nasser himself. In short, the Middle East was congested by ideas and emotions which were always capable of eruption. The war was caused not by a single event, but by the general denial of Israel's historic personality and sovereign destiny.

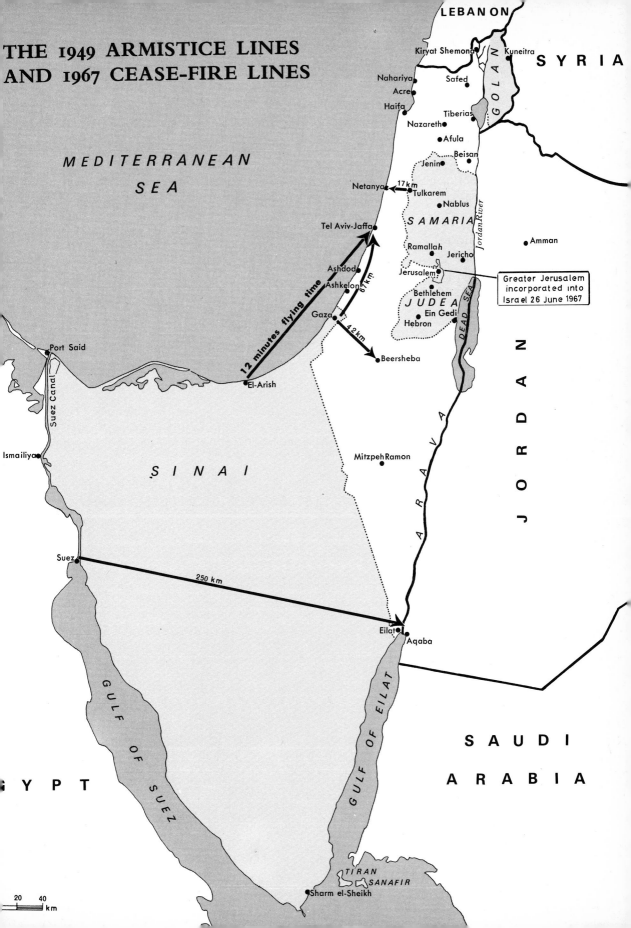

THE 1949 ARMISTICE LINES
AND 1967 CEASE-FIRE LINES

LEBANON

SYRIA

Kiryat Shemona • / Kuneitra

Nahariya •
Acre •   Safed •
Haifa •

Tiberias •

Nazareth •

Afula •

Beisan •

Jenin •

Netanya • — 17 km — • Tulkarem

Nablus •

SAMARIA

Tel Aviv-Jaffa •

Ramallah •   Jericho •   • Amman

Ashdod •
Ashkelon •   Jerusalem •

67 km

Greater Jerusalem
incorporated into
Israel 26 June 1967

Gaza •   Bethlehem •
             JUDEA
             Ein Gedi •
42 km   Hebron •

• Beersheba

El-Arish •

12 minutes flying time

MEDITERRANEAN
SEA

Port Said •

Suez Canal

Ismailiya •

S I N A I

Mitzpeh Ramon •

J O R D A N

Suez • —————— 250 km ——————

D E A D   S E A

A R A V A

Jordan River

G U L F   O F   S U E Z

Eilat • • Aqaba

G U L F   O F   E I L A T

S A U D I

A R A B I A

E G Y P T

TIRAN
SANAFIR

• Sharm el-Sheikh

20 40
|—|—|
km

Beyond Nasser's adventurism one must look at the attitudes of the Powers and the United Nations to understand how the war had come about. Nasser was acutely sensitive to international situations. His discovery of Israel's solitude and of Western diffidence played a major role in his developing audacity. The other side of the same coin was his confidence in Soviet support.

For in any study of the 1967 war Moscow enters the cycle of causation at every important stage. The Soviet Union had given the Arab states what appeared to be an invincible superiority of armament. It had blocked all attempts to formalize the armistice lines as permanent boundaries. It had closed the Security Council to Israel by its veto, so as to make it a sanctuary for Arab belligerency. It had virtually banished the United Nations as an effective guarantor of Middle Eastern security. With the 1956 experience in mind, Egypt had relied on Moscow to neutralize armed intervention by the Western Powers. The Arab leaders had convinced themselves that it was the Soviet threat, not American pressure, which had frustrated British and French intervention in the Suez campaign of 1956. They now relied on Moscow to perform a more daring service – to ensure that the United States would not intervene militarily no matter what injury might be done to the credibility of her commitments. On 29 May Nasser had stated publicly that his War Minister, Shams ed-din Badran, had given him a message from Premier Kosygin stating that the USSR 'supports us in battle and will not allow any power to intervene until the matters are restored to what they were in 1956'. This version, which was never denied, emphasizes the Soviet Union's responsibility for Nasser's decision to impose the Aqaba blockade. There are no grounds for believing that the Soviet Union ever disapproved of Nasser's blockade decision. It is possible that the USSR would not have advised Nasser in advance to take the fatal step. But once it had been taken, and the heavens had not fallen, Moscow might well have thought that its own robust stand would confirm Nasser in his gains, deter Israel from resistance and force the United States to reconcile itself, despite President Johnson's displeasure, to the acceptance of Nasser's *fait accompli*. It seemed clear at the time that the Soviet Union was confident that Israel was weak, trapped and paralyzed. When the Soviet Ambassador in Cairo told Nasser on 3 June that Israel's non-resistance was assured he was faithfully reporting Moscow's appraisal. After all, Israel was abandoned by its friends, encircled by its enemies, betrayed by the Security Council and, in the Soviet view, domestically divided and militarily inferior. Resistance does not usually spring from conditions such as these. The Soviet contempt of Israel until 1967 was beyond remedy. Russian diplomats and agents had swarmed over Israel for two decades, learning more and more – and understanding less and less. Israel, in the Soviet conception, is small, geographically indefensible, dependent on outside forces, incapable of autonomous decision and, when all is said and done, Jewish.

Thus the 1967 war was very largely a child of Soviet misconceptions. The Arabs who were meant to be the beneficiaries of Soviet protection became its victims. Moscow's policy had provoked the Arabs to make war; but this did not mean that the Soviet Union would ensure that they won it, or would even take risks to help them recover their losses after it. In the Soviet conception, the race is to the swift and the battle to the strong. When Arab governments and armies had proved their impotence, the Soviet Union limited itself to political and propaganda support.

Despite its reputation for deliberate and prescient calculation, Soviet diplomacy committed many faults. In the first place, Soviet leaders overestimated the importance to themselves of protecting the Syrian régime from the consequences of its 'revolutionary' activity. They behaved as though a blow inflicted by Israel on Syria would shake the Soviet international system to its foundations. Later, this was to be proved quite untrue. Similarly, the Soviet report to Cairo on an imminent Israeli drive to Damascus was decisive in spurring Egypt to adventurous deeds.

Once the Tiran blockade had been imposed, the Soviet leaders did not probe its full consequences. Finally, and most crucially, the Soviet Union misjudged the military relationship between Egypt and Israel. It believed that Israel without allies could not break out of a siege and that if it tried to do so there would be an Arab victory.

Through these failures of judgment and control, the Soviet Union suffered a defeat of its global interests and prestige. Everything went against its dogma. 'Progressive' Arab states were routed by a 'reactionary' Israel. Clients and allies of Moscow were defeated by a little state which, in Soviet eyes, was a mere puppet of Western imperialism. And the pride of Soviet arms was brought low by the inefficiency of Egyptians and Syrians in their use. The most massive investment of effort and technical skills ever made by the Soviet Union outside its European sphere of influence was squandered in a single week. Soviet power and realism would henceforth be held in lesser awe across the world. In order to give a reassuring picture of the USSR as an ally, Moscow hastily rebuilt the Arab armies and air forces and stationed thousands of experts on Egyptian and Syrian soil. But the halo of Russia's might and majesty has not shone as brightly in the world as before.

The United States had better fortune than the Soviet Union in adapting itself to the evolving crisis. Yet Washington, too, was taken by surprise at many stages. The United States had grown so accustomed to periodic eruptions in the armistice system that it had ceased to believe that any outburst could destroy the entire structure. When Nasser concentrated his troops in Sinai between 14 and 16 May, American officials were emphatic in asserting that nothing more was at issue than a demonstrative show of strength on behalf of Syria. The first American statements in Washington and in the Security Council were of routine placidity. There was no attempt to disguise American disapproval of Nasser's decision to expel the UNEF; and on 23 May, President Johnson spoke in very stringent terms of Nasser's blockade as 'illegal and potentially disastrous to the cause of peace'. The President had gone on to say that 'the United States is firmly committed to the support of the political independence and territorial integrity of all nations in the area'. Yet for a full week the main American effort was to counsel Israel to hold back.

This advice was to have far-reaching results. By restraining Israel with inhibitory messages, Washington was bound to assume serious responsibility if the passing weeks and days brought no remedy. The urgent appeal for restraint probably had much to do with habit. There is a spontaneous Great Power reaction to crises. Even when America's own national security was at stake in the Cuban Missile Crisis of 1963, President Kennedy and his advisers had first drawn a long, deep breath and played for time. Yet the deeper motives of the American appeal for Israeli restraint must be sought in the condition of the American-Soviet relationship. The true extent of the Soviet commitment to Egypt had never been fully or precisely appraised in Washington or, for that matter, in Jerusalem and elsewhere. Might not an Israeli attempt to free the Straits of Tiran involve the Soviet Union in military support of Egypt? If so, the United States would face a fearful dilemma. It could either come to Israel's aid and risk confrontation on a global scale; or it could leave Israel to its fate and incur the collapse of all credibility in American commitments everywhere in the world. Each of these was a nightmare prospect. The United States recoiled from them and sought time to probe Soviet intentions. It may not have fully understood that a Great Power which asks a small nation to take no action in defence of its vital interests assumes a heavier moral burden than one which abstains from such a request. Once President Johnson had asked Israel to hold its hand pending further consultations, the United States was involved in the crisis in a way that it had never been during the 1956 Suez war. And as the days rolled on, its dilemma became sharper.

In the years since 1957, the concreteness of the American commitment on Tiran had faded in the official memory. On 24 May, a leading American newspaper commentator wrote: 'The decision-making machinery is busy making decisions, unaware of a fundamental decision made ten years ago.' Consultations with President Johnson and the Israeli invocation of the 1957 guarantees gravely enlarged the American anxiety. For only the second or third time since the end of the Second World War, the authenticity of American commitments was being put to the test. There is no doubt that President Johnson was sincere in the assurances which he gave on 26 May and which he ratified even more strongly on 28 May, about his desire to take all and every measure to open the straits. The idea that Nasser might be forced to retreat under international pressure did not, at first, seem fantastic in Western eyes. Egypt, after all, was not the most terrifying of military powers; and the United States, Britain and their friends had a virtual monopoly of force in Red Sea waters. The Soviet Union was strategically distant and politically cautious; and if the Western Powers had sailed together with Israel through the blockaded straits, the humiliation of Nasser might have had dynamic results in the Arab world and in Egypt itself. It could have led to the overthrow of a humiliated Nasser régime. The integrity of international commitments would have been affirmed and the primacy of the Western Powers in Middle Eastern waters impressively proved. These brave thoughts may have glowed in the minds of President Johnson and Prime Minister Wilson between 24 and 28 May. Yet on closer contemplation, the prospect grew steadily less inviting for them. For international and domestic reasons, the United States wished to have some UN support for its efforts; and the Security Council was already a broken reed. Nor was much support coming from America's allies outside the United Nations. Few were willing to join the international escort or even to sign the declaration on free passage in the Straits of Tiran. In the United States itself, congressional opinion shrank from a military involvement, however limited, unless it fulfilled three conditions: it had to be multilateral; it had to have congressional sanction; and it had to be proved that there was no other way of solving the problem and that Israel's survival was really in peril. The administration convinced itself and the Congress that Israel did have a capacity for effective defence.

The difference between 1967 and 1956 was Israel's success this time in getting the President of the United States to admit that Israel was the victim of an aggressive Egyptian act. Yet as the days went on, the American and Israeli time-tables fell out of accord. By early June, Israel was more concerned with the Arab troop concentrations on three frontiers than with the Tiran blockade. However difficult it may be to recall these fears in the light of the subsequent military result, the apprehension of Israelis was that they would soon be at the mercy of an Arab surprise attack which could well have a knock-out effect. And as Israel's plight became more urgent, the American capacity for action became reduced. By 3 and 4 June, the administration in Washington was probably hoping in its heart that Israel would confine its call on the United States to an appeal for political aid and not for anything that would risk American military involvement. When it became clear that this was Israeli policy, American and Israeli hearts began to beat in unison, and their harmony grew deeper when the results of the war were known.

President Johnson's difficulties before the war were compounded by a parallel growth of caution in London. The Foreign Minister, George Brown, had reacted to the news of Nasser's blockade with Palmerstonian ferocity. One could almost see him personally on the deck of an aircraft carrier sailing up the Straits of Tiran in righteous pugnacity. The only trouble was that he had no aircraft carrier anywhere near the straits. By the end of the third week in May, many voices seem to have been raised in the British Cabinet asking if the United Kingdom was really in a position to blaze away heroically in emulation of ancient habits. The discovery that the nearest British forces were far away pointed to the immense change that had come over Britain since the days of its dominance in the Middle East.

At any rate, when President Johnson and Prime Minister Wilson met in Washington on 2 June, they would have been less than human if they had not asked themselves, whether explicitly or in glances of private understanding, if it would be all that disastrous for Israel to solve her own problems on her own responsibility. It is the anomaly of our times that small countries defending their own interests sometimes have more mobility and resilience than greater powers whose eyes are always fixed apprehensively on each other's potential reaction and on the perils of Armageddon.

Of all the figures in the 1967 drama, none acted more unpredictably than France. True, some reticence and inhibition towards Israel had previously been noticed in Paris. But nothing quite prepared Israelis for the jolt which shook their confidence and emotion between 24 May and the outbreak of hostilities. After all, the solemn French commitment of 1957 to support Israel's navigation rights in the Straits of Tiran had never been abrogated or even questioned. Nor had France criticized the motives or results of Israel's resistance to Syrian terrorism during the 7 April air engagement or thereafter. The flow of French arms to Israel for seven years after the end of the Algerian war had convinced most Israelis that the French interest in Israel was inherently durable and not a mere child of circumstance. Israel believed that she and France were hand

One of the expressions of Israel's interest in its past is the Bible Contest, which is closely followed by almost the entire population and attracts participants from all over the world

in hand not only because they had had a common adversary in the past, but because they had common ideals and interests in the present.

The collapse of this Israeli hope was a powerful stimulus to Nasser as he advanced towards war. For one thing, President de Gaulle's attitude ensured that there could be no united Western stand. It nullified the prospects of the Anglo-American maritime declaration becoming an international document. And the arms embargo imposed on Israel by France must have given Nasser vast encouragement as he weighed the potential gain and loss of his adventure. Here was a tangible sign that a weakened Israel might one day be at his mercy. The embargo told Israelis plainly that they had already reached the peak of their power, and that the balance would decline as Arab arms poured in while Israel's main source of supply was closed down. It can never be forgotten that General de Gaulle's embargo was imposed on Israel before, not after, the outbreak of war. It cannot, therefore, be described as a 'reaction' to Israeli armed resistance. By the time the embargo became known to Israel on 3 June, war was probably inevitable. But General de Gaulle's embargo helped to secure unanimity in the Israeli Cabinet in favour of armed resistance. From 3 June onward France had ensured that time would henceforth be working against Israel. This completely cut the ground under any possible argument in favour of further patience. In short, President de Gaulle had faced Israel with a 'now or never' dilemma; if that were the case, the answer had to be 'now'. The French decision to leave Israel isolated and desperate must be included among the most formative causes of the Six Day War.

The change in de Gaulle's attitude has never been convincingly explained. It is certain that French policy, liberated from the Algerian conflict, was seeking to restore a place for France in the affections of the Arab world. But the deeper reasons for France's new policy probably lay outside the Middle Eastern context. It had become an axiom of de Gaulle's policy that 'Western solutions' were no longer feasible and that Soviet support must be engaged for the repair of all the disruptions which cut across the life of the twentieth century. He believed that international equilibrium required that France throw herself on the Soviet side of the scale. He may also have been haunted by the spectre of a nuclear conflict arising from the engagements which Washington and Moscow had taken towards Israel and the Arab states. When he said 'Ne faîtes pas la guerre' ('Do not make war'), his tone was not arbitrary or authoritative, but full of anguish. He was not thinking of a local war alone.

The primary victim of the events which unfolded in the summer of 1967 was the United Nations. It is hard to know who does the United Nations

Levi Eshkol succeeded Ben Gurion in 1963 and remained Prime
Minister until his death in 1969, achieving with dexterity the
political unity that defied his predecessor

more harm – those who believe that it is everything or those who believe that it is nothing. In the test of conflicts, such as those in Vietnam, Biafra, Czecho-slovakia and Pakistan, the sceptics have been vindicated more than the hopeful supporters. But even those who had been most reserved about the real weight of the United Nations could never have foreseen the humiliating abdication that actually occurred. The spectacle of a docile United Nations hauling down its flag in Sinai to make way for Egypt's impending war; the callous-ness with which Nasser reduced U Thant's visit to futility; above all, the fiasco of the Security Council meetings in New York marked the lowest point which the United Nations had reached in the first two decades of its existence. As time went on it became less and less likely that it would play a formative role in a region which it had abandoned in the decisive hour to the fate of war.

The chief drama of May and June 1967 was the evolution of Israel's mood. This went through a sharp transition in the three weeks of suspense. At the beginning of that period neither the military disposition nor the national temper was geared for a decisive struggle. It is doubtful that any nation has ever passed so quickly from relative repose to a desperate battle for life. In later weeks the Soviet Union and the Arab governments, stunned by the blast and fury of Israeli resistance, constructed a theory of Israeli premeditation. The reasoning was that since the war had turned out so well for Israel, it must have willed it in advance.

   Nothing could be further from the truth. One of the few consoling facts in modern history is that wars are often won by those who have tried hardest to avoid them. Israel's lack of premeditation can be proved by many items of evidence. First, there was the absence of mobilization. Nasser himself said on 26 May: 'We sent reconnaissance aircraft over Israel: not a single brigade was stationed opposite us.' This extraordinary confession does not support the theory that an Israeli conquest of Sinai had been planned or even envisaged in advance. In point of fact, there was a relative vacuum of force on the Israeli side of the armistice line with Egypt up to the very last days of May.

   Then there was Israel's serious, but vain effort to maintain the United Nations forces in their original positions. When this failed there was an attempt by Israel to ensure that Sharm el-Sheikh, at least, remained immune from Egyptian control. Finally, there was a readiness to give President Johnson a long chance to overcome the difficulties which he faced in his efforts to concert some international action. Not one of these attitudes can be explained unless the assumption is accepted that Israel was willing, up to the very end, to give Nasser some room for retreat. Even the multiplication of verbal warnings to Syria by Israeli spokesmen in mid-May points away from, and not towards, the assumption that Israel was bent on war. If it really wanted to overthrow the régime by war on 17 May, Israel would hardly have wished to stimulate vigilance several days ahead by making speeches which put their main accent on Syria.

But more decisive than all the other proofs of Israel's lack of warlike intent was the message sent to King Hussein through General Bull on 5 June, giving him the opportunity to save his kingdom from what both sides knew would be a resounding defeat. Israel knew that it could take the Old City and much of Cisjordan by war. Eshkol's message said, in effect, that the avoidance of war was an aim worthy of immense renunciations. One returns to the truth that by the end of May the Arab leadership had lost its head in the intoxication of tactical successes. The position was exactly as Heykal described it then:

Israel must reply now, it must deal a blow. We have to be ready for it and to mini-mize its effect as much as possible. Egypt has exercised its power and achieved the objectives at this stage without resorting to arms so far. But Israel has no alternative but to use arms. This means that the logic of the fearful confrontation now taking place between Egypt, fortified by the might of the masses of the Arab nation, and Israel, fortified by the illusion of American might, dictates that Egypt, after all it has now succeeded in achieving, must wait, even though it has to wait for a blow. I say that Israel must resort to arms. I say that an armed clash between the UAR and Israel is inevitable.

The French philosopher and historian Taine wrote: 'The aggressor is he who makes war inevitable.' Egypt, by its own confession, had created a situation in which 'an armed clash between the UAR and Israel [had become] inevitable'. The result was that in early June Israel found itself rushing to victory in a battle which not a single Israeli had believed to be on the horizon three or four weeks before. The transition from danger to triumph was too swift for the sensation of it to be felt at once. As the armies returned home, Israeli emotions were overwhelmed by the force of the change that had come about in their fortunes. Henceforth, Israel would face history in a different stature: its prospects and its dangers had assumed a larger scope.

11

The New Era, 1967–1972

*What had we gained from victory?
Everything that we would have lost
without it.*

It was Israel's golden summer. The prospect for peace and security was still obscure, but would surely never dwindle to a point as low as in early June. After six days of fighting, Israel's population centres were separated from Arab forces by a belt of territory three times as large as Israel had been before. The adversary had not only been pushed into the distance; he was also shorn of military power. Much time would pass before Arab governments could re-build their armed forces; to restore their morale would be an even longer task.

Israel's diplomatic problem in the summer of 1967 was to avoid losing the victory as soon as it had been won. The Arab states and the Soviet Union were making a virulent effort to cancel Israel's gains. Their aim was to force Israel back to the old armistice lines without the conclusion of permanent peace or the negotiation of secure boundaries. In the UN General Assembly, the Israeli Government declined to accept this course. Israel's intention was to maintain the cease-fire lines until they could be replaced by peace treaties establishing territorial boundaries by negotiation. The armistice lines, after all, had been regarded by the Arab governments and by all the nations of the world as provisional and subject to change in the peace settlement. For nearly two decades the Arab states had successfully denied those lines the status of permanent boundaries. The armistice principle itself had been shattered by the Arab declarations of active war and blockade in May and June 1967. Moreover, the map of their encirclement on 4 June 1967 brought terrifying memories to all Israelis. The idea of Syrian troops again stationed on the Golan Heights, an Arab government again in East Jerusalem, and Sharm el-Sheikh again without Israeli forces was revolting both to their experience and to their instinct for security. The nation's central resolve was never to return to the edge of the precipice; it might not always be possible to pull back from the brink.

The debate in the Special Session of the General Assembly unfolded with a gravity and sharp analysis unknown in the United Nations for many years. It began with a vehement Soviet assault. Ignoring the pent-up provocation

UN envoy Dr Gunnar Jarring converses with Prime Minister
Golda Meir, Foreign Minister Abba Eban and UN Ambassador
Yosef Tekoah at the Prime Minister's residence in Jerusalem

which had preceded Israel's action, the Soviet leaders accused Israel of 'treacherous' aggression and even called on her to pay compensation to the Arab states – presumably to heal the fingers that had been bruised in the attempt to strangle us. The Israeli response placed responsibility squarely on Soviet shoulders: 'You do not come here as accusers but as a legitimate object of international criticism for the part you have played in the sombre events leading up to the war'. The Israeli defence of the 5 June action was total. 'Never has armed force been used in a more righteous cause'. I described it as being in the same category as 'the defence of Stalingrad against the Nazi hordes', 'the expulsion of Hitler's bombers from British skies' and the 'uprising of the Warsaw ghetto'. It was plain that these far-reaching analogies were approved in world opinion and that this time a universal sentiment had made its presence felt on Israel's behalf.

The strongest supporting voice came from the United States. On the morning of 19 June President Johnson had made a broadcast clearly aimed at the Special Session of the General Assembly which he had refused to attend: He did not wish to lend the prestige of his office to what he regarded as a Soviet political stunt. He called for a departure from the armistice, to which there should be no return. He admitted that there should be a withdrawal, but to secure borders, not 'fragile and oft-violated armistice lines'. He emphasized that the nations which lived together in the Middle East should sit together to work out the conditions of their coexistence. He called for free use of the international waterways and a just settlement of the problems of refugees. The whole atmosphere of the speech was one of innovation, not reconstruction. Opposition to the Soviet-Arab campaign spread into Europe, Latin America and most of Africa. It became evident that the Soviet Union had made a serious miscalculation in convening such a spectacular diplomatic assembly and engaging its prestige in the outcome. The truth was that Israel's military success had aroused relief around the world: the attempt to condemn it was an embarrassing failure. Nasser's boasts of victory and his threats to 'destroy' Israel were still remembered. When he fell flat on his face there was the quiet satisfaction which usually accompanies the downfall of bullies. To announce an 'active state of war' at one moment and then to complain that the intended victim of the war had dared to hit back was to invite derision. It is far worse for a statesman to be ridiculed than to be reviled.

So the withdrawal resolutions fell to the ground; and all that the General Assembly managed to do was to resolve by vote on 4 July to oppose the union of Jerusalem, which Israel had enacted on 26 June. This exotic insistence on keeping Jerusalem divided did not destroy the taste of Israel's political victory.

The abstention of the United States from the vote gave a clear indication that the resolution was not going to be enforced. The United Nations was merely adding new layers of anomaly to a bizarre record on Jerusalem. Since 1948, whenever the city had been besieged or bombarded, the United Nations had looked on inert and silent. When all the synagogues in the Old City were destroyed under the Jordanian régime, it had maintained a total reticence. Yet it had always withheld recognition from anything that the people of Jerusalem had done to ensure the administration of the city or to express the national sentiment of its population. The resolution was not expected to have any effect. The dividing walls had crumbled and no international injunction could build them anew.

For Israelis the resolution on Jerusalem was a cloud in an otherwise bright sky. The important fact was that the debate initiated by Prime Minister Kosygin on 19 June had recoiled against him. Israel was able to rally forty-six states to vote against all resolutions for withdrawal before a peace settlement had been secured. There were another two dozen states which abstained from supporting the Soviet-Arab offensive. The delegate of a small Latin American republic had shouted exultantly at the Soviet Foreign Minister: 'You got eight votes, Mr Gromyko' – for this, astonishingly, was all that the Soviet-Arab bloc had been able to add to its basic voting strength.

Israel's resolve not to return to the old situation was upheld with special ardour in Jerusalem. It was at the Western Wall, more than anywhere else, that Israelis came to terms with the fact of their victory. For nineteen years the Jordanian Government had barred Jews from access to the most sacred and venerable of their shrines. It had also destroyed all the houses of Jewish worship in the Old City. In a final burst of contempt and rancour, it had used the tombstones of Jews buried on the Mount of Olives to pave army latrines. Israelis were afire with resentment at this disrespect for ancient sanctities. They were also astonished by the apathy with which the world community had indulged the sacrilege. Under the Jordanian régime there had been deferential protection for the interests of Islam, a somewhat wayward and grudging treatment of Christian rights and a total violation of everything that Jews held in respect. When Israeli leaders came to the Western Wall on 7 June and vowed that the nation would never again be sundered from the cradle of its birth, their words re-echoed strongly in Israeli hearts. A month before, a song called 'Jerusalem the Golden' had been introduced at the Independence Day Music Festival. Its haunting and nostalgic tune and its almost sensual descriptions of Jerusalem's sites and landscapes spoke deeply to the national mood. A few weeks after the Six Day War, it had acquired something like the status of an anthem and was played v. ith greater frequency and emotion than *Hatikvah* itself.

It was in Jerusalem, too, that Israelis had the experience of standing in line with Arabs to get on buses, of jostling with them in markets and in some rare cases of visiting them in private homes. The Mayor, Teddy Kollek, responded imaginatively to the falling of barriers. The old 'Mandelbaum Gate', at which the Israeli and Jordanian parts of Jerusalem used to meet, with soldiers glowering at each other from each side, was pulled down to nobody's regret. For two decades few people had managed to discover who Mandelbaum was; now it did not seem to matter. The scar slashed across the city's face by the war of 1948 was healed.

On 12 July 1967 Israel told the United Nations that it would not claim 'exclusive jurisdiction or unilateral responsibility' in the Holy Places of Christendom or Islam, and would be willing to discuss with those traditionally concerned arrangements for giving effect to this principle. It was the first time in history that a government controlling Jerusalem had been satisfied with anything less than the application of its unreserved sovereignty to every part of it. All previous régimes, including the most recent – Jordan, Britain and the Ottoman Turks – had considered that their prestige required the world to place confidence in them for the management and safeguarding of the Holy Places. Israel felt itself more likely than any of them to be meticulous on this principle for, alone among them, it had suffered from the violation of it. But Israelis felt that a gesture to Christendom and Islam would evoke a universal interest in the union of the city and might even contain a seed of a political settlement with the neighbouring Moslem state.

The war and the first round in the political struggle had ended with no certainty about the ultimate outcome. But one consequence was already at work. Hereafter, Israel would project a new vision of itself to its own people and to the world beyond. It had given proof of resilience and determination; it had shown the qualities that glow most brightly in adversity; and it had carried its banner forward in an atmosphere of intense world sympathy. Wherever Jews walked the streets anywhere in the world, there was a new confidence in their step. Israel, after all, was not a Great Power. It would always be small in size and material strength. Surely, then, its victory bore witness to special qualities of spirit. Israel's example had something to say to small, threatened and oppressed countries everywhere. A sense of spiritual vigour went out from its shores and set imaginations astir in many lands.

West Bank Arabs receive instruction in improved agricultural methods. Despite the absence of a peace settlement, Arab-Jewish cooperation in Israel and the administered territories has grown

In Israel itself the sudden change of fortune was met with a level head.
But there was also a consciousness of having lived a unique and elevating
moment. The psychological impact of the victory had been very deep. Israelis
thronged by the tens of thousands to the Western Wall and the Temple Mount
to gaze incredulously on the stones that symbolized their ancient glory. For
nearly twenty years Israelis, or indeed any Jews, had been brutally barred
from any access to East Jerusalem. Now Israelis moved to reconstruct the
synagogues destroyed in the Old City of Jerusalem. They also came into Arab
towns and villages west of the river in Judea and Samaria, from which they
had been cut off by the war of 1948. Their demeanour, strangely, was of
deference, not of triumph. They were touchingly eager for some communication with Arabs. Israelis had been closed up for two decades within the wall
of their regional isolation. They were now in contact with the stream of Arab
life. They felt that the Arab and Israeli peoples, for all their conflicts, had a
common origin and a common destiny. So Israeli visitors moved awkwardly
into Arab towns and villages, absorbed the swift colour and variety of their
movement, listened to the cacophony of their market-places and inhaled the
characteristic smells of strong coffee, donkey's dung, nargileh smoke and
Arab bread. They were somewhat alien and remote to all of this, yet they
responded with respect to the evidence of a solid, earthy way of life. Those
who had been mature men and women in Palestine before 1948 had known

what it was to be in daily contact with Arab life at many points; but the armistice boundary had separated Arabs and Israelis into hostile ghettos. Now, at last, Israelis had elbow-room for movement. They were out of their cage. Many places with great resonance in Israel's history—Hebron, Shechem, Shiloh – were within their access, and they came to them in a strange ambivalence of humility and exaltation.

Yet there was still a twinge of melancholy. The victory had been glorious, but the peril that had preceded it vibrated more strongly in their memory than the triumph itself. Above all, there had been a heavy price. Bereavement and mutilation had darkened hundreds of homes. Soldiers returning from the battlefield to their kibbutzim gave astonishingly candid interviews about their emotional and moral dilemmas. Some of their conversations were collected in a volume called *The Seventh Day*. It is a strong light turned on the character and quality of Israeli youth. It shatters the familiar stereotype of happy-go-lucky, superficial pragmatism. Israel's young men revealed themselves as capable of moral self-analysis. They brooded on the ultimate mysteries of life and death, as well as on the issue of their Jewish identity. Above all, they were tormented by the complexity of their attitude to the Arab enemy. Some of the conversations are aflame with national pride and free from any doubts about the legitimacy of Israel's struggle. But many others are full of discomfort at the idea that Jews should have domination over hundreds of thousands of Arabs. Common to most of them was a revulsion from bloodshed, a moral torment about killing even in the highest national cause and a compassion for the defeated foe. And when Jerusalem entered their discussion, the secular Israeli youth showed an unexpectedly tender concern for the unifying memories of Jewish tradition.

The first task at home was to establish a viable order of life and law in the new territories. The government wished to avoid binding commitments about the political future of Arab populated lands. These would be held under military administration, and existing municipal and local leadership would be maintained. Israel would apply the previous law, as international conventions required. The result was that a traveller to Arab villages in Judea and Samaria would hardly have known that an 'occupation' had taken place. The Israeli Army stayed unobtrusively in the background, while Arab mayors and officials went on with their tasks; hardly any of them fled or resigned. With Israeli markets open to perishable goods, Arab agriculture flourished.

The Palestinian Arabs had been caught up for the second time in a war provoked from outside, more specifically from Cairo. They seemed to have had enough. Their chief concern was to avoid the disruption of their social and municipal routines. Not all of them were free from panic. The uncertainty of what would lie ahead for them under a non-Arab régime, together with the shock and peril of the war itself, had caused some 200,000 Arabs from the West Bank and the Gaza Strip to move east of the Jordan. After all, their propagandists had told them that Israelis were wild beasts with horns and tails. They knew that there would have been a massacre of Jews if there had been an Arab victory. Why should not the opposite be true? One of their apprehensions was to be cut off from the other Arab countries – from a brother in Beirut, a bank account in Kuwait, schools and universities in Cairo. When the Israeli military administration gave evidence of liberal conduct and of understanding for their desire to maintain contact with the Arab world, the flight was stemmed.

The Israeli administrative policy was to limit the military presence to a minimal strength required for effective security; and this restrained approach had positive effects. Most of the Arab schools functioned, and a profitable commerce developed. The sense of rootedness and stability, the experience of having solid, concrete interests to defend gave birth to an attitude among West Bank Arabs quite different from that of the Palestinians in Beirut and Cairo who lived exclusively with their grievances in a world of violent slogans and revolutionary ideas. The majority of the Palestinians, who were unmolested in their peaceful homes and soil west of the Jordan, in Judea, Samaria and even Gaza, hardly welcomed the terrorists who came to summon them again to a life of explosion and suffering in the cause of Israel's 'liquidation'. The Palestinians west of the Jordan did not seriously believe that Israel was just a temporary boil that could be excised from Arab flesh. In their eyes it was clearly a stable, if undesirable, reality. And it gave no sign that it was about to disappear.

In Israeli domestic political life there was a brief period of tranquillity. The pre-war contentions were silenced. The polls indicated the overwhelming popularity of the national leaders, including those who, only a short time before, had been under vehement assault. Those in charge of defence policies and foreign affairs were sustained by staggering percentages, well into the eighties, while Prime Minister Eshkol quietly celebrated the emphatic endorsement of his policies and personality, which had often been the target of fierce criticism. While the relief and advantage of victory were intensely savoured, there was also a consciousness that victory had its limitations. The Arab governments still refused to give it any lasting acknowledgement. Israelis looked anxiously into their political crystal ball in an attempt to predict how the Arabs would grapple with the problem of their defeat.

It was cruelly difficult for the Arabs to come to terms with what had befallen them. During a few hours in June their mood had plunged from high exuberance into a shock so deep that the impact of it would never be fully absorbed. Only a few days before, millions of Arabs had felt that they were on the brink of a triumph unblemished by doubt or risk. The fall from hope was correspondingly hard. Even while their planes were being blasted from the airfields and the skies, the fantasy of triumph had lingered. One minute they were being told of huge Arab triumphs. A few hours later the sensual images of victory had faded into the afternoon air like a brief mirage. One day the truth would come to them like an awful spasm of pain; but meanwhile a stunned and disordered leadership did everything to ward it off. All the Arab world was face to face with a defeat of which the sting was sharper because of the anticipation that had gone before.

There now began a deep searching of hearts. What had gone wrong? Who and what was to blame? The literature of the 1948 defeat had begun to dwindle in recent years; now it was to be renewed in a higher key. 'A greater disaster than in 1948 has happened', wrote an Egyptian commentator, 'and it therefore demands a greater measure of frankness and criticism'.

It is difficult even for the adversaries and intended victims of the Arab assault to read the literature of their defeat without emotion. The wicked enemies, 'Zionism', 'Imperialism', and 'Reaction', still hold the centre of the stage. But with them, the Arab nation itself stands this time under a searchlight focussed on its own imperfections. We find Arab writers and thinkers castigating their people as superficial, frivolous, excessively individualistic, prone to illusion, recalcitrant to the recognition of facts, in short, deficient in the qualities by which nations guard themselves against disaster. The central theme is that failure comes not from outward circumstances alone, but to a much greater degree from elements in the Arab social nature. Every section of Arab opinion had its own, particular answer to the riddle of failure; but nearly all of them came back to the human issue: the failure was not of Arab arms, but of Arab men. Unless the Arab himself came out of the debacle with new attitudes and capacities, there would be no recovery. It was not a matter of technical competence alone. 'We cannot build a modern army', writes Jubran Chamieh, 'capable of wielding modern weapons out of a backward community'.

The Arab leaders by now had an ambivalent approach to Israel. They still portrayed their enemy as in the pre-war caricatures, the oily, curly-headed, hook-nosed monster with horns and tail. Yet they also had a hostile respect for Israel's achievements. Indeed, it was only by assuming the qualities that had brought Israel success that Arab nationalism would ever be able to rise above its failures. At no stage in their thinking did Arab writers make an honest attempt to ponder the motives which had forced Israel to break out of siege. Our 1967 action was fantastically portrayed as having nothing at all to do with Nasser's policies in May 1967. It was attributed to a long-planned, deliberate design of 'Israeli aggression'. According to this mythology, the Israeli Government and army had sat around for months and years until, for no special reason and under no particular provocation, they had broken out in military action on an arbitrary date, 5 June 1967.

The Arab 'establishment' faced a sharp dilemma. If it accepted the criticisms it would, in effect, be disqualifying itself from the right to continue in power, for it would be confessing that Arab leadership had been either too moderate, or too subservient to Communism, or too traditionalist, or not traditionalist enough. Arab governments were bound, for their own sake, to reject any radical diagnosis of Arab troubles. Their only course was to affirm that everything in Arab leadership was basically sound and that the disaster had come through episodic, accidental causes. These could be remedied without a fundamental change of policy or régime. The Arabs would simply have to organize themselves better. The enemy should be regarded with contempt and yet with a higher appraisal of his capacities.

So the Arab failure in the war was attributed to historic causes, to defects in education and social development, to excessive subservience, to Islam – or inadequate observance of Islam – to the treachery of imperialists and reactionaries, to Israeli devilry – to anything except the mistakes of Gamal Abdul Nasser. And since an Arab military defeat by Israel did not fit the picture of a contemptible, narrow-shouldered Israeli dwarf, it was essential to attribute it to other forces. With a cynicism unusual in modern history, Nasser, with the reluctant aid of King Hussein, invented the myth of direct American and British participation in the bombardment of Egypt. This caused Washington and London to break off their relations with Cairo on 7 June 1967. The charge was so preposterous that even the Soviet Union refused to give it any support. The explosive malice of this lie could not be underestimated, however. If Nasser could prove that the United States and Britain had taken part in a regional war, he would be forcing the Soviet Union to review its own responsibilities. In Nasser's ethics, a short-term propaganda gain was more important than abstention from increasing the dangers to all mankind.

The system of argument which eliminated Nasser from all the causes and factors of defeat came to expression in the episode of his 'resignation'. On hearing the true story of his debacle, Nasser, on 9 June, announced his willingness to step down from the direction of the nation's affairs. There came into action an organized wave of protest. Some of it was undoubtedly spontaneous. The Egyptian people had taken Nasser into its possession. It was proud of his prestige. As their world fell about them, Egyptians might have thought that this was the only asset that remained in their hands. There was a sentiment that in putting the blame for defeat on Nasser, they would be humiliating and censuring themselves. In addition, of course, all the capacities of a one-party system came into play to bring about a strong expression of consensus. Crowds in the streets, deputies in parliament, military leaders and others joined in urging Nasser to reconsider his resignation. He 'bowed' to the public opinion which he himself had created and inspired.

Yet many scars were left behind. If the fault was not with the political leaders, surely it must lie with inefficient army commanders. Nasser shifted the blame from his own shoulders to those of Air Marshals and Generals, whom he now placed on public trial. In a society that insisted on some degree of truth and justice, the failure would have been sought not in military incompetence but in a reckless political decision. Nasser had gambled and lost. He had violated an Israeli interest in the defence of which Israel had vowed to fight. He had not made an accurate estimate of his adversary's capacity. He had deluded his people and himself with the legend that Israel was impotent unless the armies of the Great Powers stood with it in the field. He had also exaggerated the military effects of Arab unity and alliances. Against all these indictments, however, we must set his success in being able to transcend his failure. He had won a domestic success in the midst of a military and international debacle.

This fact had far more than personal consequences. A new leader might have been free to criticize the war and to set Arab nationalism on a path of regional conciliation. By sticking to its old leaders, therefore, the Egyptian people committed itself to the old policies. Sure enough, within a few weeks Nasser was at a meeting of Arab heads of governments in Khartoum proposing the old irredentist slogans: 'No peace with Israel; no recognition of Israel; no negotiation with Israel; no territorial bargaining with Israel'. How peace could be extracted from such unpromising ingredients was difficult to understand. By fidelity to its old leadership the Egyptian people had lost the chance of a new direction.

Indeed, the first reactions of Arab nationalism to defeat was not to assume that the anti-Israel ideology had failed but rather that it had not been sufficiently

applied. This doctrine was synthesized and formulated by the terrorist organizations, especially El Fatah. After some eruptions of military action in
1968 and occasional acts of spectacular but facile piracy against airlines, these
movements shifted their emphasis to the political domain. Their device was
to elevate the concept of 'Palestine' to the point at which 'Israel' would disappear. They must have seen that as long as the struggle was portrayed as lying
between Israel and the Arab world, sympathy went to Israel. It was enough
to compare Israel's sparse territory with the huge expanse of Arab lands in
order to conclude that Arab nationalism did not have much to complain about.
But when the contest was presented as being not between Israel and the Arabs
but between Israel and the Palestinians, the perspective changed. All the gains
of Arab nationalism in fourteen states outside Palestine were taken for granted
as though they had no effect on the balance of equity between the rights of the
Arab and Jewish peoples to independence. If the actors in the drama were Israel
and the Palestinians, previous roles were reversed. Israel could be portrayed
as powerful, sated, established and recognized, while the Palestinians were, by
contrast, dispossessed, dissatisfied, irredentist; above all, their problem was
unresolved. By this ingenuity Arab nationalism was making an unprecedented
claim to total self-determination. Wherever there was an Arab community of
any size, there had to be an Arab state, as though the existence of so many
Arab states were not enough to justify a few hundred thousand Arabs being
a minority in a non-Arab country. For the Arabs, as for no other people,
ninety-nine per cent of self-determination and sovereignty was not adequate.
Arabs must be sovereign everywhere; Jews nowhere.

The substitution of the 'Palestinian' for the 'Arab' image thus had confusing
effects on those sections of opinion which tended to give their support to
the victims rather than to the survivors of history. Many who had felt a sense of
chivalry in supporting an embattled Israel against Arabs now found that their
sentiment was better served by supporting the down-trodden Palestinians
against a victorious Israel. The anti-establishment current is strong in contemporary culture. It was now flowing away from the victor and towards the
defeated. Israel was transformed from David into Goliath overnight. It had
committed the dark sin of survival.

In the summer debate of 1967, the United Nations had declined to denounce
Israel at the behest of Egypt for having had the temerity to exist. When the
international discussion was resumed in October the approach was serious
and pragmatic. For one thing it was held in the Security Council, not in the
General Assembly. All United Nations discussions are subject to the disease of

constant publicity, which is particularly lurid when the conflict is as dramatic as this one had become. But in the Security Council, with its fifteen members, there are more barriers against demagogy and prejudice than in the 130 member General Assembly. The veto power acts as a deterrent to the more extreme absurdities; and the general aim is to secure the consensus of all the Major Powers. Israel could feel that a resolution weighted heavily against it would be opposed by the United States; and that even if it were adopted without American consent, it would lack compelling political force. But Israel did not have to rely on Washington alone. There were several other members, including the United Kingdom, Canada, Denmark and two Latin American states, which had opposed the Soviet proposals for immediate withdrawal without the establishment of peace. The resolution adopted by the Arab Summit Conference at Khartoum in September had alienated world opinion without intimidating it. When the Security Council debate got under way, the major objective was to formulate a set of principles on the basis of which a UN representative could assist the parties in arriving at agreement.

When the United States representative, Ambassador Goldberg, took the floor on 15 November, it was plain that Israel had achieved a major breakthrough. For the first time a Major Power advocated not only a revolution in the political relations between Israel and the Arab states, but also a doctrine of possible territorial change. Analyzing the boundary question with juridical precision, the United States delegate presented the Security Council with the singular nature of the territorial situation in the Middle East. He pointed out that there had never been agreement on any lines as the permanent territorial boundaries between states; that the armistice demarcation lines of 1949 had been specifically defined by the signatories as provisional lines based on purely military considerations; and that according to the Armistice Agreements they could be revised in the transition to peace. He pointed out that neither the armistice demarcation lines in force on 4 June 1967 nor the cease-fire lines that emerged from Israel's victory could be regarded as permanent territorial boundaries: 'Since such boundaries do not exist, they have to be established by the parties as part of the peace-making process.'

When the British delegation came to formulate a proposal for the Security Council consensus, its draft was based strongly on the need for innovation. It made a preambular reference to the principle of 'the non-admissability of the acquisition of territory by force', but it said nothing about a need to return to the armistice lines, and it did not rule out the determination of new boundaries by agreement. The draft presented by the United Kingdom on 22 November called primarily for the establishment of a just and lasting peace to be based on

Participants in the annual Three-Day March pass along the walls of the Old City of Jerusalem. The march attracts people from every walk of life and from all over the world

two principles: withdrawal from occupied territories and the renunciation of all forms of belligerency, blockade or organized warfare. Attempts by the Soviet Union and the Arabs to secure a provision for withdrawal from 'all the territories' were resisted by the original supporters and sponsors of the draft. Not only were the dimensions of the withdrawal left unspecified; it was also stated that peace included 'the right to live in peace within secure and recognized boundaries'. For Israel there was the further safeguard that the objective of the UN's representative would be to 'promote agreement' between Israel and the Arab states to achieve a mutually acceptable settlement. Thus the principle of an externally imposed solution had definitely been ruled out.

The Security Council resolution was necessarily ambivalent as a result of the need to secure the support both of the United States and the Soviet Union, as well as the acquiescence of the Arab states and Israel; but it marked some progress for Israel in three directions. First, withdrawal was conditionally linked to the establishment of peace. Second, the peace would have to include the establishment of secure and recognized boundaries. Third, the settlement would have to be the subject of agreement, not of external adjudication.

The question whether the Security Council's resolution of 22 November 1967 authorized territorial revision was to be the subject of unceasing discussion in the months and years ahead. Two years later, on 9 December 1969, the American Secretary of State, William Rogers, whose government had invented the term 'secure and recognized boundaries', said:

The boundaries from which the 1967 war began were established in the 1949 Armistice Agreements and have defined the areas of national jurisdiction in the Middle East for twenty years. Those boundaries were armistice lines, not final political borders. The rights, claims and positions of the parties in an ultimate peaceful settlement were reserved by the Armistice Agreements. The Security Council resolution neither endorses nor precludes those armistice lines as the definitive political boundaries.

As the British Government had sponsored the resolution, special weight was attached to its interpretation of the territorial provisions. In the House of Commons late in 1968, the Foreign Secretary, Michael Stuart, made it clear that the withdrawal envisaged by the resolution would not be from 'all the territories' but only from those which lay beyond whatever boundaries were agreed upon between the parties under the peace. He pointed out that the omission of the word 'all' before the word territories had been 'deliberate'.

U Thant had appointed as his representative for the Middle East, the Swedish Ambassador to Moscow, Dr Gunnar Jarring, who set out for the area at the

Golda Meir, Prime Minister since 1969, has led the government
and the nation through the trials of attempting to achieve a
meaningful and lasting peace settlement for the Middle East

end of December 1967. Dr Jarring established his headquarters in Cyprus and embarked with persistence on what seemed an endless round of political talks in Cairo, Amman and Jerusalem, with visits from time to time to Beirut and New York. Between December 1967 to December 1968, he visited Jerusalem twenty-two times for meetings with the Foreign Minister. The position that he heard from Israel was that in order to achieve a peaceful settlement, the principle of agreement had to find full expression; and agreement on all the elements contained in the resolution could be reached through negotiations between the parties concerned. Israel, therefore, suggested that Dr Jarring convene representatives of the respective governments. It also presented an 'Agenda for Peace' covering the political and territorial problems which would have to be discussed during the negotiations. Jordan and Egypt rejected these propositions. They wanted neither negotiation nor detailed discussion. Their case was that before anything else could be done Israel must withdraw its forces. Between March and May 1968 Dr Jarring made a purposeful attempt to bring about a meeting of the parties under his chairmanship, along the procedural lines that had been followed in the Rhodes armistice negotiations in 1949. This proposal was rejected emphatically by Egypt in March 1968 and more tentatively by Jordan which, whatever its own views were, felt it necessary to follow Egypt's lead. In the absence of any direct contact under Jarring's auspices, the mission degenerated into a public exchange of positions, which only served to emphasize the wide gap between Arab and Israeli policies. The Egyptian position was defined by Nasser on 23 July 1968: 'The following principles of Egyptian policy are immutable: no negotiations with Israel; no peace with Israel; no recognition of Israel; no transactions will be made at the expense of the Palestine territories or the Palestine people.'

The Egyptian case was that Israel should simply withdraw and then take part in a discussion about peace. The Israeli policy was set out by the Foreign Minister in an address to the General Assembly of the United Nations on 8 October 1968. The main elements were: the establishment of peace; the establishment of secure and recognized borders by mutual agreement; a special status for the Holy Places in Jerusalem; a declared policy for regarding the conflict as permanently ended. It was clear in this statement, as would be more specifically stated ten months later, that the Israeli forces would withdraw from the cease-fire lines to whatever boundaries were fixed by negotiation and agreement with the Arab states. In April 1969 Dr Jarring again took the temperature of the rival positions by asking for specific replies to a questionnaire. It was evident that Egypt and Jordan, on the one hand and Israel, on the other, remained as far apart as when the mission had begun.

Dr Jarring now ceased his regular visits to the Middle Eastern capitals. In the meantime, the United States had agreed to join with the Soviet Union, Britain and France in Four Power discussions at the United Nations. It seemed to be no easier to arrive at agreement between the United States and the Soviet Union than to obtain it between Israel and Egypt. The Soviet Union identified itself blindly with the Arab position, while the United States was not similarly tied to all the Israeli positions. On the territorial issue it clearly envisaged less substantive revision of the previous lines than Israel thought essential for its security. On the other hand, it was firm on three major principles: there should be no withdrawal from the cease-fire lines until peace was established; the peace would have to be agreed upon between the parties and not imposed from outside; and there would have to be a negotiation of the boundary and not a mere restoration of the previous armistice lines.

By the summer of 1969 the work of the Four Powers was going forward under the unpromising accompaniment of thunderous battles; for in March of that year President Nasser had openly repudiated the cease-fire and embarked on what he called a 'war of attrition'. While battles between Egyptian artillery and the Israeli air force raged almost daily across the Suez Canal, a parallel campaign of violence was being launched from the east across the Jordan River and from the Golan Heights. And even when armies were not in movement, persistent raids by El Fatah and other terrorist organizations kept the fires burning. Nasser was clearly placing his chief reliance on military success and his secondary hope on a solution to be imposed by the Great Powers. The situation on the eve of the cease-fire in August 1970 was closer to the renewal of major war than to progress towards permanent peace.

It became fashionable in later years to say that on the morrow of victory everybody in Israel had believed that peace was near. This is not my recollection, nor do the records bear it out. Israel had occupied no Arab capitals; overthrown no régimes. She could not, like the victorious allies in the Second World War, bring the vanquished leaders to railway compartments or the decks of aircraft carriers and instruct them to sign whatever her will or interests dictated. She could, if necessary, impose her own security on them; but she could not impose peace. Here they still had an effective veto power. In the summer of 1967 there was more fear of international pressure for a return to the old lines than serious hope of a negotiated peace.

And yet the hope of peace, if still qualified, was greater than before. Israel had cards to play. She had something in her possession that her neighbours wanted very much. She could give them significant restitution of territory if they would give her peace, security and a negotiated and permanent territorial structure.

That Arab-Israel relations might not always be impossibly savage first dawned on Israel in the light of contacts with the Arabs in the administered territories. By the middle of 1969 most industrial enterprises in the West Bank were in full operation. Israeli exports were pouring into the administered territories, while merchandise from these territories to countries outside the region flourished with Israel's encouragement. The Israeli administration cooperated with the United Nations Relief and Works Agency to serve the needs of the Arab refugees. The mutual currents of commerce and movement between Israelis and Palestinian Arabs had deep symbolic effects. Above the slogans of hostility and revenge the spectacle of thousands of Israelis and West Bank Arabs in normal and fruitful contact proclaimed a fundamental community of interest. More than anything else this new reality gave the idea of peace a tangible incarnation.

But there were also negative impulses at work. While farmers and workers gained much from the new stream of contact, the Arab intelligentsia, professionals and former Jordanian officials found themselves deprived of their previous authority. The Arab intellectuals formed a background of sullen discontent. Far graver were the activities of El Fatah and other terrorist organizations which were sharply alarmed by the prospect that peace might evolve through coexistence between two peoples whom the 1948 war had separated and the 1967 conflict had brought together. Demonstrations, terrorist attacks, strikes and murders became frequent. The Israeli response included curfews and occasional punitive destruction of terrorist hide-outs. In spite of some ugly clamour in parts of the Israeli press, the death penalty was avoided. El Fatah and other terrorist organizations, being unwelcome in the administered areas, turned the brunt of their assault towards the pre-1967 Israel territory. Their casualties were high and their rate of capture higher. They had been able to create some centres of physical insecurity in the few parts of Israel which were accessible to attack from across a cease-fire line, principally in the Jordan Valley between Beisan and the Sea of Galilee, and later in the Israeli townships close to the Lebanese border. Some Israeli reactions, such as that against the village of Karameh on 21 March 1968, caused unexpected Israeli casualties and abrasive international reactions. But it soon became evident that Israel's existence could not be menaced by terrorist movements. The threat was not to Israel as a state, but to individual Israelis whose tragic lot put them in the way of the mortar shell or bomb thrown into bus stations, markets, agricultural villages and university cafeterias. The El Fatah movement struck progressive revolutionary attitudes in its propaganda; on the ground it took discreet care to insure that its opponent should be school children in buses, students on university campuses and workers and shoppers in supermarkets. El Fatah and the Palestine Liberation Organization had a passion for fighting vulnerable moving targets, such as travellers in unarmed aircraft.

The Palestinian terrorist movements were acting under the pretence that their position was analogous to that of the Mau Mau in Kenya or the FLN in Algeria. This was fallacious. The FLN had expelled the French from Algeria the Mau Mau had helped to get Britain out of Kenya. They had not expelled the French from France or the British from the United Kingdom. In Israel the Palestinian organizations were trying to expel Israel from Israel. They were not operating against 'settlers' with their home country behind them, but against a recognized and deeply rooted nation which belonged nowhere else and which had no intention of ever being uprooted again. El Fatah stirred open revolt against the Jordanian régime and embroiled Lebanon with Israel. This was a tragic result, for Lebanese governments had managed to keep out of three Arab wars. Lebanon had a particular vocation which Israel had good reason to respect. It is, of course, a part of the Arab world; but it is also distinguished by unique links with Christendom and with Mediterranean civilization. In Lebanon itself many understood that what was at stake was the existence not of Israel but of Lebanon in its true and historic personality.

In the end it turned out that the El Fatah movement was not so much an instrument of war as an impediment to peace. Frustrated in their hopes of paralyzing Israeli life or creating permanent convulsion in the administered territories, El Fatah leaders sought more spectacular enterprises abroad. In 1969 and 1970 the capture and hijacking of aircraft and the explosion of bombs in Israeli offices kept them in the forefront of the news. Their cause was embraced by sections of the 'New Left' and by others who found respectable grounds for the new 'progressive' anti-Semitism, which acknowledges

During the civil war in Jordan between the Palestinian terrorists and the Jordanian Army, many terrorists sought refuge in Israel, the country they had vowed to destroy

the right of Jews to exist as individuals but considers·that the right to build a state in accordance with their own culture must be reserved for non-Jewish nations alone.

All the Palestinian organizations, and especially El Fatah, were active in the 'Palestine National Council' which assembled in Cairo in July 1968 in order to amend the Palestinian National Covenant which had originally been adopted in May 1964. The object was to codify the 'rights of the Palestinians' in a manner which excluded Israeli sovereignty from any part of the Middle East. The main principles set down in the covenant are:

In the Palestinian State only Jews who lived in Palestine before 1917 will be recognized as citizens (Article VI).

Only the Palestinian Arabs possess the right of self-determination and the entire country belongs to them (Articles IX and XXI).

Warfare against Israel is legal, whereas Israel's self-defence is illegal (Article XVIII).

In Article V the 'Palestinians' are defined as 'the Arab citizens who were living permanently in Palestine until 1947, whether they were expelled from there or remained. Whoever is born to a Palestinian Arab father after this date within Palestine or outside it is a Palestinian.' The draftsmen of the Palestine Arab Covenant were therefore willing to 'accept' a handful of Jews who could trace their Palestinian residence to 1917. In a more ambitious bid for external opinion, some in the Palestinian organizations were sometimes willing to compromise to the extent of 'accepting' those Jews who had been in the country before 1948. Since these had numbered only 650,000, the most 'moderate' Palestinian definition left about two million Jews in Israel to be 'disposed of' by expulsion, disenfranchisement or other methods on which speculation is unpleasant but not particularly difficult.

From the Palestinian organizations came two leaders whose names were to become celebrated outside the Arab world. One was Yasser Arafat, the El Fatah leader. He lacked dignity and eloquence, but he enjoyed the most precious advantage to which a politician can aspire – an insufferable predecessor. Compared with Shukeiry, he appeared to the relieved world as a serious, if somewhat fanatical man. There was much illusion in this picture, for on closer scrutiny he was quietly venomous. More monstrous was the leader of the Palestine Liberation Organization, Dr George Habash. His doctrines combined mediaeval Arab militance with modern Marxist phraseology. He scornfully rejected 'effeminate' compromises such as the Security Council Resolution of 1967, which was based on Israel's sovereignty and right of security and defended the action of his followers in setting fire to civilian aircraft on the ground or in the air with indiscriminate slaughter of men, women and children.

One day in March 1970, we stood before twenty coffins containing the symbolic remains of civilians murdered in a Swiss air plane by Dr Habash's gangsters. The fearful cries and tears of a hundred relatives, tortured by grief, went up in Jerusalem's air. We could feel the demoniacal doctor's presence gloating over us, and we could have no illusions about the fate which would befall us if 'Israel' were ever to become 'Palestine'. The same thought occurred to us as we saw our children burnt to death in a school bus at Avivim in May 1970 amidst sounds of joy from Dr Habash, and later still when twenty-six air travellers, mostly Puerto Ricans, were mowed down in a river of blood by a group of Japanese fanatics hired by the 'Palestine Liberation Organization' for an attack on Lod airport. A deadly evil was abroad in the world and, as in the 1930's, the Jewish people was the target of its rage.

By the early months of 1970 it had become obvious that in his 'war of attrition' Nasser was suffering more attrition than he could inflict. The result of the fighting across the Suez Canal was to leave Israel's positions intact, while the oil refineries and the inhabited areas of Ismailia, Suez and Port Taufiq were made uninhabitable and desolate. Nasser's choice was hard: he could solve his dilemma either by making peace or by maintaining his belligerency with Soviet aid. He opted for continuing the war, and Soviet involvement was invited and received. The SA-2 anti-aircraft missiles were followed by SA-3 missiles. Weapons of such electronic sophistication had never been seen in the Middle East before, and their dispatch to Egypt was accompanied by the arrival of thousands of Soviet advisers, technicians and military personnel.

In April 1970 an even more ominous development provoked a shock across the world. Soviet pilots took over expanding responsibilities for Egyptian air action. The prospect of hostile contact between Israeli and Soviet forces raised international apprehension to a high peak. The United States, in particular, faced a dilemma. If it abandoned Israel to the mercies of the Soviet Union, the credibility of the Americans' commitments to other states in the world would be undermined. Since American security depended on the deterrent effect of her alliances and partnership, Israel's peace and security had become a condition of the security and peace of many nations, and especially of the United States. This theme came to growing recognition in the statements and policy of President Nixon. He enunciated the doctrine of a balance of strength and moved to reinforce Israel's military power. Late in 1970 he asked the United States Congress for an appropriation of $500 million, and then of

$300 million, to finance a part of the arms and military equipment which the United States had made available to Israel that year.

The choices posed for the United States by Soviet involvement were so unattractive that Washington made every effort to blunt their edge. To abandon responsibility for Israel would be unthinkable; yet to exercise it would invite a Great Power confrontation. Only if the fighting across the Canal ceased would there be relief from the choice. The restoration of the cease-fire had thus become a major international objective. In the summer of 1970 the escalating conflict was brought to a halt through a successful diplomatic initiative by the United States. On 19 June American Secretary of State Rogers approached Israel, Jordan and the United Arab Republic with a three-point proposal. They were invited to appoint representatives to confer through Ambassador Jarring on the establishment of a just and lasting peace; to indicate their acceptance of the Security Council's Resolution of 1967; and to observe the Security Council's 1967 cease-fire resolution for at least ninety days.

This initiative set new currents moving across the whole Middle Eastern scene. On one side were the fundamentalists who opposed any negotiations with Israel or recognition of her existence. On the other side were those who grudgingly understood that the old slogans had faded and that the Middle East would never have a destiny which did not include Israel. Of the neighbouring countries, Syria maintained intransigence, supported by more distant Arab states whose remoteness from the scene enabled them to deploy their valour without much risk. But Egypt and Jordan could less afford such rigid attitudes.

In considering his response, President Nasser must have known that his war of attrition and siege had failed. He had not been able to persuade the United States to break the military balance by placing an embargo on Israel while Soviet arms continued to flow into the Arab states. Israel's Phantom air fleet was a major element in the regional military balance. The squadrons of Phantoms, whose purchase had been negotiated by Prime Minister Eshkol with President Johnson in 1968, had later been the subject of talks between President Nixon and Prime Minister Golda Meir. In September 1969 the air-craft had begun to arrive, and a few months later they were playing a decisive part in repelling the Egyptian artillery assault and inflicting retaliatory blows deep in Egyptian territory.

Egypt and Jordan accepted the American initiative. It was not out of military weakness that the Israeli Government came to consider its response. Acceptance of the American initiative would be difficult; it would involve the compromise of principles which had been tenaciously upheld in Israeli policy up to that time. The proposed negotiation would be indirect, at least in its first phrase; and the cease-fire was to be temporary, with the result that every prolongation of it might have to be bought by concession to Arab pressure. These disadvantages, however, were outweighed in the minds of the majority by the urgent necessity to set a dialogue afoot. And the Israeli Cabinet could not ignore the effects of its response on its relations with the United States. For the first time in Israel's history, a Major Power was dedicated to the maintenance of its strength, as well as to the political deterrence of external intervention. A negative response by Israel would not only be interpreted in much of the world as a retreat from a traditional readiness to negotiate; it would also imperil the understanding on the basis of which American reinforcement was flowing in. In addition, the cease-fire, however temporary, had important benefits not only for Egypt but also for Israel, where the daily toll of loss was arousing poignant echoes. Accordingly, on 4 August 1970, the Israeli Cabinet accepted the American initiative and agreed to nominate representatives to meet under Ambassador Jarring's auspices and discuss the establishment of a just and lasting peace in accordance with the Security Council resolution.

This decision amounted to a rejection of the faith which had been maintained with consistency and talent by the Herut leader Menachem Begin and his colleagues. For them a peace treaty was only acceptable if it were clear in advance that all the territory in Israel's hands must be retained, at least in the area west of the Jordan. Most Israelis doubted if peace could be achieved without any territorial compromise. Nor did they like the prospect that Israel would no longer be a predominantly Jewish state, but a bi-national entity with a dissident Arab population of 1,500,000 liable to increase in relative strength through the intensity of the birth-rate. The decision of 4 August 1970 accepting the American proposal raised deep conflicts of principle which the Israeli

Menachem Begin, former head of the IZL and leader of the opposition Gahal Party, which left the Cabinet after Israel accepted the US peace-initiative proposal in August 1970

Government had not faced since 1967. Begin led his group of six Ministers out of the coalition, took his seat on the opposition bench, and brought the memorable period of the great coalition to an end.

In August 1970 some observers wondered if the Middle East was on the eve of a new hope. Instead of military escalation and political deadlock, Israel and her principal neighbours had come to agreement on three points. There was a cease-fire with a military standstill; a common formulation of the principles on which peace negotiations should be based; and an agreed procedural framework. Nobody was simple-minded enough to believe that these omens were enough to herald a final peace. The basic divergence between the parties remained acute. Israel demanded complete peace with substantial but not total withdrawal; the Arab states demanded total withdrawal without total peace.

Indeed, the modest hopes of the summer were soon eclipsed. On the morrow of the cease-fire agreement Egypt began to move up missiles into zones where their presence was forbidden by the accord. It is certain that this violation was endorsed by the Soviet Union. Cairo had exploited Israel's acceptance of the cease-fire to gain an illicit military advantage. Israel was also concerned with the political and psychological implications of the Egyptian move. The question was asked in Jerusalem whether any purpose would be served by negotiating a new accord with Egypt when an existing agreement was being flagrantly torn up. The credibility of Egypt as a negotiating partner had been brought into question. The Israeli Cabinet unanimously decided to suspend participation in talks with Egypt until the previous situation west of the cease-fire line was restored. In parallel and sympathetic action, the United States called on the Soviet Union for 'rectification' of the violated status in the stand-still zone. Washington not only refrained from pressing Israel to negotiate under intimidatory conditions; it expedited and increased arms supplies to Israel in an effort to restore the equilibrium. In September 1970, when Prime Minister Meir visited President Nixon in Washington, the common interests and views of the two countries were given strong emphasis. Moscow and Cairo had inadvertently helped to draw Washington and Jerusalem closer together, although American and Israeli policies were still not identical.

In the last few months of 1970 dramatic changes succeeded each other at a rate unusual even in the history of the Middle East. A violent civil war erupted in Jordan, where the Arab terrorist movements, led by El Fatah, attempted to gain control of the kingdom. Unable to resist the counter-attack of King Hussein's army, the terrorists called upon Syria for aid. In the third week of

September 1970, the Syrian forces invaded Jordan in the area of Irbid. It seemed likely that they would move southwards to overthrow the Jordanian Government and install a régime composed of the terrorists and their supporters. This would, of course, have aggravated Israel's security position; but it would also have established a new centre of Soviet power in a part of the the Arab world where Western influence had always been predominant. This would have been an unacceptable change of the international equilibrium from the viewpoint of the United States. Israel and the United States, without taking any military action, managed to convey to Syria and the Soviet Union their view that an attempt to take over Jordan might well have grave results. These warnings, together with unexpectedly effective counter-attacks by King Hussein's air force, caused the Syrian troops to retire without much saving of face. The Jordan Government had come successfully out of its ordeal and the reputation, as well as the strength, of the terrorist organizations was sharply diminished.

The Arab heads of government now embarked on the intense series of meetings by which they always register their sense of crisis. On 28 September 1970, a day or so after a conference of Arab leaders called to heal the breach between Syria and Jordan, President Nasser was overcome with fatigue and succumbed to a heart attack. The news of his passing cast the Egyptian people and the whole Arab world into a shock of grief. There was a strange reaction in Israel, which had got used to its adversary and had hardly known what life was like without him. It was believed that a new leadership might possibly, but not inevitably, open out new prospects. Gamal Abdul Nasser had begun his career of leadership in 1952 amid sympathies which had gripped most countries in the world, including Israel. His slogans of national liberation, economic development and a nationalized Suez Canal serving the international interest had seemed to augur a new epoch in Arab political leadership. All these high aims, however, were frustrated by his implacable hostility towards Israel. Since he could not express this rancour effectively with his unaided force, he had come increasingly under the control and, eventually, the military occupation of the Soviet Union. He had banished the traditional dominations of Britain and France only to let in the presence of a more powerful and tenacious imperialism. War against Israel had also diverted Nasser from his social aims. In twenty-two years the Middle Eastern states were to spend $20 billion on war. The region could not simultaneously mobilize resources both for this kind of waste and for economic development. Israel alone, with a sophisticated economy and constant partnership with world Jewry, had been able to combine a burden of defence with an unceasing momentum of development.

The truth is that by emphasizing the anti-Israel element in his programme, Nasser had condemned his better ambitions to failure. But beyond this frustration he was the author of an achievement which could not be assessed in rational terms. No Arab leader in his generation, and few in Arab history, had cast so strong a spell over millions in his own country and in the Arab domain beyond. After every failure and defeat his popularity seemed to rise. He had assumed a symbolic dimension that placed him beyond the necessity to succeed. The Arab people granted him an indulgence which politicians hardly ever receive; they forgave him, and even cherished him the more, for having lost a war of his own making. When the passion of grief began to wane it seemed as if a new opportunity might eventually spring out of the transition in leadership. Nasser's successor as President, Anwar Sadat, could never hope to emulate him in the arenas of international diplomacy. It was possible that he might not even try; but there seemed to stretch before him and his colleagues a chance of competing with the dead leader in the social and economic tasks which Nasser had neglected. For the first time since the early 1950's, cautious voices were heard in Egypt hinting that the priority of national concern should be given not to war with Israel, but to the battle against the backwardness which had condemned the Egyptian people to poverty and weakness.

As 1970 went by it would become apparent whether dialogue had replaced polemics or whether the world must resign itself to a seemingly endless Middle Eastern deadlock punctuated by bursts of fighting. Early that year the Israel Government invited Dr Jarring to Jerusalem and set out the principles by which peace could be promoted and maintained. The Egyptian response was unyielding, but so long as the dialogue continued, hope was not dead. A military solution was clearly beyond attainment: the chance existed that by sheer elimination of alternatives Arab leadership would come to understand the compulsions of a future to be shared with Israel in peace.

Nineteen sixty-seven was a revolutionary year not only for Israel but for the Jewish people everywhere. The success of Israel's arms and the Arab failure to win a political victory in the international arena gave all Jews a consoling idea of their place in history. In the United States thousands came out of a timid anonymity to proclaim their association with the Jewish fate. Many assimilated Jews in the West who had always been at pains to stress the distance between them and Israel suddenly made lavish contributions to the organizations which expressed solidarity with Israel. There was a kind of Jewish 'vogue' in large metropolitan centres in the West; to be identified with

Jewish destiny was now a badge of prestige. 'It's in to be Jewish' ran a popular night-club tune. Immigration of young Western Jews to Israel, although still small, showed a sharp relative increase.

The feeling that Jewish identity was, after all, a matter of great significance burst with special force on the oppressed Jewish communities of the world. In the Soviet Union Jewish life was now charged with tension. The drab, dark air in which Soviet Jewry lived contrasted with the strength and pride which were now characteristic of Jewish life elsewhere. In addition, Soviet Jews lived in the country whose government had become the spearhead of hostility to Israel's security and, therefore, to Jewish preservation.

At the beginning of 1971 there were some three million Jews in the Soviet Union. In formal terms they were regarded as a separate and recognized nationality; but none of the privileges and rights of other national groups were enjoyed by them. Jewish schools and theatres did not exist; and the only organized expression of Jewish identity was to be found in the one hundred synagogues which still survived. There was no central religious community and no institutions to give the dispersed religious congregations a co-ordinated identity. Matzot could rarely be bought for Passover, and anything written in Hebrew was considered hostile to the Soviet Union, as if a state of original sin resided in the language itself. The thin boundary between anti-Zionism and anti-Semitic prejudice was breached at many points. In his book *Ostorozhno–sionism* ('Careful–Zionism'), published in 1969 by the Political Literature Publishing House of Moscow, Yuri Ivanov designated 'the international Jewish bourgeoisie' and the 'ruling circles of Israel' as Enemy Number One. The rest of this tract was full of expressions taken directly from *The Protocols of the Elders of Zion*. The official Soviet press and radio lavished their praise on this book. Trials for 'economic crimes', by coincidence, always seemed to concern Jewish embezzlers. Everything that Jews held up to pride and emulation, either in their historic past or in their present reality, was the subject of official calumny.

None of this was new. The innovation after 1967 was not in Soviet policy, but in Jewish reaction to it. The old fatalism and docility had given way to a rebellious courage. Thousands crowded into Moscow's Great Synagogue during the High Holidays. It is certain that for most of these the attraction lay not in religious ceremony but in the opportunity to exchange a warm but silent solidarity with other Jews. Soviet Jews also took heart from a growing international interest in their cause. By 1970 the problem had emerged from underground and stood irrevocably on the international agenda. A moving expression of Soviet Jewish sentiment came in November 1969, when eighteen

Jewish families from Soviet Georgia published a petition to the United Nations Human Rights Commission. Their plea was formulated with dignity and authentic passion. They emphasized that they felt no hostility to the Soviet Union. They wished it well. But historic memory and national emotion made them part of another people whose homeland was far away. They asked for nothing except to join that people in its era of freedom. They said that a voice of history spoke to them from six million graves.

Expressions of sympathy for this moving document came from all over the world. In Jerusalem the Knesset devoted special sessions to the expression of solidarity with Soviet Jews. This sentiment came to a head in more sombre circumstances when, on Christmas day 1970, news was published of two death sentences and harsh judgements of imprisonment passed on nine Jews alleged to have planned the hijacking of a Soviet aircraft from Leningrad to Finland, with the aim of subsequently immigrating to Israel. The defendants were not accused of having performed this crime, but only of having intended it. They had not inflicted harm on any human being or done injury to any property. In these conditions the secret trial and savage sentences sent a shock of protest throughout the world. Governments, parliaments, heads of religious organizations, trade unions, writers and even Communist parties in Europe urged the commutation of the sentences and a more realistic acceptance of the Jewish right to leave the Soviet Union. The volume of protest was so intense that the Soviet authorities found it expedient to yield. The harsher sentences were commuted; but the Soviet predicament was not at an end. What had been kindled in world opinion was not only a humanitarian concern for victims of judicial cruelty, but a sense that the national sentiment of Soviet Jews was beyond suppression.

Some hundreds of Soviet Jews had arrived in Israel since the suspension of exit in 1967. Western statesmen rarely visited Moscow without pointing out that a revised Soviet policy towards the Jews was essential if the Soviet Union were to improve its relations with the non-Soviet world. The strength of Jewish persistence has never had a more vivid illustration than in the growth of the movement for the emancipation of Soviet Jews. After all, fifty-four years had passed since the Communist régime was established. For nearly all that time the expression of Jewish cultural and national identity had been suppressed. Two generations had grown up within the assumptions and dogmas of the Communist revolution which sought to deny Soviet Jews the quality of nationhood. The Zionist idea had never won a greater victory than in that community, for nowhere else had it been called upon to rise above so many circumstances calculated to bring about its eclipse.

A crack appears in the hitherto almost impenetrable wall surrounding Soviet Jewry. Georgian immigrants disembarking from an El Al plane at Lydda airport

By the end of 1970, the question what to do with Soviet Jews stood high among the predicaments of Soviet policy. To keep them imprisoned would mean continual repression with adverse effects on world opinion. To let them all go would be to compromise the idea of a closed society and put a heavy strain on Soviet-Arab relations. A middle course was taken. Enough satisfaction was given to the aspirations of Soviet Jewry to take some steam out of the pressure; yet not enough was done to violate the 'closed society' or pose a serious difficulty for Soviet-Arab relations. Nevertheless, many thousands of Soviet Jews reached Israel in 1971 and 1972. One of the most cherished ambitions of Israel was coming to fulfilment.

The period after 1967 was tragic for the small Jewish communities that had lingered on in Arab countries. Some of the great communities had solved the problem of their alienation from Arab society by immigrating to Israel – from Iraq and Yemen during the early 1950's and from Egypt in the crisis after the 1956 Sinai Campaign. The few thousand who had been left behind were the target of Arab hostility that did little to distinguish between antagonism to Israel and comprehensive anti-Semitism. The Arabs argued that Zionism was the central movement in Jewry; therefore their opposition to Zionism meant, in effect, the suppression of all efforts to express Jewish identity.

Early in 1969 the cause of the Jews in Arab lands seized the world's attention when nine Iraqi Jews were publicly hanged in circumstances of squalid brutality in a place called 'Independence Square' in Baghdad. The international protest was deep and strong. Hundreds of Egyptian Jews had been held in concentration camps in the sequel to the 1967 war, while the Jews of Syria were harried and persecuted with the special ferocity which Syrian governments had always shown in their external and internal policies. But the Iraqi hangings exceeded all other outrages, and late in 1969 an influential committee, under the Presidency of Alain Poher, the President of the French Senate and a former candidate for the Presidency, with the participation of many leaders of science, letters and world opinion, came together in Paris to raise the cry 'Let my people go'. There was some success in moving the Egyptian Government to allow detainees to leave; and later Jews contrived to get out of Iraq. In Syria, however, Jewish distress continued with only trivial abatement in 1972. Yet world opinion was not entirely impotent. If before 1967 the cause of these tiny communities had seemed lost and forgotten, thereafter there was hope that their liberation might only be a question of time.

Many of the newspaper headlines about Israel from 1967 onward dealt, as was natural, with armed conflict and political struggle. The prominence given to war and diplomacy obscured what could well turn out to be a more significant development. The minimal hope of Israel's Arab adversaries was that even if they won no decisive military or political victory, they could keep Israel cut off from international support, ostracized and boycotted in the world community. The danger was real; an Israel isolated from the main stream of international life would have had great difficulty in surviving. It would certainly have lost its special character. It was important to prove that in conditions of siege Israel could not only survive, but grow. If Israel had been so obsessed and paralyzed by neighbouring hostility as to do nothing except to ensure its military defence, it would have ceased to be Israel in the deeper sense of the term. The characteristic dynamic of Israeli life is one of constant growth. An Israel that is not cultivating, planting, sowing, building, establishing rural and urban settlements, broadening its educational structure, creating new resources in science and in technology would have lost the élan which gave it a special quality in the life of its age. After five years of attempted siege it seemed that success had been achieved. Israel had managed to grow at a rate which made the word 'siege' invalid as a description of its condition. Between 1967 and 1972 the Jewish population had risen from 2,383,600 to 2,650,000; exports had grown from $554,453,000 to over $1 billion; the gross national product which had been IL 11,972 million in 1967, had become IL 22 million in 1971. In military strength Israel was a more impressive force than that which had displayed triumphant qualities in 1967. The links of the Jewish community with Israel were more passionate; and the measure in which Israel was not sundered from the rest of the world could be gathered from the fact that 1972 was a peak year in tourism and pilgrimage:

some 750,000 people visited Israel, fifty per cent of whom were non-Jews. It seemed that nothing could separate Israel from its sources of support in the Jewish world. The nation's democratic institutions continued to work with characteristic turbulence, and the rhythm of social advance was intense. This was perhaps Israel's most notable achievement in the post-war years. It had been a fighting nation; but it had not become a warrior state. As they looked over their frontiers, the Arab governments, in their cooler moments, must have understood that they were having little impact on the processes which gave Israel added strength from year to year.

A new phase in the country's leadership had opened with the death of Levi Eshkol in February 1969. His calm temperament contrasted strongly with the spectacular movements which he was called upon to direct and control. Many leaders in Zionism and Jewry had been more flamboyant and colourful; but none had been called to a responsibility equal to his, and none in his life-time had celebrated such vast transformations. He had brought about unity in the labour movement, an achievement which had eluded his more eminent predecessor; he had been at the helm during Israel's most spectacular military success; and he had seen his nation reunited in Jerusalem with the cradle of its birth. After the war there had come nearly two years of political struggle which ended with Israel's positions intact and the hope of a more secure future unimpaired. His adversaries and rivals found it hard to forgive him for his success. He never pretended that he had been the unique agent of all these events; but it is certain that if there had been failure the responsibility would have been laid at his door. His tolerant captaincy was congenial to the free interplay of diverse forces. His revulsion from excessive authoritarianism brought out the latent energies in the community. His temper expanded in an atmosphere of harmony. He had little time or talent for abstract slogans; his gnarled farmer's hands were firmly plunged in the soil of practical achievement. The developing economy of which he and the Finance Minister, Pinchas Sapir, had been the main architects was the basis on which Israel's military strength and political stability had been erected. When he died suddenly in February 1969, the Jewish world felt that a gentle presence had been borne away, and the appreciation of his qualities grew stronger as the months rolled on.

There was the danger of a disruptive combat for leadership. It had been widely assumed that the Labour Party would be torn by a contest between the Minister of Defence, Moshe Dayan, and the Minister of Labour, later to be Deputy Prime Minister, Yigal Allon. Each of these had made his mark in

Israel's military contests before turning their energies to the political arena. Yet many doubted whether the issue was really drawn between them alone. The Israel Labour Party, after all, was a federation with its central bulk in the Mapai Party, and with two smaller wings formed by those who had seceded from it during the past two decades. Allon belonged to the Achdut Ha'avodah group, which was clearly a minority within the Labour camp, and Dayan represented the Rafi Party, which, despite Ben Gurion's leadership and his own participation, had secured only ten out of 120 Knesset seats at the height of its struggle for power. The main body of the party, solid, cautious, pragmatic, seemed little disposed to bequeath its inheritance to either of the groups which had been its opponents and rivals only a few years before. Within a few weeks of Eshkol's death, the problem of national and party leadership was solved through the election as Prime Minister of Golda Meir, who had resigned from the Foreign Ministry for reasons of health a few years before. The weight of her new responsibilities seemed to liberate new energies within her. Israel was thus endowed with a leadership rich in domestic authority and international prestige. Mrs Meir's defiant personality gave the nation's military and political struggle a strong dimension. Her first disappointment was the liquidation of the national coalition, but she won a vote of confidence from the electorate in November 1969 and at the beginning of 1971 her Cabinet still had a strong majority.

The new Cabinet held the middle ground. It tried to be tenacious but not dogmatic. The Prime Minister, like her predecessors, did not think that Israel's territorial structure was its only important attribute. She was not a romantic territorialist; the maintenance of Israel's Jewish character appealed to her more than anything else. It was under her leadership that Israel first enunciated, in clear terms, a willingness to accept the principle of withdrawal to secure, recognized and agreed boundaries. But her government was resolved not to be 'sold short' on its security. From December 1969 it resolutely opposed a plan conceived by its greatest friend – the United States – which would have limited it to mere 'unsubstantial' changes in the former lines with Jordan and to no change at all in the border with Egypt.

The future of the territories was still the main theme of internal controversy. The 'Greater Israel' movement, established soon after the 1967 war, exercised pressure for retaining all the territories, and especially the whole area of western Palestine. The election results in 1969 gave the Labour Alignment a majority for its more selective approach to the boundary issue. Its platform indicated that Israel would go into peace discussions with the power to focus on certain critical points, such as the Golan Heights, Sharm el-Sheikh and the approaches thereto, Gaza and on a formula for maintaining the Jordan River as a 'security boundary' without necessarily adding the populated Arab areas to Israel. This list of Israeli negotiating positions was not presented as an ultimatum; it left the bulk of the territories in Sinai and the West Bank unaffected by an Israeli negotiating directive. In March 1971 Mrs Meir told the London *Times* that she and her colleagues did not support the insistence of Gahal and the religious parties on retaining the whole of the territory west of the Jordan in a peace settlement.

The fear that Israel might lose its specific cultural and national personality was among the motives which deterred many Israelis from endorsing the 'Greater Israel' programme, which would have turned Israel within a generation or two into something like an Arab state with an influential Jewish community. Partition had been upheld by its supporters since 1937 not only as a necessary political compromise, but as a defence of Israel's nationhood against the overwhelming demographic weight of the Arab environment. There was wide support for a formula devised by the Deputy Prime Minister, Yigal Allon, for a solution of the Israel-Jordanian-Palestinian problem. Allon's plan called for territorial changes which would, for the most part, be in the unpopulated Jordan Valley area, leaving the majority of the Palestinians in Judea and Samaria to be reunited with an Arab sovereignty east of the Jordan. Even this compromise was rejected by the Arabs, so that it never came to a vote in the Israeli Cabinet or Knesset; but there was strong evidence to suggest that this principle would carry great support if Arab consent could be secured.

Israel's definition of policy in August 1970 had been designed to achieve three results: the restoration of the cease-fire on the Egyptian front; the improvement of the country's international relations, especially with the United States; and a renewed exploration of the prospect for a peace settlement within the framework of the Jarring mission. As they surveyed the situation in the summer of 1972, Israelis could feel confident that the first two aims had been fulfilled. Apart from an occasional air skirmish, there were no clashes between Egyptian and Israeli forces after August 1970. President Sadat was always breathing dire threats of imminent war, but he usually had the courage and maturity to avoid repeating the errors of rash action and over-commitment which his predecessor had made in 1967.

In the atmosphere of a prolonged cease-fire, Israel's political position became less embattled. There was a remarkable florescence in her relations with the United States. As early as 1969 President Nixon had declared that the 'time was past when Great Powers used to dictate to smaller countries their future in which their vital interests are involved'. He defended the principle of non-

enforcement against Soviet and French pressure during Four Power consultations and in his 'Summit Meeting' with the Soviet Union in May 1972. His
administration, with the consent and support of both parties in the Congress,
moved to offset the Soviet rearmament of Egypt by abundant supplies of arms,
including Phantom aircraft, to Israel. In 1971 and 1972 the United States
Congress voted unprecedently large credits sought by President Nixon for
Israel in order to enable her to make the necessary purchases without economic
and financial ruin.

Israel's acceptance of the cease-fire and of the American peace initiative
brought relief in other sectors of its international relations. The attitude
of West European countries, other than France, had usually been respect-
ful of Israel's basic interests. For a year, between 1970 and 1971, a note
of reserve had crept in. Europe was also more vulnerable than America to
Arab economic pressure; and there was no Jewish community of sufficient
strength there to have an influence on political opinion. Fighting in the Suez
Canal area was more audible and ominous in European ears than in those of
more distant continents. In 1971 a French initiative among the six members
of the European Economic Community (France, Italy, West Germany,
Belgium, Holland and Luxembourg) nearly brought about a united position
in favour of complete withdrawal within the framework of a peace settlement.
Israel was able to recoup its position when the cease-fire proved its stability
and when most of the Foreign Ministers of the Community countries visited
Israel. Israel's declared readiness for territorial compromise was an essential
element in any understanding with Europe. In 1972 agreements on Berlin and
on the new European post-war structure seemed to add weight to two of Israel's
contentions: the substantive results of direct negotiation and the legitimacy of
territorial modifications in the transition from war to peace.

Israel was not markedly successful in its efforts to improve the French
approach, but it was able to ensure a more balanced attitude on the
part of other European states. Britain, which had refused to sell Chieftain
tanks to Israel in 1971, did not deny its intention to sell submarines in 1972.
Rumania, which was the only East European Communist country to avoid
breaking relations with Israel in June 1967, elevated its Legation to Embassy
status in 1969 and received an official visit by Prime Minister Meir in May
1972. The Organization of African States, in which Arabs and Moslems were
heavily represented, usually adopted hostile resolutions; but, with the excep-
tion of Uganda, none of them weakened its practical cooperation with Israel.
When four African Presidents visited Israel in November 1971, they issued
a report which paid tribute to Israel's desire for peace and showed a positive

Former West Bank residents return to visit their families and tour Israel in the summer of 1970 as part of the 'Open Bridges Policy', which also seeks to encourage commercial links over the Jordan River

attitude to some of its positions. Yet Egypt, as a member of the OAU and of the African family, could usually obtain anti-Israel resolutions in African Conferences, at which Arabs predominated and Israel was absent.

The fifth anniversary of the Six Day War was celebrated in Israel on 5 June 1972. The balance-sheet revealed a substantial improvement since 1970. Two years before there had been no cease-fire along the Suez Canal line; vast quantities of high explosives were being exchanged between Egyptian artillery and Israeli aircraft, with heavy human losses on both sides. The world had then lived under the daily nightmare of a globalization of the war through the involvement of Soviet personnel. Arab radicalism had been on the ascendant, especially during 1970, when the terrorist organizations carried out successful hijacking operations. Many across the world doubted whether Israel would be able to maintain its balance of strength in view of the question mark permanently poised over United States military supplies. There were those who thought that even if Israel held its political and military positions, it would not be unable to sustain a constant rate of growth.

Two years later the cease-fire had held firm except for sporadic encounters. Accordingly, the danger of Great Power military involvement had receded, especially after the Moscow Summit Conference. The terrorist organizations had suffered defeat in Jordan, a decline of their status in Lebanon and a lack of influence or activity in the administered areas and in Israel itself. There was also a decline in their resonance, and Arab governments no longer felt them-selves compelled to bow to their intimidation. In Judea and Samaria, municipal elections had been carried out with wide participation against the explicit veto of El Fatah and the Palestine Liberation Organization. The success of the 'Open Bridges' policy and the multiplication of contacts between Israelis and Arabs had reduced the air of abnormality. There was more assurance of Israel's ability to maintain its balance of strength in view of the United States commitment, which had become firmer than before. In Israel itself the rise in the gross national product, in exports, in tourism, in building and public works, as well as the sharp rise in immigration, proved that the strategy of attrition had been successfully resisted.

Against these achievements we had to set the lack of progress towards a settlement. In February 1971 there was a flurry of excitement when Egypt agreed, in a communication to Dr Jarring, to 'enter into a peace agreement' with Israel. This new terminology was welcomed in Jerusalem. It was realized, however, that its value was annulled by other provisions in which President Sadat demanded the full restoration of the armistice boundaries and the absence of any territorial negotiation with Israel. He also used language on navigation in the Red Sea and the Suez Canal which was equivalent to the formulas under which Egypt had blockaded those waterways in the past. As the weeks went on it became apparent that the phrase about a 'peace agreement' was probably a manoeuvre. Egypt was willing to conclude an 'agreement' with Israel provided that Egypt could write all the clauses of the agreement, including those concerning the boundaries.

Dr Jarring requested Israel to agree in advance to accept the proposal for a withdrawal to the previous international boundary. The Israeli Government unanimously declined to do so. It would, among other things, have ruled out any solution for Sharm el-Sheikh which would have involved a continuing Israeli military control. It would also have debarred Israel from having any changes in her favour in the military or territorial balance compared with that which existed under the armistice régime. Israel regretted Dr Jarring's willingness to identify himself with a position of one of the parties. In its view the Egyptian request for total withdrawal and Israel's position on negotiated boundaries should have been put on the table with equal weight, while negotiators tried to bring them into harmony. After Dr Jarring's February memorandum there was a long period of deadlock. In November 1971 four African Presidents tried to extricate the mission from its frozen state by suggesting that replies given by Israel and Egypt to their own memorandum be regarded as sufficiently positive to justify the mission's resumption. But when the General Assembly convened, its majority, including many African states, rejected African statesmanship in favour of a fundamentalist position supporting Dr Jarring's February memorandum. The UN General Assembly seemed to be illustrating an affection for deadlocks and an aversion to pragmatic solutions.

New immigrants from the US at the Absorption Centre of Mivaseret Zion in 1970. Since the Six Day War, the number of Western professionals settling in Israel has risen sharply

This did not mean that Israel abandoned its efforts to find a path towards dialogue. European and other Foreign Ministers went between Jerusalem and Cairo clarifying respective positions. Israeli leaders felt that when the history of the peace effort came to be written, it would be shown that Israel had not neglected any opportunities for contact or clarification with Arab leaders.

During this period many in Israel and in the world began to doubt whether the transition from complete deadlock to total peace could be made in a single ambitious leap. It seemed more likely that progress would have to come in phases. If this was so it seemed obvious that the first stage should be disengagement at the Suez Canal cease-fire line, where the broadest international interests were at stake. The United States, with the consent of Cairo and Jerusalem, exercised its good offices to clarify this prospect. Egypt would have gained a tangible asset in the form of the open Canal under its management, and the restoration of Egyptian civilian life along its banks without any renunciation of Egypt's position on the final settlement. It was hoped that, despite initial rejection, Cairo would regard one step as better than none.

As the pressure of war and political struggle died down, some of the latent tensions in Israeli society came to the surface. The turbulence took many shapes and expressions; but the common factor was the growth of dissent. There was a sudden tendency to ask searching questions, to be sceptical of the routine answers and to reject the idea that external dangers justified inertia or apathy towards domestic imperfections. Some observers at home and abroad held

this to be a sign of weakness and danger. Was Israel losing the special cohesion, discipline and inner unity which had helped it to survive its ordeals? Could its adversaries take comfort and hope from the air of rebelliousness and self-doubt which afflicted the nation as the years of cease-fire and semi-normality grew longer?

The question arose in the context of constant labour disputes in which government and Histadrut authority were defied in a series of wildcat strikes. Sometimes vital services, such as hospitals and airports, were paralyzed on behalf of what seemed to be trivial claims. A social malaise found expression in street rioting with an ethnic background. There was even a movement called the Black Panthers, which expressed protest against poverty. Furthermore, in 1970 the Government was challenged in its foreign policy, not as heretofore by the fundamentalists, who considered it too flexible, but by professors, university and high school students who were worried lest it was not assiduous enough in the search for peace. When an unauthorized military action led to the displacement of thousands of Bedouin in the Rafah area, the wave of protest was led by kibbutzim who resented arbitrary treatment of their neighbours. Irregularities in a government-owned oil corporation were investigated by a commission headed by a High Court Judge; but the public sentiment favoured an even more rigorous criticism and conclusion than the commission itself agreed upon.

The secular community became increasingly restive towards restrictions arising from the religious *status quo*. An attempt to prevent television on Fridays was defeated by civic action in the courts. There was anger at rabbinical conservatism which prevented the solution of acute human problems arising from rigid interpretation of personal status, such as refusal of marriage facilities to children born out of wedlock. The Labour Party was sympathetic to these libertarian trends, but it had pledged its word and honour to the *status quo* as a condition of partnership with the National Religious Party in the coalition. That party took a sober and central line in security and political matters, so that partnership with it was an asset for which it was worth paying a price in terms of less crucial issues. Within the Labour Party itself, the generation gap was reflected in a demand for more constant discussion and for less decision by hierarchical authority. Immigrants from North Africa protested against what they considered to be excessive and discriminatory facilities offered to Soviet Jewish newcomers. Young couples asked why new immigrants should receive immediate housing while they – the native-born citizens of Israel – had to wait months or years for similar accommodation. In the Hebrew literary movement and parts of the press there was an earnest spirit of moral agitation about whether enough justice was being done to the Arabs under Israeli control.

It was easy enough to show disquiet about these evidences of dissatisfaction. The Israeli tradition had been to argue fiercely at election time about who should run the nation's affairs, but thereafter to accept decisions and rulings with docility. The anti-establishment trend was new and, to some, disconcerting. On a deeper view, however, these stirrings can be seen as a sign of vitality, not of disease. Some of them were exaggerated, and in most cases they did injustice to governmental achievement. The steep growth in economic resources and the almost unparalleled expansion of social services bore witness to the progressive emphasis in Israel's planning and direction. But the more vigilant and exacting mood of the public towards its representatives had a stimulating, not a narcotic effect. The current phrase was *ichpat li* – 'I care'. The loyalty of the electors to their representatives remained higher than in in any other free country: but it was accompanied by an exigent demand for explanation and assurance about the efficiency and integrity of national and local leadership. History shows that those societies are most resilient and durable that are open to the expression of dissent. Israeli society tends to have a monolithic aspect only when it faces urgent external danger. But it is essentially a diverse, turbulent, sophisticated organism, recalcitrant to paternalistic authority and more and more disposed to seek consensus by lively debate.

It could be said as pertinently of Israel as of the ancient Greeks that 'this people was born to have no rest itself and to give none to others'. The outside world, whether fascinated or infuriated by Israel, could not fail to acknowledge a special quality in its life. Amid much evidence of nihilism and ferment in contemporary culture, Israel was still a nation in which affirmation counted for more than protest. And there was one thing that all Israelis understood: adventure and decadence are the only choices offered to mankind. Sometimes their spirit would fall amid the stress of bereavement and the toll of suspense; and then it would seem that victory itself had been nothing but a summer's dream. But in a more authentic mood they would take their memory back and give a resonant answer to the question that lurked in every mind: 'What had we gained by victory?' The answer was: 'Everything that we would have lost without it. Everything – home, life, honour, purpose and the special destiny which our fathers had conserved and which this Israeli generation had been able to renew.' As the twenty-fifth anniversary came near, Israelis could feel that they had not betrayed their triple trust: to serve the central interests of the Jewish people; to safeguard its legacy; and to guarantee its future.

12

This Is Our Land

> *To be or not to be is not the question.*
> *We all want to be. How to be and how*
> *not to be is the essence of the question.*
> Abraham Heschel

She has been not only the high road of civilizations and the battle-field of empires but the pasture and the school of innumerable little tribes: not merely an open channel of war and commerce for nearly the whole world but the vantage-ground and opportunity of the world's highest religions. Men who looked at life under that lofty imagination did not always notice the details of their country's scenery. What filled them was the sense of space and distance, the stupendous contrasts of desert and fertility, the hard straight coasts with the sea breaking into foam, the swift sunrise, the thunderstorms sweeping the length of the land: and if these great outlines are touched here and there with flowers or a mist or a bit of quiet meadow or a quiet pool or an olive tree in the sunshine, it is to illustrate human beauty which comes upon the earth as fair as her wild flowers and as quickly passes away.

Few Israelis could describe their country as eloquently as George Adam Smith, whose *Historical Geography of the Holy Land* was published in 1891. But most of them believe that the land itself is worthy of their special devotion. Israel's rebirth has been a constant ecological drama; rarely are the literature and rhetoric of a national movement so full of tender concern for a scarred, devastated and neglected landscape. Far away in their cold, dark ghettos, with never a glimpse of the sun or of anything green and growing, the early Zionists built an idealized picture of the country's natural beauties. Many of them in later years would tell how they slept under a clear sky on their first night after landing and how they met the early dawn as it came up amid a riot of yellow and purple radiance which repeated itself in the evening twilight.

This, of course, was not the whole story, or even the greater part of it. The hard truth is that when the early Zionists arrived, the country was a neglected estate. No human violence or folly could deprive it of its coastline, or the light playing on the hills, or the immense variety, within a compact space, of mountain country and lowland, shimmering lake and bleak desert.

The view from Mount Carmel onto the Bay of Haifa has
inevitably been impaired by industrial progress. Israel has
come to terms with the necessity to pay a price for development

But beyond this, history had done the worst of which men are capable. Invading armies, improvident farmers and the ubiquitous goat had destroyed the forests. Orchards had given way to scrub and cactus, the old terraces had fallen into disuse and the sand encroached and invaded everything like a yellow plague. The total effect was of a land that seemed to reject human settlement. Seldom was there shade from the sun or shelter from the driving winter rains. In many areas stagnant pools of water hissed and buzzed with the fever of malaria. Jerusalem was the biggest town and more developed than any other part of the country. Yet even here the contrast between the romantic memory and the real view was hard to bear. In 1856 a European writer described the city as being like 'a pilgrim grey with age who has come here and sunk down to die: his pain has turned into stone like that of the mother whose children had been throttled by the wrath of God'.

The first impact of Jewish settlement on the landscape was one of gentle rehabilitation. The early Zionist village was never affluent, but it had a rustic charm and gave an air of rootedness and tranquillity. Zionists across the world were particularly obsessive about trees, which were subscribed for, purchased and eventually planted in such profusion that by the 1930's the boundary between a Jewish and an Arab area could be discerned by colour. It was simply the line dividing the green from the yellow.

The early urban development, such as it was, gave a less uniform satisfaction. But in Tel Aviv and elsewhere the claims of speed overrode all ambition of refinement. Many immigrants came from the East European *shtetl* environment. Hebrew and Yiddish authors have tended to idealize *shtetl* life, but not

even the most affectionate of them ever pretended that the *shtetl* was aesthetically inspiring. Something of its cosy disorder can still be seen in the main streets of the first *moshavot*, as well as in the Jaffa suburbs that became Tel Aviv. By a stroke of ill fortune, the first major impetus to urban building came in the 1920's and 1930's, when Central European domestic architecture was at its worst. The unsightly cubes of 'white' cement on their inevitable stilts, with peeling façades and a withered, jaded air, still linger on with depressing tenacity. And the sea-shore at Tel Aviv is almost too unsightly to be believed.

Yet on total balance, it is not flattery to describe Israel as a country of many beauties, and Israelis showing their country to others – which is one of their major pleasures – can point to sharp maritime landscapes, intense concentrations of verdure, gracefully tinted patches of cultivated earth in the Jezreel Valley, vistas from Mount Carmel that rival San Francisco or Table Mountain, a uniquely volcanic grandeur of ravines between the Dead Sea and Eilat and two points of scenic climax: the Sea of Galilee, with its surounding ring of farms, and Jerusalem, more spread out and diverse than in the old paintings and engravings, yet still majestic in its general effect.

But the struggle to keep Israel beautiful still has to be waged against a relatively dormant public consciousness. The Zionist pioneers came from places in which men were more interested in what things are than in what they look like. There is more public display of laundered underwear on balconies and roof-tops than almost anywhere else. Manufacturers of beer, coffee and other admirably exportable commodities are inclined to commit outrages by advertising along the highways. There are problems of air pollution in the crowded coastal plain. It is theoretically understood that in Jerusalem aesthetic standards must have a higher place than elsewhere in determining the pace of development. But there are sharp controversies about whether speed or beauty comes first in the construction programmes. The struggle against ecological carelessness and plain ugliness will have to be joined with full intensity in the next generation.

Of the Jews in Israel today, sixty per cent were born on its soil. If we add those who came as children we must revise the common image of Israel as an 'immigrant society'. It is not true today, as it was two decades ago, that most Israelis are searching for their roots or making a transition from one environmental memory to another. Of the minority not born in Israel, about half originated in European countries and half in countries of Asia and Africa. Israelis of non-European origin have a more prolific birth-rate; but in recent years the Western component among new immigrants has grown rapidly. The debate

far left Water buffalo in the Lake Huleh Nature reserve
left The Jordan River as it enters the northern end of the Sea of Galilee

about whether Israel will be 'European', 'Western' or 'Oriental' overlooks the certainty that it will be none of these, but simply Israeli. Some writers, despairing of any Arab reconciliation with a 'Zionist' Israel, have drawn false comfort from the prospect that Israel might become increasingly orientalized until it loses the qualities which separate it from the rest of the Middle East and becomes absorbed unobtrusively in the surrounding Levantine region. There is no chance of this coming to pass. Israel will always be non-Arab in its speech, thought and shape of mind; and its Jewish connections will always be stronger than anything else. It learned in 1948 and again in 1967 that its survival depends on its relationship to the science, technology and the democratic structure which marked it off from its neighbours. The qualities which it did not share with them were those that enabled it to withstand their assault.

This is not to say that Israel is a finished product in terms of its human composition. Every few years a new thread appears in the tapestry. The arrival of tens of thousands of Soviet Jews has set up a new focus of social influence. Their main gift, in addition to a high educational level, is the simple ardour with which they cherish their new freedom. They take a special pride in a Jewish identity which for many years was a source of inferior status. There is even a danger of exaggerated reaction. Some are so resentful of the 'socialist' régime under which they suffered that they become hostile even to democratic and voluntary forms of socialism. Moreover, they come from a country in which the government defined each citizen's needs and rights. At first it was not easy for all of them to face the multiplicity of decisions and personal initiatives that fall on a citizen of a democracy. Since this is the first sizeable transfer of manpower from a Communist to a democratic régime, the results will evoke interest far beyond Israel and the Middle East.

To a lesser degree, but more significantly than once seemed likely, Israel's human geography will be affected by immigrants from the West. The Six Day War had a powerful effect on Jews in free countries, especially on the youth among them. Some 7,500 volunteers from forty countries were in Israel at the beginning of 1968. The war in which they had wanted to take part was over almost before they could register their intention; but the concept of a living link between Western Jewish youth and Israel has never been lost. Immigration from Western Europe and the Americas has never exceeded 12,000 a year; but if this rate can be sustained or increased, its qualitative effects will be significant. At any given moment there are 9,000 or 10,000 Jewish students from abroad in Israeli universities, scientific institutions and *yeshivot*.

The ability of each citizen to pull his weight is anxiously appraised by Israelis – for the simple reason that there are so few with any weight to pull.

This has always been the pathos of Jewish history – the few against the many. It was aggravated by the holocaust, which ravaged the nation's human resources. The value attached to each individual gives enrichment to a small society; there is no danger of being lost in a nameless crowd. It is natural to find Israelis constantly counting themselves, calculating the birth-rate and immigration trends and anxiously asking when their numbers will put the issue of Jewish survival beyond doubt. Another effect of this numerical weakness is to make most Israelis sceptical about political solutions that would obliterate the country's Jewish identity. Israelis cannot evade the question of whether a large map is more important than an irrevocably Jewish population.

It is easier to examine the statistics of the Israeli people than to probe its inner world. At first sight the spectacle is one of anarchic diversity. What is there in common between the youngster born in Degania or Ramat Gan, the orthodox youth from Georgia, the banker from Amsterdam or Zurich, the doctor from London, the scientist from Harvard, the silversmith from Yemen, the lawyer from Egypt or Iraq and the small shopkeeper from Morocco or Algeria? The answer is that whatever they have in common is strong enough to have brought all of them to Israel and nowhere else. Israeli society appears to be marked by pluralism and diversity; yet the overriding impression is one of coherence. The Israeli scene is often turbulent, contentious and effervescent, but when danger threatens, when the news comes that the neighbour down the road has lost a son in action or when something happens to revive memories of Jewish martyrdoms, the ranks tighten, and all manner of disciplines and restraints are accepted with sudden docility.

For one part of the Israeli population, the hostility of the Arab states is something that can never be put out of mind. When Israel was established in 1948, some 165,000 Arabs and Druze declined or failed to join the exodus. Their national and cultural loyalties made them an integral part of the Arab world which had concerted its efforts to bring about Israel's destruction; but they managed to transcend the hostility by giving first place to their private or family welfare.

The Arabs of Israel have lived at a high rate of growth. They now number some 450,000. They combine the Arab tradition of large families with Israeli social and health services that keep the death-rate low. Thus they have become the most rapidly growing community in the world. They have full citizenship, with representation in the Knesset, and the Israeli Government and parliament accept vigilant responsibility for their security and welfare. Israeli Arabs are not expected to fulfil any military service since this implies a duty to take up arms against their fellow-Arabs. The Druze join the army with fierce devotion and are among Israel's most passionate defenders. Until 1964 the border areas in which most Arabs lived were under special military control, subject to surveillance and restrictions of movement. With the abolition of the 'military government' system, their equality became more real. The Israeli policy is not one of assimilation: it does not aim to de-Arabize the Arabs or to force them into identification with Zionist aims. It conceives educational autonomy as the key to the maintenance of their national identity and pride. The Arab sector of the Israeli educational system shows a constant increase in the percentage of those attending primary school. There is also an expansion of the secondary school network. The Arab village and township in Israel are not luxurious but they give an impression of solid agricultural and mercantile growth, with modern amenities coming to them in a degree than the citizens of most Arab states do not yet enjoy.

Israel is likely to be more affected by its encounter with the million Arabs in the West Bank and Gaza than by those who have lived in Israel for twenty-five years. Whatever the political destiny of the territories may be, both peoples will be different for the experience of having come together in 1967. The most durable result is the encounter itself. From June 1967 Arabs on the West Bank and in East Jerusalem were allowed to cross the Jordan eastwards with permits valid for one or several journeys. Nearly half a million have used this facility. In the other direction, Arabs from abroad, Palestinians and others have been permitted to visit the administered territories. At first this liberty was granted to summer visitors; later it was extended for the whole year. Arab students whose families live west of the Jordan and in the Gaza Strip can come and go between Arab countries and the administered territories. There is a constant flow into Israeli towns and villages of Arabs from Cisjordan, Transjordan and more distant parts of the Arab world. The number of Arab workers from Judea and Samaria entering Israel daily leapt from 9,000 in 1969 to 24,000 in 1970 and to about 35,000 in 1972. With the addition of workers from Gaza, the Israeli economy employs about 40,000 Arabs from beyond Israel's previous borders.

Against these benefits on both sides of the line, some long-term dangers have been adduced. In Israel there is a fear lest the ideal of a Jewish country in which all forms of work are performed by Jews will suffer dilution. The statistics today are marginal, since the Arabs form only five percent of Israel's labour force. But should the numbers increase steeply there is a danger that a society will emerge in which Jews perform the skilled and highly paid functions, while the simpler, rough work is carried out by Arabs. There is thus a possible conflict of interest between the short-term necessities of the economy and the broader social aspirations of Israeli society.

But while there is considerable opinion in Israel in favour of controlling the Arab entry, nobody wants to go back to the old ghetto-like separation. Some processes of integration have grown up which it will be impossible to annul. The former armistice lines reflected a military result and a demographic division. They became a frontier of political jurisdiction, but made no economic sense. Until May 1948 the area of Palestine west of the Jordan had been a single economic unit. Suddenly it became divided into two entirely separate economies, one oriented westwards across the Mediterranean and southwards to the Red Sea, the other entirely directed eastwards and northwards towards Arab countries. The elimination of the armistice lines in 1967 was like the falling of an artificial dam: water simply flowed to its natural levels. By the end of 1970, the Arab territories west of the Jordan were sending to Israel some sixty per cent of their exports and receiving from Israel nearly eighty-five per cent of their imports. The natural interdependence of two economies was free to assert itself.

Yet while a positive relationship grew up between Israelis and West Bank Arabs in the administered areas in commerce, agriculture and normal human exchange, the fact remained that the central problem of political self-expression for the Arabs of the territories remained frozen. Here were a million people with an undefined political future and with no institutional expression for their political aspirations. There is no recent example of a community so numerous in comparison with those ruling over it, so clear-cut in its cultural and national identity, living quietly for long periods without any outlet for its national self-expression. It is one thing for Israel to accommodate an Arab minority less than one fifth of the size of the Jewish population. It would be quite another thing to maintain a state in which some forty per cent of the population would direct its deeper sentiments and devotions not towards Israel's flag, but across the boundaries to neighbouring states. Yet this will be the situation by 1990 unless a way is found to ensure a separate political destiny for the majority of the Arabs in the West Bank and Gaza.

It is more conventional to praise Israel's military exploits and her fight for international recognition than to speak rhapsodically of her economic achievement. The starting point of Israel's economic history is a land with few natural resources and, little apparent hope of swift development. Many of the reports and surveys of the pre-state years are full of reserve about the country's potential. Israel's economic drama is dominated from the beginning by an atmo-

sphere of struggle with budgetary deficits, increasing taxation and a pro-
liferating debt. By its very nature economic recovery can only come slowly.
There cannot be exhilarating moments of sudden victory as on the battlefield
or in dramatic votes in international organizations. If all the adverse factors
are taken into account a historian might reach the conclusion that Israel's
economic performance in her first decades comes near the top of her achievements. The fact is that in 1950 Israel's GNP was IL3,325 million, her total
industrial output $18 million, the number of tourists visiting her 33,000, and
exports and invisible exports $46 million. By 1971 the GNP was IL 21.9 billion,
export earnings, including tourism and invisible exports, amounted to
$1,713 million, the number of tourists was over 657,000, spending $155 million,
and exports accounted for forty per cent of her total foreign currency income.
No other economy has shown so steep and constant a rate of growth; and
nowhere else in the developing world has an economy passed so quickly
from relatively primitive levels to such intense productivity both in agriculture and in industry. European countries now find Israel a growing and
dynamic market, receiving more goods from the countries of the European
communities than all the contiguous Arab countries put together. To have
achieved by 1970 an average per capita consumption of IL3,920, which is
higher than the corresponding figure in Japan and many European countries
or any country in Latin America and Africa, testifies to the pace of Israel's
achievement.

These achievements would have been more impressive, if the Israeli people
had been willing to accept greater restraints in the standard of living and
in the import of consumer goods. There has been a constant tension between
economic realities and the exigencies of a people determined to maintain
advanced social services. There is also no readiness to put up with austerity
except in critical emergencies.

As we look back we find many things that could have been done better.
But the general conclusion must be that the spectacular increase in resources,
productivity, fertility, commercial activity, the infrastructure and apparatus
of industry and the utilization of a favourable position in world communications all add up to an achievement of remarkable quality which no other
developing state has rivalled. Somebody who knew what Israel looked like
in its first year would have difficulty in recognizing it in its twenty-fifth.

Whether this progress can be sustained depends largely on Israel's educational
enterprise. Israel's schools are called upon to consolidate the national culture,
cement the social union, stimulate intellectual excellence and sharpen the

Students of electronics at the Weizmann Institute of Science. Emphasis on the development of science-based industries has been particularly marked during the past few years

nation's capacity to survive in a region where all the material calculations work heavily against it. It is a heavy and complex task, and the instruments created for it are impressive. There were 140,000 pupils in Israel's schools and universities in 1948. The figure today is 960,000. Education has expanded at a far higher rate than the increase of population. There is probably no similar rate of expansion in educational history. The primary school system, including kindergartens, comprises 477,379 pupils. The expanding post-primary network, including vocational and agricultural education, provides schooling beyond the compulsory age of fourteen to 189,905 pupils. The 1970's will be the era of the student explosion arising from the expansion of the university network inaugurated in the early 1960's. Today there are 45,000 students in Israel in six recognized university-level institutions. Apart from defence, the education budget ranks first amongst the items of governmental and public expenditure.

Israeli schools developed at first in close contact with political parties. One of Ben-Gurion's early audacities was to break away from this pattern in order to give the educational system a national framework under a highly centralized system of governmental control. The old differentiations have not been completely eliminated. At the primary level, the State provides either general or religious schooling, according to parental preference; some thirty per cent of households opt for the religious trend. The same division runs through the secondary school network.

Education in Israel is surrounded by an atmosphere of challenge. There is an understanding that the national character is still in formation, and that some of the stimulating forces at work in the intellectual history of the Jewish people are not operative in the safer but narrower context of statehood. The Jews alone, of all historic nations, have lived intimately with every one of the intellectual currents in recorded history, from ancient prophecy to modern science; from the dim roots of man's past to the shining possibilities of his future. It will not be easy to keep the targets high and the vision broad. It cannot be denied that there was an anti-intellectual theme in pioneering Zionism. The object was to convert an excessively academized people into a nation distributed into normal categories. The hero of the Zionist saga was the scholar or mathematician who had left his studies or research to milk a cow on a Zionist farm. There was reason and method in this process some decades ago. Today it would spell ruin for Israel's security and economy.

There has been a special scientific ambition in Israel since its earliest days. Many find it startling to come across a small state on the western fringe of Asia endowed with research reactors, accelerators, computers, laboratories, hospitals and clinics, aircraft-repair facilities, electronic factories and other indications of scientific progress. The result is not to be measured in economic welfare or security alone. When Weizmann founded his Institute of Science at Rehovot, he was as much concerned with Israel's intellectual level as with any 'practical' consequence. The climate of scientific enquiry, its rational spirit, objective judgment, emphasis on reason and order, constructive scepticism and universal solidarities have all gone deep into the texture of Israeli life. A society in which a family of research workers takes part in the universal scientific enterprise is intrinsically different from a society in which no such family exists. There are many elements in Israeli culture and history which tend towards a mystic, metaphysical and intensely emotional attitude. The scientific community contributes a balancing dimension of rationality. Apart from this, Israel's scientific role has enlarged her position in the world. She has come to be regarded by developing nations as the natural point of contact between the world of national freedom and the world of scientific progress.

In the next two decades Israel's scientific community will have to face three of the country's most difficult challenges. There is the scarcity of water, which could be compensated for by a break-through in the economics of desalination; there are demands for increasing quantities of power, which could be met by a successful development of nuclear fuels; and there is an insistent need to break loose from the servitude and dependence created by defence procurement needs. The uncertainty about where the next tank or aircraft was

The 'Arava', designed and manufactured in Israel, in flight off the coast of Tel Aviv coming from has had an obsessive effect on Israel's diplomacy for much of her first three decades. If Israel were able to reach a position similar to that of Sweden or Switzerland and become independent in the main items of arms manufacture, it would not be exposed to periodic pressures and would breathe much more freely in its international relations. This prospect may not be as far from view as it seemed a decade ago.

But Israel's eyes are not directed only forward to the future. It is not a new synthetic nation writing its history on a clean slate. The past follows it wherever it goes. The revival of the Hebrew language in daily speech, its steady growth in conceptual precision, the spectacular results in archaeological discovery, the role of the Bible in secular as well as in religious education, the privileged status of religious tradition in some domains of personal law are all symptoms of the profound yearning for continuity. The Shrine of the Book housing the Dead Sea scrolls and the Yad Vashem Memorial to the holocaust, a few kilometres away, are two institutions which could not exist anywhere but in Israel. They stand out on Jerusalem's skyline the one in testimony to Israel's ancient origins, the other in mute and painful witness to her people's martyrdom.

One of the Dea Sea Scrolls, the Manual of Discipline, on exhibit at the Israel Museum, Jerusalem. As a primary link with the past, the Hebrew language is one of Israel's dearest possessions

With all its outward signs of modernity, Israel is still a nation haunted by memories too powerful to fade.

For this very reason the Hebrew language is one of Israel's dearest possessions. On the political level, it causes immense confusion to Arab adversaries who seek to argue that modern Israel has no authentic connection with the Middle East. The truth is that Israel is the only nation in the world that speaks the same tongue, upholds the same faith and inhabits the same land as it did three thousand years ago. Its language unifies the nation on two levels. It links Jews all over the world in a common legacy: and it joins all of them to the Israel of antiquity, whose bequest to mankind was primarily in the form of a literary heritage.

In the past twenty-five years the Israeli nation has not merely used the Hebrew language: it has also enlarged its capacities. Few Israelis are aware of the strides that their language has taken since the beginning of statehood. It is not only a question of adding new vocabulary to meet modern technological concepts. The structure and syntax of Hebrew have advanced to a point at which no conceptual subtlety or technological sophistication is beyond it.

One of the major themes of modern Hebrew literature is the drama of conscience arising out of the spectacle of Arab frustration and defeat. The new authors were all involved in war, of which they write in sombre memory without a single note of glorification. In the writings of S. Yizhar, Haim Guri, Aharon Meged, A. B. Yehoshua and Amos Oz we find attempts to come to terms with the moral paradox in Israel's rebirth; the feeling that every Israeli victory is an Arab defeat while an Arab victory would mean Israel's annihilation, so that in the last resort there is no alternative to victory. This does not mean that Israeli writers reach a negative conclusion about their nation's legitimacy; nor do most of them have any political conclusions to draw from their searching of the nation's soul. What concerns them is not political attitudes towards Arabs, but Israel's moral relationship towards itself. They seem to be arguing for a constructive humility, for an understanding of the pathos and contradiction of the historic process and, consequently, for a more modest national style in relations with Arabs inside Israel and beyond.

It would be wrong to assume that the literary movement is entirely taken up with qualms of conscience. At its other extreme it conveys a feverish pride, arising from a traumatic reaction to danger and victory. Every war in every land throws up some literary exponents of 'manifest destiny' and of acute self-righteousness, and some eminent Israeli writers were driven by the 1967 experience to paroxysms of national pride. The dominant atmosphere in post-war Israel is one of sobriety, not exultation. The victory is absorbed with a balanced understanding both of its opportunities and of its dangers.

A Hebrew aphorism compares Israel to 'the stars of the heavens and the dust of the earth'. It has been a people of abrupt contrasts, pulled upward and downward by elements in its own nature. The movement of men between nobility and decline takes up a great part of history, literature and, above all, drama. There is little fear that Israel will be the least among the nations in vitality and creative force. But will it go further and fulfil its founders' highest hopes? The question mark hovers over three of Israel's challenges: its relations with the neighbouring world, the nature of its democratic society, and the degree of its fidelity to Jewish values.

There is a constant debate about whether Arab hostility could somehow have been avoided. One of the legends is that the early Zionists were not 'aware' of the existence of the Arabs or, at least, were oblivious of the intensity of Arab resentment. This begs the question whether Arab resignation to a Jewish State could really have been promoted by a larger dose of Jewish awareness. There is room for the belief that an Arab attempt to keep every acre of the Middle

East Arab and not to want a single inch of it to be Jewish was in human terms inevitable and even normal. If this is true then the question of Jewish awareness is very important for the moral health of the Jews, but of almost no consequence in relation to the conflict itself.

The fact is that Zionist leaders were unbelievably persistent and sometimes naïve in the constancy of their search for Arab consent. We find them in all the history books, Congress protocols, memoirs, and newspapers, button-holing every Arab who came into sight or earshot and besetting them with pleas, assurances, formulas and programmes for coexistence. Sometimes these encounters kindled a spark of hope, as in Weizmann's 1918 talk with Feisal or the contacts with Abdullah of Jordan in the early 1950's. For the most part, they were necessary to appease the Zionist conscience or to reassure friends in the world that no remedy was being overlooked. But it is counter to history to believe that diplomatic charm or persuasiveness or assiduity could generate Arab consent to something that was manifestly beyond their power of accept-ance. These are conflicts of interest so deep that they can only be adjudicated by authority or power in favour of one party and against another, and not brought to reconciliation by prior voluntary consent. If this were not so in civil life there would never be courts of law. In international relations, too, there is no escape at times from judgments of one sort of another, which leave one of the litigants unsatisfied. Professor Talmon, who is often amongst the most critical voices raised against Zionist and Israeli diplomacy, reaches the correct historical appraisal:

Was the Arab Jewish conflict inevitable? Can one put one's finger on sins of com-mission or omission, on points of no return, and say that had this or that happened or not happened, been done or not been done, things would have taken a radically different course? The more I ponder these questions, the more confirmed I become in the grim conclusion that although in detail, in style and tone, the Jews might have acted more wisely or more tactfully, it would not have made much difference in the final analysis. The same cannot be said about the Arabs. On very many occasions they could, by making concessions, have arrested or very significantly slowed down the growth of the Jewish National Home so as to prevent its transformation into a Jewish State. By adopting an attitude of absolute and total intransigence, they reduced the Yishuv's alternatives either to giving up Zionism or to carrying out its programme to the full extent in the teeth of Arab opposition. Since no give and take was possible, since even such modest forms of Zionism as a measure of immigration and settlement encountered maximum resistance, there seemed no choice but to aim at maximum strength. God had hardened the heart of Pharaoh (Jacob Talmon, *Israel Among the Nations*, page 147).

This is the heart of the issue. If the argument had been about the dimensions of the National Home or the State of Israel a natural negotiating position would have existed. Once Israel was discussing its own size, while the Arabs were opposed to the sheer principle of its existence in any shape or form, there was bound to be a 'dialogue of the deaf.'

Yet since 1967 the conditions for a dialogue have been radically transformed. After more than five years of unavailing reliance on foreign powers and international agencies, there may well be those in Arab states who see no way out except in a negotiation with Israel. The challenge for Israel is sharp. The majority of its population understands the need for a compromise under which Israel would have better boundaries than before the 1967 war, but a much more compact configuration than the cease-fire lines. It is one thing to live without peace while this is inexorable: it would be quite another to renounce a prospect of peace which, apart from the independence of Israel itself, appeals to the highest of all Jewish visions. In the summer of 1973, with Egypt disengaging itself from Soviet domination, Israel's moment of truth and higher statesmanship seemed to be drawing near.

At the end of a generation scarred by war and nourished by many triumphs, some of Israel's original values are in doubt. The dilemma can best be illustrated by a series of questions: will the tolerant, humane, empirical theme in Israeli thought triumph over tendencies of extreme nationalist fervour? Will ortho-dox Jews stretch their imagination to find solutions to urgent human pre-dicaments without opening a destructive conflict about the special place of religion in Israel's history – a conflict that cannot possibly end in their favour? Will the pioneering and collective ideals of early Zionism temper the wild rush for affluence and individual welfare so as to maintain a society with a special accent on human worth? Can Israeli democracy show a better solution than in recent years to problems of a rising crime rate, a high level of road accidents and a widening social and economic gap between sections of the population? Will intellectual, scientific and artistic excellence be given due preference in Israel's order of priorities? In short, will the temptations of parochialism and apathy be overcome by appeal to a Jewish legacy, which is universal in space and eternal in time?

The tension between national particularity and broad universal vision runs through the whole of Jewish history. Israel's task is not to ensure the total eclipse of one by the other, but to bring them together in creative alliance. If it succeeds, the ceremony in the little museum hall in May 1948 may loom larger in the human story than any of its participants could have dared to dream.

Index